STEFAN AND FRIDERIKE ZWEIG

BOOKS BY FRIDERIKE ZWEIG

PASTEUR
Forscher und Menschenfreund

STEFAN ZWEIG
Companion of My Life

WUNDER UND ZEICHEN
Grosse Gestalten des Hochmittelalters

GÜTE, WISSEN UND VERSTEHEN
Drei Lebensbilder grosser amerikanischer Erzieher

ERIK NEERGARD UND DIE SCHWESTERN
Novel

STEFAN

AND

FRIDERIKE

THEIR CORRESPONDENCE
1912-1942

TRANSLATED AND EDITED BY

HENRY G. ALSBERG

WITH THE ASSISTANCE OF

ERNA MacARTHUR

HASTINGS HOUSE
PUBLISHERS   NEW YORK

The correspondence published in this volume might be regarded from different points of view by the reader: as a document contributing to the understanding of the trends of modern
literature; as throwing some new light, perhaps, on certain
phases of the history of our tragic era; or simply as a novel in
letter form—the story of a spiritual wingéd love, friendship and
marriage. Perhaps the first impression—due to the fact that
the woman's impetuous letters take up most of the early pages
of the book, will be that this is a record of personal relations
for the most part. Unfortunately the letters written by Stefan
Zweig from 1912 through 1916 have disappeared; some of them
were stolen; some (together with those of 1938 and 1939) were
destroyed during the German invasion in France.

That so many letters were saved is largely due to the courage
and determination of my beloved friends, Magda Grasmayer
and Josefine Junger, who remained loyal and devoted despite
the danger to which their loyalty and devotion exposed them.
Both these dear friends have died; and in a way this book is a
memorial to them, too.

Both Stefan Zweig and I cultivated the habit of keeping the
letters we wrote each other while we were separated, and bringing them home with us when we returned from our various
journeyings. Although the letters were despatched from the
furthest corners of the globe during a period of some thirty
years, there are only a comparatively few gaps in the correspondence, accounted for by the occasions when we were on
trips together or both at home. To eliminate repetitions (except those that were symptomatic of recurring attitudes), and

certain personal details, some letters have been omitted. On the other hand, no textual changes have been made in those included here for publication.

Stefan Zweig's life was significant to many people through its great and important literary achievements and the convictions that inspired everything that he thought, wrote and did. That is why I have not hesitated to unveil so many intimate circumstances of our relationship. I felt that my own objections to doing so were not of primary importance, for his image and tragic destiny will be illuminated and even transfigured in these letters.

There is something more to be said concerning the letters of the years 1912–1917. Here the man's figure is discerned only through the woman's voice as its echo. The only exceptions are the two poems he sent her. These early letters, written by the woman, these letters of devotion—and self-assertion, too—will reveal her in her own sphere of activity, her daily life and creative impulses, and throw light on the abiding friendship between the two that was to weather every storm.

I am deeply indebted to Mr. Henry G. Alsberg for an excellent translation and for his sympathetic understanding. I also extend my heartfelt thanks to Mrs. Erna MacArthur for her very able cooperation in connection with the translation of the letters written by me. My sincere thanks go also to Mr. Walter Frese, my esteemed publisher, for his very great kindness.

Friderike Zweig

STEFAN AND FRIDERIKE ZWEIG

July 25, 1912

Dear Mr. Stefan Zweig:

Perhaps I don't need to tell you why it is so easy for me to do things that are generally considered "improper," at any rate this is not the time to tell you *why* I don't think them shocking.

Yesterday I came to Vienna and spent half a day and night there. I had left my gentle countryside behind me, and my mill beside the brook in the forest—where I live entirely without benefit of city-civilization.—And then, by chance, something very nice happened.—I had seen you a few years ago, on a summer evening, at Stelzer's [1] when Girardi [2] bade farewell to Vienna. Somebody said: "That's Stefan Zweig over there." I had just read one of your stories and also some sonnets (those possibly later) whose sound pursued me. It was a charming evening. I believe you were with some friends and there was, or seemed to be, a sort of rapture among them. At that time I had reached a kind of crisis in my life. Late that night we drove back to Vienna in a smart carriage with fast-stepping horses.— And yesterday you sat next to me at the Riedhof [3] and an acquaintance of mine brought me your *Hymns to Life*. I read them to the accompaniment of rolling wheels on my trip back to my summer home early the next morning. Out yonder the fields were bathed in bright sunshine. And then it seemed the natural thing for me to send you my greetings. The hymns are so beautiful. Some of them I had known before. "The Word" is especially dear to me. When I am all alone I often turn to it in the "Insel" [4] Almanac and read it out loud. Yesterday as I sat beside you it occurred to me that what a person translates is not without significance, whether it be Peladan and Strindberg and Shaw he devotes his whole life to, or, on the other hand, Verhaeren. Tell me what you translate and I'll tell you what you are. But, of course, the *how* is important too. It is glorious to "recreate" the original in one's own poetic rendering of it.

1

I write poetry too. Perhaps you've recently read or noticed something of mine. Would like sometime to send you something as a greeting from my dear world out here.

Why are you in town? One should be in town as little as possible. It is so lovely out here. It would be wonderful for you.

I got your address from someone who told me about your veranda. He was looking through my list of books for Christmas, which included *Thersites*.[5] I imagine you won't want to talk about this stupid letter to anyone. I am not writing because I expect a reply, though I'd like one very much. If you should want to, write to Maria von W., General Delivery, Rosenburg am Kamp.

Many greetings!

[1] Garden Restaurant near Vienna.   [2] Famous actor and singer of Viennese folk songs.   [3] Restaurant in Vienna.   [4] The Insel Verlag which published Stefan Zweig's works.   [5] A drama by Stefan Zweig.

Mannigfallmuehle near Gars
July 30, 1912

Dear Dr. Zweig:

It was so wonderful to hold your letter in my hands. And to read your words which were what I had secretly hoped for.

Will phone you tomorrow morning, because I want to hear your voice. And, since you wish it, I shan't hesitate to drop my anonymity. I believe you find it hard to understand what might appear to be so banal; but perhaps you will understand why I couldn't let you know my name before hearing from you. If you are really curious, please ask me yourself. Undoubtedly I can answer all your questions. Your kindness has touched me very deeply.

I must tell you of two odd coincidences. After dining that evening at the Riedhof, I slept in town for the first time in many years. And the place where I spent the night happened to be in your street, only a few houses away from you. Then, during the weekend, one of our friends (who was staying with us) had some visitors, some people who arrived by auto and stayed with us overnight and went swimming at our beautiful beach. Although I don't believe there could have been any connection, I imagined that you might have alighted from the gray car and confronted me with a miracle—a very wonderful miracle.[1]

Should I venture to make myself known to you by some outward, visible sign? Certainly not in the midst of a crowd of people. In your eyes is so much beauty. You see everything with such "illuminating insight." I dare not face your scrutiny.

With cordial thanks, yours,

Friderike Maria von Winternitz

P.S. Perhaps you'd like to know whether I sign myself "Mrs"? I do.

[1] Stefan Zweig's answer informed me that he had been invited to take part in the excursion to Kamptal, but had declined. Actually the auto mentioned in my letter belonged to his cousin. And so Stefan Zweig might easily have been one of the passengers.

Mannigfallmuehle
August 3, 1912

Dear Doctor Zweig:

Perhaps my wire puzzled you a little. It was sent because of a letter I received yesterday which made it impossible for me to get away from here next Monday or Tuesday. It had never been very likely that I could have, anyway. Since I can't make it, here are my best wishes for a happy trip. I am looking forward to clasping your hand in mine when you return.

With affectionate admiration, yours,

Friderike von Winternitz

P.S. Sincerest thanks for your offer to stay in Vienna a few days longer. I am almost—but not entirely—free to do what I please.

(Stefan Zweig had asked me to meet him in Vienna before he departed for Belgium to visit Verhaeren. My wire had suggested that he should come to Gars instead. In answer, he sent a very cordial message and some books as a farewell gift. Later I received several letters from Belgium.)

Mannigfallmuehle
August 7

Dear Doctor Zweig:

Yesterday it was as if gracious flowers were showering upon me. How dear and kind you must be. Thanks for everything. You accuse me of being too reserved, reticent. Yet, I, for my part, feel my emotions are quite exposed to, or at any rate only very thinly veiled from you. And this "reserve" is no mere maneuver, never believe it. Cleverer people may resort to that kind of thing, and when they do you may be sure they will dress it up in fine words and still "have more cunning to be strange." But I am sure you never believed me capable of anything like that.—I am bothering you with this letter because it occurred to me that you might be passing through Munich. I expect to be there for a few days in about four weeks. The purpose of my trip is a visit to a very sick friend, Karl Borromaeus Heinrich; perhaps you know him through his writings. I am somewhat attached to Munich, and it would be wonderful to see you there.

Isn't it strange that Erich Stoerk, my intimate friend for the past thirteen years, mentioned your dear name for the first time last Saturday? Evidently he knows you quite well. We were remarking on the way his youngster talked. I was happy to think you knew the little fellow, too. He has been staying with me for the last few weeks. Again many thanks!

With all my admiration,

Friderike Maria von Winternitz

Mannigfallmuehle
August 29

Dear Doctor Zweig:

So you are back!

Now I have a confession to make. I read *Thersites* and after the first transports of delight had passed, I was brought up short by a guilty feeling that I had no right to lay violent hands on your time. I don't know whether my awe-inspired mood of self-denial would have lasted, for you decided the issue for me. It was good of you to bolster up my courage. And so, hastily and somewhat fearfully, I have selected a few old and new things. Among them verses that have never been read by anyone, while some of the other work has been accepted for publication. A novella and a recently completed novel would have taken up too much of your time. I'll send them after they "come out."

4

Will you be in Vienna next Wednesday or Thursday? I'd like to phone you then.

Let me add the sincere wish that the rehearsals [1] won't be too exhausting.

With many greetings from my radiant garden, yours,

Maria Friderike von Winternitz

[1] The rehearsals of Stefan Zweig's play *The House at the Seashore* had begun at the Vienna Burgtheater.

Doebling
Friday, September 6, 1912

After a brief spell of reflection:

You will have begun to wonder whether I was as sure of myself as you thought. But the thing is this: I am altogether shut up within myself and I can never tell when this mood is imminent, how long it will persist, or when it will disappear. And though I have a quiet conviction that it will be dispelled by your presence, still I am afraid that this and my other inadequacies will cause you to regret the loss of an hour, though it would be a radiant hour, indeed, for me. Yet I'd like so much to come to you, for it will be wonderful for me and will rob you of only as much seclusion as you are willing to sacrifice. I am convinced that you will not think it strange that I don't do a bit of play-acting and refuse to come because of the "impropriety." I would gladly have invited you to my house, but considered that would be presumptious, the more so, because the place is still in disorder. Also a walk in the woods would have been nice, but possibly something you are not in the habit of doing.

So, tomorrow at six, I shall greet you, holding your dear hand in mine.

Maria Friderike von W.

(The visit did not take place because of my little daughter's indisposition.)

October 6, 1912

I want to tell you about two things that happened in the past few days. I read the *Karamazov* and thank you very much for the book. Will your essay contain something about Dostoievski's attitude toward children?

Secondly: I am carrying a play around inside me.

October 12

Dear Doctor Zweig:

May I break in on your harried hours and thank you very much for all you said and for the poem whose words mean so much to me, and which also transported me again into the novel's intoxicating nocturnal atmosphere.

> *And books like flowers may be loved*
> *For the fragrance that lingers long after them.*

(I read this recently in Eulenberg.[1]) Your beautiful poem has the same lingering fragrance.

I intend to spend one or two weeks in Berlin and Hamburg between November 5 and 25, with two days' interlude at the beach. Up to now, there's no reason why this plan shouldn't work out.

Again many thanks and many greetings, dear, honored Doctor.

Yours, Friderike Maria von Wint.

[1] Herbert Eulenberg, German poet and writer.

October 14, 1912

Dear Doctor Zweig:

I've just had an unexpected though not unhoped-for offer; I am to write a review of the Burgtheater's next premiere [1] for the *Hamburg Fredenblatt.*

Hastening to inform you of this charming little miracle, I am your devoted

F.M.W.

[1] This performance happened to be the premiere of Stefan Zweig's play *The House at the Seashore.*

Saturday

Dear Dr. Zweig:

Please come on Monday! I am anticipating your visit with great joy.

Your devoted

Maria Friderike von W.

6

My dear Doctor Zweig:

I am still tempest-tossed by the joy you have given me. I have already drunk deeply of the first part. Now I'm off to bed brimful of all this beauty. And tomorrow I can go on reading it. Thanks, and again thanks for the verses.[1]

Did you say "judge"? If that were so, it would be a crown too heavy for my head. How could I ever presume so greatly?

One may expatiate on beauty; that is not sitting in judgment on it.

I greet you in heartfelt admiration.

Your devoted Friderike Maria W.

[1] Written after Stefan Zweig's first visit to my house in Doebling. He had brought me his volume of short stories *First Experience.* (Erstes Erlebnis)

October, 1912

It would be cowardly to refuse to show you the little novel,[1] since you were good enough to ask to see it. I don't care for it any more because it is too worldly to be worth much for a wide circle of readers. Perhaps I would be less afraid to have this book published if I were better satisfied with it myself. It isn't so much the fear that the novel might be misconstrued as a "Confession." Now, as the date of publication draws near, I am aware of a certain misgiving. Doubtless, through custom and use, I shall eventually lose this feeling, but I am not at all sure that that will be a good thing. I have also been thinking about what you said about our children who will read what we have written in the days to come.

I venture to present you with a silly little piece that was my first literary venture.[2] I really believe it can't be read seriously now. But I was very young then.

Please forgive me for being so taciturn the whole evening (about which I won't write inexpressive words). I was worried about my baby, now, fortunately, back to normal again.

Many greetings from your

Friderike M. Winternitz

1 The novel *Those Who are Dreaming* which appeared in the *Pester Lloyd*.
2 A story whose title, "Love Is the Danger of the Lonely," was taken from Nietzsche's works.

November 12

Dear Doctor Zweig:

Am I condemned to lie here anticipating the pleasure of our next meeting? Or shall I be disappointed, should you have to leave sooner?

Were you angry that I extolled you in my feuilleton in the *Fremdenblatt?* Maybe I should have asked your permission. But I didn't want to bother you—and felt so much like writing it.

If nothing crosses my plans, I'll leave for Germany around November 15. I'll go to Berlin first, then to Hamburg where I hope to see you.

Cordial greetings from your devoted

Friderike Maria Wint

The following bad verses came to me Wednesday evening, inspired, to a certain extent, by the words *Burgtheater* and *Sham Traditionalism.*

They do not serve the poet's word
Or so it seems to me,
But always flaunt themselves.
Delving deep down, they merely disinter themselves.
And if the picture they present
Is scarcely what the poet had intended,
We hardly are aware of that.
For you can murder words more easily than people,
And leave no trace behind,
And then go mincing carelessly away,
Strike up another tune
With viola and shrill flute.
But underneath it all is heard a note
Trembling at first, confused,
That soon becomes a swelling resonance,
A keystone of the poet's throne.
And yet the actor's pose still holds the stage,
His cloak disposed in careful folds

To show his nimble limbs.
Critics applaud and shout:
"The part doth fit him like a glove."

(These words refer to the tradition-bound "hamming" prevalent at that time among the actors at the Court-Theater.)

Berlin, 11/19/1912
(To Berlin)

Dear Doctor Zweig:

After spending a marvelous day in Dresden, I arrived here in excellent spirits and find everything very amusing. I believe the air here is turning somersaults and makes people dodge around like mad so as not to get clouted over the head.

I shan't disrupt your schedule by coming to see you.

Cordial greetings from your devoted

F. M.W.

Grand Hotel Four Seasons
Hamburg, Alster Basin
November 22, 1912

Best thanks for your greeting. I was a little afraid that I had misunderstood you. How I envy the people who will hear you lecture tomorrow. I feel a bit dejected. Yesterday, during *Michael Kramer*[1] I wept. And now, after *Gabriel Schilling's Flight*[2] I am anything but calm.

Is there anything I can do for you at the *Hamburger Fremdenblatt*? Or do you know the editors?

Am looking forward to Tuesday. But please don't pin yourself down too unconditionally.

Cordially,

Fri. Maria W.

1 and 2 Plays by Gerhard Hauptmann.

(Stefan Zweig had asked the stage manager of the Hamburg Playhouse, where his *House at the Seashore* was to be performed, to accompany me to the above-mentioned Hauptmann plays. Zweig begged me to stay away from his lecture, because my presence would make him self-conscious. However, I was to spend the day following the premiere in his company and return with him to Vienna, if that "would be compatible with my domestic duties.")

Hamburg
November 23, 1912

My dear Doctor Zweig:

You are heaping up so much happiness in my heart!

I'll gladly travel with you. (I must be in Vienna on Friday, or at the latest, on Saturday).

Everything shall be as you wish it, even if I should suffer by it. My house? It is truly mine; I am free to do as I wish in it. No Paul Pry or Mrs. Grundy can harass me. I earn my own living and have been entirely independent for a long time. I want you to know this! But I can give you so little. I am so diffident, so shy when I am with you.

I couldn't get to sleep before two o'clock last night, either. I would have liked so much to have looked down on the Alster with you for a few minutes longer. I try, with baited breath, to be no more to you than you wish me to be. But so much at least I long to be, out of the depths of my soul, my whole being.

Friderike Maria W.

(From this point on the letters use the familiar form of address: *Du*.)

Vienna
December 6, 1912

I might have been with you yesterday in spite of everything. Unfortunately, I had not realized how easy it is to make such a wish come true if one only wishes it hotly enough.

I am amazed at myself and much too happy to be self-critical. I only know that it is uncanny how quickly, as if under a very hot sun, much in me has ripened, much that I knew nothing about until now, except as a precocious child might be aware of it. But precocious children are perhaps stupider than other children, because they assume an aura of omniscience, when actually they are merely in a state of self-corrupted innocence.

I see your dear image before me, and I look upon it with tenderness and awe. However you interpret what I have written, be assured you have naught to fear from me. Be it joy or sorrow that you bring me, I shall embrace either joyfully. You needn't spare me. I am strong.

Many thanks for the card. Just read an account of the Munich [1] performance. Oh, why couldn't I have been there?

Fri Maria

1 *The House at the Seashore* had also been performed in Munich, where Stefan had written the postcard.

XIX, Kreindlsgasse 19
Vienna, December 19, 1912

My dear:

Am writing in haste. Come on Saturday if you feel like it and are not too much rushed with Christmas. I was not aware of any unfriendliness. I myself had had a few bad days (extraneous matters) and was probably not very nice either. Please don't think I am reproaching you.

F.M.

(Reality made itself felt. It was decided to put an end to a situation that was too tense to be maintained. Both of us wanted to get away for a time. My little daughter's ill health, moreover, made a change for her advisable in any event.)

1 9 1 3

January 5, 1913

My dear:

I must leave now and perhaps you will phone, though it's almost too late to hope for that. I don't want to bother you today. You can read my letter in the train, when you have more time.

I didn't know yesterday whether I would still be here when you returned. Something is happening inside of me and to me—and who knows where it will lead me? I believe it is one of those *tristesses fécondes* which have their paradoxical origin in a kind of gladness, and perhaps I shall burst the bonds that would otherwise hold me and escape somewhither—where I think I could be yours more completely than I had ever hoped to be—some lonely haunt, without any of the amenities to remind me of people, without a house, alone with my work which will belong to you.

You know how much I wish you joy of your faring forth into the light. May no evil or injustice befall you, no injustice, that is, to the true you. Forgive me for saying this. In the book on Romain Rolland [1] there is a passage (on page 156) that might be applied to you: "Rolland does not instruct, he limits himself to understanding. His power of understanding is profound and marked by the fervent sympathy of a deeply religious soul. (God is Life.) He has a freedom of spirit that preaches no dogmas; and is truly aware that man is a single entity, spirit and flesh, greatness, passion and weakness; and that art reflects man's image."—I wish some woman would write about Rolland and tell all the things men do not discern in him.

The fruit is for the journey, dearest!

Affectionately yours,

F.M.

1 Probably the biography by P. Seipel.

January 6, 1913

For a moment I thought of calling you up myself, but was prevented by the same emotional block. It wasn't that I felt distrustful, because I'd consider it impertinent to be too trusting. So whatever comes will be in the nature of an unhoped-for miracle.

If you own Droste-Huelshoff's [1] *The Christian Year,* look up the poem "On Palm Sunday." "On New Year's Day" is also very beautiful. Occasionally I take refuge in these prayers. These days I find my everyday duties very hard to bear. I'll cry for joy once I am seated in the train.

Will you come?

Tomorrow I'll surely see your dear face. Forgive me if my words are not as calm and reserved as they might be. You, my dearest, I know will forgive and forget.

Your Fri. Maria

1 Annette von Droste-Huelshoff, German poetess.

Bozen, Hotel Greif
January 17, 1913
8:30 in the evening

My dear:

We had an excellent trip.[1] Your fear that the radiators might freeze were quite justified. But an official of the Railroad Ministry (in which my two brothers have important jobs) brought us to the station and installed us in a comfortable compartment. The journey through the snow-covered mountains was marvelous. The Semmering[2] in the moonlight was as bright as day. I might have gone to bed and slept soundly, but I couldn't, being aware of all the beauty outside. I let my big girl stay up and look at the magic splendor which she enjoyed as if it were a fairytale. Pustertal,[3] flooded with sunshine, welcomed us when we woke up: You are enraptured anew every time you see it again, although you may have forgotten it altogether back in the city. The night was very beautiful. When I closed my eyes I dreamed of our last trip together and seemed to become painfully aware again of revolving wheels relentlessly hurrying us to our journey's end. I strained my ears to hear my beloved's breathing. The children's low breathing was inaudible because of the rumbling of the wheels. Bozen lapped us about in gentle breezes, turning damp towards evening. The hotel is homey, but not too comfortable. I think of the two hotels in Germany. Now that I am away, being so seems altogether unreal. What drove me to it, made my leaving not only possible but even imperative?

Tomorrow I'll go up to the Ritten.[4] It's only one hour from here. Your beautiful books will serve to make me less lonely up there. And many thanks for the letter. I took the Bible along. I don't consider it my property, because I'd rather think it still belonged to you, and besides, ever since my childhood, it has somehow been painful for me to accept gifts. This surely is just a bit of the Philistine but I am not yet spiritually free enough to shrug it off—it and a lot of other such notions. Perhaps I never shall be able to.

Read some beautiful passages in Lenau.[5] So much was left out of the biography of him we studied in school. I have had to reconsider a lot of my ideas about him. Do you believe that Sophie, had she known of his illness, would have wanted him any the less? I believe it would merely have added to her happiness, to give herself to him and suffer for his sake. And he would have been justified in accepting her apparent self-sacrifice. A man of Lenau's stature or of his caliber! I have recently been reading some books on eugenics. Are we to breed for healthy bodies only—just a race of healthy animals, and call them human beings? Yet how much greatness has come out of puny bodies that eugenists would never have permitted to be born!

But now I am so sleepy. The last hours of my stay in Vienna were very tiring: saying farewell to my mother and others whose devotion to me is truly touching, a devotion I can't reciprocate in kind (although perhaps sometimes in better kind). Then traveling and getting settled here was exhausting; but the children's gayety made up for it all. Also the baby seems better and happier than she has been for weeks.

Forgive me for bothering you at such length with my affairs. If I could only tell it all to you in person instead of writing. The old houses here are so beautiful. Even after Luebeck.

Affectionate greetings from your

Fri Maria

[1] The party consisted of myself, my two daughters aged three and five, and a nurse who had followed Susi to Vienna from the Munich Sanitarium where the child had spent several weeks.   [2] Mountain-pass near Vienna.   [3] Main Valley of Southern Tyrol.   [4] Mountain resort near Bozen.   [5] German-Hungarian poet who was often discussed by Stefan Zweig and myself. Later we edited the exchange of letters between him and Sofie von Loewenthal.

Bozen, January 18, 1913
9:45 in the evening

My dear:

Just received a letter from the Deutsch-Oesterreichischer Verlag. It was written so eloquently that the editor might as well dispense with authors and write his own books. In a way, I agree with him. I find society novels (and mine might possibly be regarded as such)[1] tiresome, too. In the meantime, Dr. Wengraf has asked me to submit the book to the Westermann Verlag.

Returned from Oberbozen a little while ago. My cheeks are still burning from the mountain air and sun. It is really beautiful up there. I had marshaled all the arguments against making the move, but Schlern, Rosengarten, Latemar and Presanella [2] made an overwhelmingly effective rebuttal, looking down on me from their snow-clad heights gleaming in sunset splendor. The air here is like deliciously pure water and you gulp it up eagerly as if you were terribly thirsty. I imagine I couldn't stand this sort of rapture all the time; it grips and holds me almost against my will. Despite the snow, the forest birds are singing as if it were spring. And the pussy-willows touched the windows of the cable car that carried me up. From time to time the sound of Bozen's church bells breaks through the crystal clear silence. I've rented a small apartment. It will be easy to work up here. Brand Buys (the composer) lives nearby and Hans von Hoffenstal[3] in Maria Himmelfahrt, where the Bozen patricians have their castles—ancient houses with, it is said, magnificent interiors and furnishings. No one who doesn't "belong" is allowed to settle there. These old families considered the railroad an intrusion on their privacy and fought to keep it out of their village.

While drinking a solitary cup of tea, I read from the "Poet's Workshop" and thought that you, too, had heard these words. But I thought also "Oh! Save them from the city's guilt, where all is stale, dull and bewilderment."

I believe Rilke says something like that.

Just said goodnight to my jolly children.—I'll take them up to the mountain heights on Monday.—After which I went to the café to read the papers. As I was glancing at an article about Romain Rolland, a bell-hop comes in and hands me an unaddressed envelope. Inside it there was a card which I enclose, because it might amuse you.[4] At first I tried to refuse to accept the envelope, but he laid it down and disappeared. I let it lie for a time, but finally my curiosity got the better of me and besides the waitress might have picked it up after I left. God knows who this Torero is and why he pretends to know me. There are a lot of people here whom I might suspect of being the author of the Torero note. I opened the note after the half hour had elapsed. Oh José, you lost paradise.

From Monday on my address will be the following: Oberbozen, Villa Holzner. Mail is delivered four times a day. But I don't promise to write that often.

Many greetings to the dweller in the Low Lands from

Fr. Maria

1 The novel *Dream People* which had appeared in the Pester Lloyd.
2 The Dolomite mountain ranges.   3 Tyrolean poet and writer.   4 The

visiting card of a certain José M. who begged for the favor of meeting the "esteemed lady" in half an hour.

Oberbozen
Wednesday, nine in the evening

Your card from the Semmering made me very happy. It is not good to enjoy things that others, with whom one would like to share them, have to forego. I wish you could have had as wonderful a day as the one that has been bright all about us. We drink our fill of light and fresh air! And it never seems to want to get dark these full-moon evenings. I've never seen such a huge moon. It pops up out of the trees, as if by magic, as early as six o'clock, and climbs up into the sky where it hovers pallidly among the equally pallid stars. Rosengarten and Schlern loom up in the distance, clear and bright to my eyes, veiled in the thinnest of silvery clouds. To please the children, who never get enough of my silly tales, I have peopled the mountains all around us with King Laurin and other mountain kings; and now this company of spirits whirls round and round about me and holds me under a faery spell and will not let me go until the rising sun makes loud protest. And then it gets so warm that we can do without our overcoats. When my ski-stick hits a branch in the forest, the snow shower that follows feels wonderfully cool.

Several times a day a handsome black steer is led past our house. Oxen pull wooden sleighs driven by peasants who fit right into the general picture. Today I am sending some snapshots taken up here. Later on you'll get one showing me on my skis, since that's what you wanted to see. Have also copied out my play and shall gladly send it. But as a matter of fact, I can't send anything, or anyway only to the Kochgasse: for I don't know just where you live. Actually I think of you always as being on a mountain top in your beloved yellow fur coat, which I sometimes look for up here.—Suddenly just now an ugly flame of jealousy blazed up within me, because others look upon you when I can't. No one looks at me here, which rejoices my sluggish fish-blood.

Affectionately yours,

Maria

My dear:

So now I have read almost all of your books. I have also finished four volumes of the Romain Rolland.[1] I'm eager to know what you will write about them. I find their psychological insight quite perfect. But the ferocity of point of view at times frightens me. Christophe doesn't endear himself to me by kicking people and making an uproar. And then: *il n'est pas intelligent.* His genius seems too much a physiological phenomenon, and, therefore, I can't admire it for its own sake, whatever fruitfulness it might develop. I worship genius that is the man himself, his very self, through and through. And to such a man, such a God (for what else is God?) all things are permissible.

The place where I live is called Maria Schnee. Maria Himmelfahrt is even more beautiful. Yesterday I went there again. Did I tell you that Hoffensthal wrote a novel about it? He sometimes goes out walking around here and almost scares me away. The thing is that he wears a light-colored fur coat very much like yours, which I can't forgive him for. Who knows if otherwise we might not have become acquainted? We are the only two human beings for miles around who could understand each other. He sometimes looks at me with a sort of intense astonishment out of bright childlike eyes set in a razor-sharp, handsome face. A friend had asked me to remember him to Hoffensthal. But isn't it more wonderful just to pass each other like this in this vast, snow-white solitude? To be able to do it!

In Maria Himmelfahrt the Ritten suddenly becomes a park with noble trees. It is as though nature had built a terrace from which the Marmolata [2] can be viewed whose graceful turrets rise in the far distance. Deep down in the valley one occasionally hears a shot or a rumbling as of an avalanche. Maybe it's the Vienna train which perchance passes you on your way to Baden [3] for a Sunday outing. My thoughts are always wanting to take wing—and yet I must tell you of Maria Himmelfahrt. Here there are about a dozen huge, weatherproof, patrician houses encircled by galleries. All the shutters are down. Only the church is open. I like to go inside, partly to get warm, and partly because I love country churches. The holy water is frozen, and the Saints on the walls seem to shiver. Especially one pale woman à la Tiepolo. Nevertheless, I feel warm up in there. Yesterday it was already dusk. The eternal light in the red chalice sparkled like a ruby or a drop of blood. I am always upset, when I'm in a church, to see it flicker so, seem so bewildered. The eternal light should be steady, unvarying. But though it flickers, it never, never goes out. After leaving the church I walked about among the baronial mansions. The sun dials, on which Saints are painted in Filippo Lippi colors, cast no shadows. But the Presanella still loomed up on the horizon in a rose-tinted haze.

Good morning, dearest!

Fri.

(Postcard showing the Rittenberg railway with Dolomites in the background.)

[1] *Jean Christophe.*   [2] Mountain range.   [3] A resort town near Vienna.

2/6/1913

My next greetings will come from Meran where I'll settle down shortly. I am looking forward to seeing a place so much beloved by you.

I don't know when I am going to write another long letter. Here my pen is just as obstreperous as I am myself. The *Lamb* [1] has departed hence and is far away and I can't feel a trace of it in me now. Perhaps it has stayed behind on your mantel and you absent-mindedly run your fingers through its wooly coat now and then while reading. Or maybe it has taken to the mountains.

I kiss you lightly on the forehead.

M.

[1] Stefan called me his "lamb". For almost thirty years he kept a tiny wooden lamb I had given him, on his desk.

(Card with view of Wolfsgrube and Schlern.)

(Written in French)

Thursday

I am taking your good letter that came this morning along with me to Meran. It came just in the nick of time to give me

18

some comfort and gladden my soul so downcast because my little daughter has lost so much weight up here, at Oberbozen. I hope she will improve in the valley whither I go in search of the sunshine you left behind there. It will be a pilgrimage with two objectives, then. I'll write you from there. I am in love with the place even before I see it. Thanks for the books. I'll return the ones I have finished. I read "Nju" and shall discuss it in my next letter.

Fr. M.

Meran, February 13, 1913

I thought that I wouldn't write you for a long time. If you are just "someone or other," as you say, then to whom should I write? "Someone or other" is not going to get any letters from me. I am writing to my dear, my good sincere one, my true love, and if my letter does not reach him, doesn't wake him up, then "someone or other" won't read it either. Dearest, I don't want you to be good, but I want you to be "you." For you, for that "you" I would die here and now—I know not what is to come hereafter. I believe in "eternal love" just as I believe in God, Christ, Beethoven, Rembrandt, the beauty of the Meran landscape and—you. But I don't know what is to be. "Someone or other" is as indifferent to me as Monsieur Tel et Tel. Now "someone or other" may go on reading this or not, just as he pleases.

Yesterday I was at Castle Labers.[1] I walked upstairs and downstairs, rode in the elevator to the top of the ancient tower, and looked out of the windows at the view you looked upon every morning when you opened your eyes. And I dreamed that you were with me in one of the many rooms. Perhaps I was actually in the one where you lived at a time when you were still far away, quite out of my life. The rampart facing the town is covered with flowers that have the fragrance of freesias. But once they have been picked, the fragrance is soon gone. Yet it is still with me. God has given me this gift: nothing I have ever had is ever lost to me.

Your F.M.

1 A castle near Meran where Stefan Zweig had stayed at various times.

I don't know if and where my letter will reach you, but I want
to send my sincere sympathy to your friend whose sorrow
touches you so closely. And then I must tell you how much I
rejoice in the thought that you will soon be with your great
friend.[1] A few days ago, when I wanted to feel closer to you,
I went into a bookstore and ordered *Rembrandt*.[2] I know a
good deal about him, have delved deeply into his works. I
thought the book was marvelous. And then to know that these
were your very own words! Dearest, dearest: work and write,
then I shall never be poor. And many other people will be
enriched through you too, even though you won't know that
they are, as you do know I am.

What you mentioned in regard to helping me with my
own books has made me quite happy. And I don't want you to
get over it.[3] I have come to realize that it doesn't matter in
the least whether one's external life is a bit more or less difficult. We create our own measure of happiness and grief. One's
outer life and what one does in it, and disregarding what happens to one from outside, is just a seeming, without significance, provided one is steadfast and secure within. And
my work? I was driven to it from childhood on. But when I
became conscious of this drive, I realized it was a flood-gate
holding back torrents that otherwise might engulf me, against
my will. Yet I know that I would be stricken dumb, if you
wished it: even though it is you who have reawakened in me
the urge to work.

My days run along smoothly here. The baby is much
better. Today is her birthday, which evokes many memories
of the past, but none of them unhappy.—Now there is this,
my happiness, for which the gods will not envy me or hold me
in their debt.—I bought her a beautiful new baby carriage;
she looks like a little princess when she is in it. And she is so
happy with her new toys. I gave them to her yesterday ahead of
time because it was such a wonderful day [4] for me, and I
wanted to share my joy with others. They sent her a doll from
Vienna which she takes to bed with her. She takes another pet
to bed with her, poor little baby, the hotwater bottle to warm
her tummy. She loves it, because it feels so good. Before she
goes to sleep, she asks: "Is 'he' here with me?"

Alix says funny things too. "Muschi" (as they call me) "what kind of children has the sun?" She knows beforehand what I am going to say, but wants to hear it again. "The stars." She beams with delight. "And who's the wife of the wind?" Now I am a little embarrassed, because I had married the moon to the sun, and the earth was the grandma. Of course, I could have cast the wind in the role of a friend. But I said: "The wind is just an uncle who's got no wife." "But where does he live?" "Nowhere! That's just it. Otherwise he wouldn't be the wind rushing around all the time." She seems to find this a little hard to believe, so she doesn't answer.—And so life goes on around here. Sometimes I read to her from the Bible, your Bible, generally while she is eating, as a reward for doing it quickly and nicely.—I am telling you all these stories because it makes me so happy that you are interested in the children.

I want to thank you for that and also for the play. I have begun *Helena's Return*,[5] although at the moment I am still reveling in *Dans la Maison*.[6] That a man can feel such things! "Now at last I am saved from myself and can forget I have a body!" Thank you again! It's a thrilling sentence. I understand why you admire him so much and I include you in my wondering admiration.

I wish you much much pleasure on your long journey.

Yours, M.

1 Verhaeren.   2 Stefan Zweig's translation of Verhaeren's *Rembrandt*. 3 His unwillingness to talk about me to others.   4 I had received a letter making me especially happy.   5 Drama by Verhaeren.   6 One volume of *Jean Christophe*, by Romain Rolland.

2/27, at night
My beloved:
I can't say anything to you about your letter, dearest. Words are too loud. I can't answer you with words, even in the silent hours of the night.

Sent you some fruit to remind you of the fruit we enjoyed on our trip together. Probably by now you have spread your wings a bit. I wish you blessed with favorable gales. I shall seek out that far country, too, in my thoughts that shall be shod in velvet, lest they sound too loud in your ear. How

I wish they could now and again fetch you back into my heart.

When shall we see each other again? I could return in April, if I knew you were back by then. I am a little afraid of this home-coming of mine. Everything would be easier if you were already in Vienna or Baden, even if I didn't see you.— I finished *Helena's Return*. It seemed to me as though at the end the poet had a hard time getting away from Helena and the struggle to get rid of her made him unjust to her. Was it that she didn't understand Zeus? I had to think of an analogy: "Wotan's Farewell," although I don't altogether know why. Yesterday I read *The Cloister*.[1] Don Marc, Aljoscha, Olivier: how I love these gentle men. But Jean Christophe gets to be more and more wonderful, too. Yet he frightens me a little. He isn't a brother to me any more.

These words live within me and always come back to me:

Oh Thou art gentle, fond, dearly beloved.
How infinitely, even in tempestuous torment,
I must hold thee dear.
Dost thou mistrust me then? Faith
And infinite goodness thou givest me to behold.
Thou makest me to harken unto holy voices.[2]

That is what he says; how beautiful it is.

My novel, which is getting to be quite voluminous, will be done in two or three weeks. I almost dread having to part with it. Dearest, now all my thoughts merge into one fervent wish that you may go forward in good spirits toward more and more happiness.

Ever your own Fr. M.

[1] A drama by Verhaeren translated by Stefan Zweig.   [2] From a drama by Verhaeren.

Meran, March 7, 1913

My dear:

As often heretofore, when I've had a letter from you, the day seemed to light up, as though the sun had hastened to anticipate you. And how sorely I needed it yesterday!

I hardly dare write you and do so only because I hope that you, with your amazing vitality, will not be too much upset by my bit of gloomy news. You can see for yourself that I am hardly able to write, my hand still shaky from the fright I had. My dear, think of it: I almost lost my baby! Her condition is still serious. But this morning there was a turn for the better. And now she is back with her toys. And today she smiled a few times and kissed me. It was pneumonia; and though it lasted only one day, the fever didn't abate right away and exhausted her so much that her poor little heart was beating madly in her breast and—oh, I can't describe it to you.

But imagine, dearest: these days have given me redoubled strength, nay, multiplied it a hundredfold. In my desperation I searched for ways in which I could help the child. I kept calm, although fully aware of the danger, the greatest I have known in all my life. You wouldn't believe that a child could be so wonderful. Even while she was in agony she was patient, intuitive and seemed to be begging me to forgive her. She never forgot her baby-pride, her compulsion to observe a certain decorum, despite her weakness and exhaustion. She bore herself so bravely that she might be an example to great heroes. And she is so good and grateful. People, many people, say that a child is its mother's flesh and blood. But flesh and blood are as nothing in comparison to a child so much beloved—. I made my body a cradle in which the child could rest while I walked her back and forth through the long hours of the night; and I came to the door that opens out on the balcony and looked up at the stars in the sky and implored them to help me, and then, lo and behold, in my anguish, my thoughts went out to you, dearest. I thought again, as I have often thought before, that these same stars shone down on you too as you walked buoyant and carefree—such was my hope— through the streets of Paris. And sometime soon you'll tell me about it. Even your postcards were so comforting.

I have a good physician, a simple, humane person who is sincerely interested in his patients and doesn't regard them as guinea pigs. I quickly got rid of the one recommended to me in Vienna. He talked nonsense and would surely have failed me in a crisis. Our present doctor is a native, no fancy resort physician. When he comes at night, as he did yesterday, it seems as if an angel were coming into the room.—Apparently nobody will be arriving from Vienna before Easter. Maybe it's for the best. "Let this heart partake alone, Of its sorrow, of its bliss." [1] In this hour of my distress, I need only my own strength, a good doctor and my love for you.

Forgive me for writing in this foolish, or rather, confused fashion. I haven't had any sleep or fresh air for a long time. This letter is my first breathing spell. Susi is sleeping peacefully beside me.

It is good to become aware of one's own strength. Weakness seems to me the most terrible danger of all. Weakness terrifies me more than anything else. You are just now, believe me, finding a certain release, as you always do, in travel (after all foreign cities may be regarded as natural phenomena too) and are conscious of the strength that is in you. I have always sensed this happy strength beneath your outer "crust." I realize you feel safe inside your shell. I quite understand now how, having been tried by the ordeal of fire, one becomes inured to every adversity. Then come what may, we shall be steeled against it.

Don't write me unless you feel like it—even if I were to tell you how much your letters mean to me. It does me good to know you are happy and cheerful.

Today I can't send you much sunshine, although for me the skies are bright, brighter than they have been these last frightful days. Of this sunshine, though it be only within me, myself, I can send you a rich store.

Be gay in your beautiful city!

Your faithful Friderike Maria.

[1] From a poem by the German poet Eduard Moericke.

AS THE SWALLOW

As the swallow swings in silvery circles,
Flashing across the drowsing waters,
And with thirsty beak rips tremulous rings in the gleam-
  ing surface,
Liquid tracks that make no wounds,
But only lightly stir the waters, lightly agitate the waters,
Oh, so my silent thoughts,
In the lonely twilight hours,
Lean down,

24

Oh, thou who art far away,
And draw close to thee.

Softly gilded by secret ardor,
Swallows of longing, to bring me solace,
With their soft wingings
Brush against my heart waiting in the silent darkness.
And I am filled with ecstasy, feeling them flutter down,
   alighting.
Joy and sadness thrill through me,
And I tremble, tremble with sweet thoughts
Of thee.

(This poem, sent to me by Stefan Zweig from Paris, was included, in 1924, in the anthology of *Collected Poems* published by the Insel Verlag.)

Meran, March 12

My dear:
   You unfeeling? You who can look deep into the heart of things? How grateful I am to you for giving me of your warmth. I have had much, oh, very much kindness bestowed upon me. But how paltry that was compared with your kindness. I used to believe I was altogether withdrawn within myself. I hardly dare tell you how now my whole being has unfolded to your warmth. Don't pay heed to what I'm telling you, dear, lest you feel obliged to show me a consideration I never asked for. And now, with nerves horribly lacerated by the black hand that reached out for my child, I have come to the same sorry pass as old Baumert in *The Weavers*[1] who couldn't eat anything at all when they set dishes full of food before him. I must take my happiness in very humble doses. Not that I am afraid of it. "Il est inhumain d'étouffer une partie de soi-même." Yes, I realize how full my life is and how you irradiate it. My life, dedicated to you and my beloved children, is very beautiful. And I can go right on living it. The visitors I expect to have at Easter won't engage me too much and won't stay at my house. I needn't give up my maidenly way of life, if I may so misuse this dear, good word. You see, my dear, how self-centered I am. But I am conscious of it and because I am, it does me good, or almost, to stand alone in grief and anguish. How much alone I was you may surmise from the fact that

25

there was some annoyance because the reports I sent were considered too pessimistic. After all, the child recovered so quickly. —But when the two physicians were alone with me, the old man called in as consultant said to me: "Dear lady, it'll be a miracle if you save the child." Don't think I am blaspheming, but I was ready to work miracles. And now there is a rosy glow on the child's cheeks. You can forgive people who are far removed from the event, for being optimistic, for making little of a critical situation, for trying to reassure. But he who has to battle through to victory or defeat (which I was spared through God's grace) must face the truth, must know the enemy.

I spoke the word "God" and you frequent anarchists' meetings? What goes on there? Do they entertain bids by bomb manufacturers and the like? You have no idea how stupid I am. And Romain Rolland, is he as wonderful as his work? Am reading *Les Amies*. Is there anything in these books that he hasn't touched upon? Will he have anything more to say?

Please, tell me about yourself. I am possessed by a conviction that you are happy; and I am too. And nothing, nothing is unimportant. You have the whole world and I but a little corner of my own, but my dreams fare forth from it and my affection reaches out to you.

Ever your own F.M.

1 Drama by Gerhard Hauptmann.

An answer came:

A FEW VERSES

A few verses at thine awakening,
Dearest, take for thy day!
To make a happy woman happier
Will be their sole excuse.
For they are too earnestly labored
And too carefully calculated
Instead of flaming, instead of glowing,
Instead of leaping wildly like the wind,
Instead of wrapping thee in flames of passion
Till thou, dearest, heart and hand,

Brow and lips, breast and cheeks
Art incandescent in ecstatic conflagration.

(Included in Zweig's *Collected Poems,* Insel Verlag, 1924)

(In answer to gay letters from Paris:)

Palm Sunday

Just received your card, my dear. I am as happy as you thought I would be, and perhaps even more so, though I am sorry that I had to write you such gloomy letters. Thanks for the book you say you are sending me.[1] I came across this poetess while cramming for my teacher's examinations. But I lost sight of her when I threw out all those dusty old textbooks. Affectionate greetings and wishes for ever greater happiness.

F.M.

[1] Poems by Marceline Desbordes-Valmore. Later Stefan Zweig wrote an essay about her and together we edited an anthology of her poems and letters. My part of the project consisted in selecting the material and translating some of the poems and letters (Insel Verlag, 1927).

Easter, 1913

Oh, my dear—what have you done to me with your *marvelously* beautiful book.

I have been reading it and am still reading it, and I am all atremble. For it has made me look back into the past—and into the future, too. Perhaps it would have done me more good had I been alone [when I read it]. But now my visitors are here. In the past three days I have come to understand many things better than in seven years [of my first marriage]. Freedom, the right to be alone and keep the children, all this was given me without my having to fight for it, without a word of opposition. Many days and hours labored on my behalf, without my knowing it, to unravel this tangled web. Now it will be easier to go back [to Vienna] for there is nothing to constrain me. Since all differences have now been resolved, I'll be able to do what I think right for the children. As yet I can scarcely realize how much this mighty breath of freedom means to me. Is this because I no longer yearn for it and am content as I am now that you have given me happiness? Happiness is a homeland unrealised, yet dares not ask for more.

My beloved, I'll write you soon again, in lighter vein, gay and refreshed.

Each day slips lightly from my shoulders,
Wings burgeon and turn me to new flights.

Rejoice, for these are the days when once upon a time blood was shed for love of Man and there was a resurrection.

Your faithful Fr. M.

To Friderike Maria von Winternitz
Neuhäuselgut, Obermais, Meran (Tirol)
We are lunching together and send our greetings

Emile Verhaeren   Stefan Zweig
Romain Rolland
R. M. Rilke   L. Balzagette

March 26, 1913

My dear:

I believe I have already thanked you for your last postcard with the many beloved signatures. It's odd, isn't it, but somehow I can't visualize you in Paris [1] just now. Nevertheless, I'll send this letter there, although I'm not sure it will get to you.

I am alone again, and so can go back to my reading and my work. All the various problems have been cleared up and settled.

I have just been reading a beautiful passage in Flaubert's letters: "Sometimes, on my great Sundays, I succumb to a sort of resplendence, exaltation, that sends an awesome shudder through my whole being, a soul-state apparently so much above and beyond that of everyday life that fame becomes meaningless and even happiness superfluous." He also says: "I have flung myself into mad emotional gymnastics. I find satisfaction in contending against my senses and in tormenting my heart. I have spurned proffered earthly bliss. In the fullness of my strength and pride I passionately commanded my two hands to uproot all that was human in me. I wanted to make the tree with its lambent green foliage a naked column and far up on the column's top I wanted to raise an altar and on the altar— I know not what sacred fires."

28

How curious: The hero in my novel is this kind of man.

My little Susi is well, or at least very happy and merry. She is gaining a little weight. The doctor still comes every day, though there's no need for it. But I don't know how to tell him so without hurting his feelings because I am so greatly indebted to him. And there has grown up a personal relationship between us and so he might feel doubly hurt. He doesn't examine the child any more, just sits and chats in his Tyrolean way, looking so happy that it seems cruel to upset him. But the trouble is that the child considers herself a patient as long as he keeps coming.

Dearest, let me know where you are. I have a feeling as if something different had come into your environment, that there is something different in you.—If I only knew that you are happy.

Your F.M.

P.S. Am reading Marceline Valmore's poems [2] again and again. I feel it would be blasphemous for me to translate them. And did she look out upon the same garden as you?

1 Actually Stefan Zweig had left Paris for a few days before returning to Austria. 2 Marceline Desbordes-Valmore had lived in the Palais Royal whose gardens could be glimpsed through the windows of the Hotel Beaujolais where Stefan Zweig was staying.

To Dr. Stefan Zweig
15, Rue de Beaujolais, Paris
March 31, 1913

My dear:

I won't be writing you any more before daybreak, for I don't wake up now till later on in the morning. I sleep soundly and when I wake up feel happy through and through. It might be otherwise if I were not sure that you were happy too. Couldn't you try, just a bit, to hold on to your happiness? Can't you think of Vienna as only a sort of way-station, a stopover for as long as you need to be there, to enjoy its beauty; you regard it, as you have said, as a sort of carnival. Yet, I believe you could make beauty grow out of beauty. Now summer is upon us. Many of the tourists who disfigure the landscape will be gone by then. And the autumn! How much you'll like it here in Meran! I so much enjoy telling you about my favorite walks. Yesterday I was in Saltaus in the Passeier. The forest lay there veiled in a haze of birch blossoms. The white crocus, tenderest of all spring flowers, was in bloom. And far below, the Passer, swollen by spring floods, rushed along foaming white. The mountains loom above the green hills in the foreground, high up in the sun-drenched sky, dazzling white from the recent snowfall. Dearest, you will discover yourself in every tree, every mountain-silhouette, every lonely cross-road, every meadow. For I have felt you and embraced you in everything I behold here. I dream of coming back in the fall; surely this is a dream whose realization no brambles of the impossible will thwart. Nor would Rolland be alien to me in this landscape. I am reading the last volume of *Jean Christophe,* who has been at my side all the time like a real live person. I also have read *The Insulted and the Injured* [1] and am pleased that you love it too. The human element is so powerful in Dostoievski that one can do without the showy, ornate phrases with which other writers so often intoxicate us as with rare music. His wonderful goodness stems not from a sensitive soul's weakness, but from virility, from strength which has a compassionate affinity for the weak, for the child. It is all so infinitely beautiful! And then this way of telling a story: how he manages to find and expose the soul of everything that happens, yet never plays the psychologist.

You know how glad I am to tell about the children. We are very happy together. Susi rejoices in the sun that we hadn't seen these last few days. On seeing it again, she said: "Me glad dat sun make shine." When she babbles such sweet baby talk, one must keep a straight face—otherwise she gets angry. It's really important to take her seriously. And Alix is so nice and tanned! I was offered a log cabin near Labers for the autumn. It would be tempting to give the children such a beautiful home. My present plan is to leave here on the 21st and break the journey at the Semmering. It would be wonderful to see you before the dust of Vienna beclouds my inner being again.

Go on having a good time; and remember I would love to hear about it.

Your Fri.

1 Dostoievski.

Dr. Stefan Zweig
General Delivery, Salzburg
End of April, 1913

Just received an undeservedly large sum of money from the *Pester Lloyd*. It must be the fee for my review of your playlet. I am ashamed to exploit you for money.

I wanted to let you hear from me before your arrival in Vienna. I have no idea whether you'll like my novel entitled *Wilgefortis*.[1] It is an agonizing thing and it tortures me. And the chapter in which I described near-insanity was a warning to me. My nerves were on fire and I only stopped writing at cock-crow, and I was more dead than alive.—Fortunately my nerves are back to normal, regular horses' nerves. The last few weeks have proved what I am made of, which is so much gained, and I can say goodbye to these weeks with a lighter heart because I am sure that what I have gained will stay with me.

Spring came as a surprise. After all, there was warmth and sunshine before. But all that was only a dim promise. Have you ever been in Meran in the spring? The air is full of fragrance till late at night and the birds' singing seems to well up out of the earth. Spring ought not to be so beautiful unless two can enjoy it together. I was pleased by what you said about your work, because I had had a shy impulse to ask you what you were doing. I often yearn to behold you soaring in the air free as a bird (not an aviator).

I send you my affectionate greetings. Write me only as little or as much as you want to.

Fr.M.

1 Was published under the title *The Call of the Homeland.*

Dr. Stefan Zweig
Vienna, Kochgasse 8
Semmering, Hotel Panhans
April 26, 1913

My dear:

Because their grandfather wished it, I sent the children to him. Now I must act the "unattached lady traveler," which is quite nice, here in your bailiwick. Thank you so much for the news from Salzburg. As always, I hope you are happy.

Affectionately your F.M.

My dear:

It is late, but I must sit down, and write you, even if that's all I have to say. Though there is something else, something I've been worrying about for an entire chilly day (alas, my southern sun).

You said, when you phoned, that something unpleasant had happened. Can't I help? Dearest, whatever it may be— I can't envisage all the dread possibilities—I surely could help. You have no idea how strong I am in my weakness. And don't believe I shall always be asking you to help me. Don't be annoyed with me for telling you this. I have been wrestling with many a problem, and do not tell you why, because if I did, I might appear to you in too favorable a light. I can keep you in the dark about the "worst" in me only if I do the same with regard to my "best." But my dear, whatever may happen, I am not at all afraid of life. Most people are afraid to abandon themselves completely to their emotions because they have a sort of fear that then they may lose their identities. But how marvelous I find this losing oneself and then being reborn! It is wonderful to go through the metamorphoses that molecules have gone through in their millennial wanderings.

The days since my return have been beautiful. I had no idea that so many people were still so fond of me.

Dearest, I am reading a marvelous book: *The Idiot*; [1] I am reading it in a sort of white heat of interest. Do you remember the peasant woman, Marie and the children? "The soul is healed through children."

Couldn't I be one of the gushing students who will be listening to you? [2]

Will you call up? I am looking forward to it.

Yours, Fri.

[1] Dostoievski.   [2] Refers to a lecture Stefan Zweig was going to deliver.

Sunday night

This evening, my dear, I saw you in Prinz Eugen Street. You were carrying a book in your hand as you walked along briskly in the twilight. I don't know why tears welled up in my eyes at your sudden apparition.

My dear, since coming home I am as one transfigured. And not even ashamed of the graceless high spirits which you unleashed in me.—I must and want to be good for your sake.

I kiss your temples and eyes.

Fri

May 11, 1913

My dear:

The evening at the theater was disappointing. I had had a very trying day. You said I shouldn't rely too much on you. It hurt me a little to hear you say that. But I don't want to make even my feeling of gratitude to you a prop to lean on, because I don't want to seem to be making any demands whatsoever on you. You said we should meet toward the end of the week. I shall keep my time free for you.

June, 1913

From Dostoievski:

"For everything is like an ocean. All things flow and touch each other."—"If you are penitent, you love; and if you love, you are God's child."—"Love is such an invaluable treasure that one may buy the whole world with it and with it redeem not only one's own sins but also those of strangers. So go in peace and do not be afraid."

Read the poems by Petzold [1] and was stirred to my very depths. If I tell you how such thoughts and imagery affect me, you will understand much in me that you might otherwise deem petty. You who rate Dostoievski so high must understand what I mean. I have always felt, with utter conviction, that we have no right to anything, that we have no right to anything at all save the bare necessities. I see quite clearly now how I came to this conclusion. Much that I have read in Dostoievski has contributed to this insight. And now that you are preoccupied with Dostoievski's God-concept, it will become clear to you too. He always contended that "earthly bread must be rejected for the sake of heavenly bread." Yet nature had endowed him with an extraordinary capacity for the enjoyment of earthly bread. Only a man who masters himself every hour of the day, who can every hour smother the thousand conflagrations in his heart, only he, whatever his station, can make his soul capable of self-denial, greatness and fruitful works. And only such a man can grasp the whole misery and the whole gladness of the world.

My dear, those who seek God in the clouds will always go astray. It is easier to worship Him as an incorporeal being than to realize the truth that we can wound Him in every living creature.

I've always longed to set mankind, myself included, free, to live the better life; it's been my consuming passion.

My dear, you fetched me down out of the rarefied atmosphere in which I dwelt, because you loved the human being in me no less than the secret resoluteness and will power. You are the only really selfless person I have ever met. Never forget, my dear, that I know who you are; especially don't forget it when you think you have done something wrong. Don't keep telling yourself that the simple human being in you is irretrievably lost. Just be patient! It is not right to give up anything as lost.

I had to tell you all this because I remembered it so clearly when I thought about Dostoievski and God. A man so tormented must have been a demon—but an angel too. Yet there must also have been antarctic moments in his life (Stavrogin)[2]. I have often felt that he pushed his works to such towering heights merely as a query reaching up to God, God whose being he explored exhaustively—if it were possible to exhaust infinity—more exhaustively than the often cunning, shallower Bible. Wonderfully poignant is the desperate longing of his people for help, literally a wild outcry, and their need to be loved. And what moves me most is the pride, the unwillingness to *take*.

Consider what the common people meant to him and you will understand how stupendous was his artistic integrity. He made it clear—and always greatly—that art is religion realized in flesh and blood, as it were, that its ecstasy is prayer: "And ever be the sage and the inspirer of ecstasy."

My dear, I would like to go on talking to you for hours. Don't you understand, then, why I can't bear to be prevented from doing so?

Your L. . . .

[1] Alphons Petzold, the workingman's poet.   [2] A character in Dostoievski's novel *The Possessed*.

34

June 1913

Stefan, dearest:

I have just been drinking in the last word of your story.[1]
It seemed to me as if I were reading with a thousand eyes and
my whole soul. My dear, the end, after the passage when he
comes home and goes to the child, is so beautiful, it inspires
religious reverence. The letter to the sister is also beautiful,
the way it dissolves and like an exhalation is absorbed into the
spring air. The beginning, at least the second part of it, is perhaps not quite alive enough. Your present mood's tempo would
be better able to express this sultriness before the storm. Yet,
for the sake of the marvelous ending (how unique that he finds
death on his beloved's lips) you shouldn't let the story moulder
in your desk drawer as it has since the year when it was first
published.

Be thanked for—yourself.

Affectionately your Fri

[1] The story *Scarlet Fever* was never published in book form.

I am very happy. I know now that the time will come
when something I create will bring you joy. And knowing this
has ended all my fretting about the meaning of my life.

I am going to Baden [1] tomorrow. Next week I shall
spend in Duernstein [2] and invite you to come along with me.
I am eager to behold again the wide river rolling slowly along
and the old buildings dreaming in the sunshine, cloisters and
gardens and the life aloof from the world, the Bibles and
manuscripts in Melk [3] and the saints' books with their naively
painted illumination.

Devotedly your Fr. M.

[1] I had begun my preparation to move from Vienna to Baden, this was to
mark the end of my old life.   [2] A town on the Danube, famous for the
castle in which Richard Lionheart was incarcerated during the crusades.
[3] A Benedictine Convent on the Danube.

Dr. Stefan Zweig
Hotel Hochschneeberg near Puchberg, Lower Austria
June 1913

My dear:

I was surprised indeed to find your little novella when
I returned from Baden late last night. Though little is hardly

35

the right word because there is a fire in it whose flames flare up beyond all limitations of space. The title is beautiful. You have captured the moon's dream-like, nocturnal, weird and somehow almost criminal essence. Its fading away into day is described most effectively at the end. And now I must tell you something. It is true that the same fire burns in all your work; but do you realize that it has never burned so brightly or so profoundly illumined the heart of passion as in this novella? One comes away from reading it as if awakening from a frenzied yet exalted dream. This creature's grotesque figure confronts or rather cowers before us like something misshapen out of an old Dutch painting. But what greatness! Not moral greatness for he will not forgive her for being so totally lost, but only for her body's sake. He knows and hopes that she—and she only—can and will lift the burden of guilt from his soul. He clings to his victim; this clinging has something of the murderer in it, a murderer who constantly returns to the scene of his crime. Redemption by propinquity, not being able to tear oneself away—in this there is more of eternity and faith than in all the oaths of the world sworn at dead of night, and this loathing of money, that makes her shudder, shakes her physically. And these passions—and that is the wonder of it— are never brutish, but flare up out of man's sacred depths where the soul is most vulnerable. Your eye has perceived it all; how wonderful you are!

"The street . . . was all night and sky"—that's how you describe it when he leaves the house. But then you have different, quite different words and images to hold us entranced and take us into the broad spaces of your real dream. At times, the leaping flames flare up beyond the framework of the story. It is not so well rounded nor is there the usual even ground-swell of sentences; perhaps in the beginning the street imagery piles up with too much repetition—but then I had to think of the Niedergasse in Hamburg, that kind of street, and my impressions of it. I'd like to say a lot more, but have been interrupted just now.

Unless you write or phone, I expect to see you Friday morning.

In haste—many thanks.

Affectionately, Fr. Maria

(The Hochschneeberg, which could be reached by a funicular railway was one of Stefan Zweig's favorite haunts when he wanted to work without being disturbed, although he often invited friends to visit him there. He had finished the story *Moonlit Street* while at this mountain-top resort and sent it to me at once.)

September 17, 1913
Baden near Vienna

My dear:

Thanks for the hurriedly written Berlin postcard. Fuerstenhof! How it recalled those November days of last year!

Things are very satisfactory here. Up till yesterday my hours were crammed full of work. But your servant was most helpful. If you ever should have to move, everything could be left to him. Today the whole place is in order. I hope you will like it. Also the children are very happy.

Will you come soon? Perhaps on Friday? And stay overnight? On sunny days the mornings are wonderfully clear.

Affectionately, Fri. M.

Dr. Stefan Zweig
Meran-Obermais, Southern Tyrol
Labers Castle
Baden, October 21, 1913

My darling:

You wanted to know how things were with me. The simple fact is that, without you, I am as frightened as a child in a dark room. I mean a child to whom the dark had been evil. I knew you were leaving, but was happy about it. How I have savored the gayety of your Paris letters. Yet when you said "Saturday" on the phone, my selfish ego felt as if thrust through its wicked, ungrateful heart. My one excuse is: I thought you would be gone much longer.

I don't want you to feel fettered or tied down in the slightest degree in anything you like to do. And I wouldn't have told you all this, had not my selfishness, this mortal fear of not hearing your voice, given way to my happiness at knowing you happy. And you can image how my joy was heightened by your card from Franzensfeste.[1] Here from my windows I can see the trains winding like golden worms through the night. I can tell what sort of train each is by the different way their engines puff and pant. I recognized yours before seeing it. It was a rather long train—and suddenly the engine seemed plunged in glowing steam and reared up like a fiery steed. . . . And so it vanished from my sight. The tiny golden streaks of the windows—one of them was yours—pursued me even in my sleep. My dear, don't call it sentimentality. I am just savoring my emotions to the last drop.—The morning and forenoon were very beautiful. I visualized every scene you now behold. And, undoubtedly, your joy was boundless. I saw you arriving, driving up the familiar road, saw the place where the roads intersect only two minutes from my house, the path to Labers, the path that always recalls your image to my mind. Am I still dwelling there? Yes, surely, except that I am no longer waiting for you there. You have arrived and are driving up the mountain to your castle.

So, my dear, I am with you again. Hope you found everything as you had expected and even more beautiful.— Forgive me for having talked so much of myself.

Rejoice in the blessed sun which now shines with twice its customary radiance upon your

M.

P.S. Just received your card. Many thanks.

[1] Town in Tyrol from which Stefan Zweig had written.

My dear:

Many, many thanks. Your lovely, good apples have just arrived. The children and I were so happy. While biting into them, we seemed to be taken back to our home of last winter. For down yonder is home, isn't it, even for us who have not, like you, a bit of southern sun in their veins. How happy I would be down there if you were near by, or if I but knew you near. I had rather not try to imagine it. I would rather try to make it come true.—I was encouraged by what you said about the pleasure it would have given you to take me along with you. And this would not have been an extravagance; for I have received some money from "Auntie" Voss [1] for my feuilleton on Fanny Elsler.[2]

Also continued with my other translations, so as not to fall behind.

Affectionately, Fri

[1] Berlin Vossische Zeitung.   [2] Famous dancer of the early 19th century.

My dear:

Something has happened to me. A friend has died who meant a great deal to me. I can't grasp it yet. All these days I had been so sleepless and frightened. It is as if he had been calling to me.—How did it happen? Out of a clear sky. Four days' illness. I hadn't seen him since August. So it came as a terrible shock, soul-shattering, like everything that's incomprehensible, irrevocable. And—I hardly dare write this—I had a premonition about it. That's the uncanny part of it.

He was so handsome and so full of strength!

F.

My dear:

Just received your good letters. You have no idea how much they mean to me, especially today. I am going to Vienna to see someone who, I believe, has a message for me from my dead friend. I'll have a lot to tell you, great and extraordinary things brought out by these latest hours.

I am overjoyed to know that there is such beauty all about you and that verses sing in you. Forgive me for my somber letters, but through all of this I do rise heavenward, whence I yearn to send down to you, my best beloved, all my benedictions.

Your devoted Frid M.

Agency of the North German Lloyd
For Dr. Stefan Zweig
Passenger on S.S. *Barbarossa*, Genoa, Italy
November 2

Dear Stefan:

Thanks for the card with the good news. Am calm and happy again. Several nice things have happened, and above all, your news. Last night was very pleasant. The nurse had her day off, and so I stayed with the children. It was so marvelous to hear their soft sweet little breathing. Since the nurse had always complained that Susi cried in her sleep and was subject to nightmares, I wanted to watch the child myself. But she slept without stirring, from half-past seven till six in the morning. Then she insisted with a good deal of vehemence on coming into my bed with me. When I gave in to her I received

39

a wet and tear-salty kiss and a "My sweet Mommy!" (her own invention).

Dearest, my father-in-law said something very nice about you: "He must be a very noble human being." For which I would have liked to give the old gentleman a little hug—something I hadn't ever thought of doing before.

Up to now I've lacked the peace of mind to do any reading. Except poetry. There's one passage in the Verlaine book [1] I want to remind you of: "When the soul is well-balanced, of what account are the body's disordered gestures, especially those of a body dragging itself wearily through so much misery?"

Sunday afternoon Emmi W.[2] and I read an endless lot of Verlaine-and Verhaeren poems. She thinks, as do so many others, that your versions are more beautiful than the originals. Many things in the *Wind-swept Wheatfields* can hardly be surpassed. Also *The Fiddler* is wonderful. I am babbling about beauty when beauty's thousand hues doubtless lie spread out before your eyes. May you have joy of them. And you being in the midst of beauty, beauty will make high holiday, too.

Affectionately yours, M.

[1] *Verlaine's Last Days,* by Cazals, which I translated; Stefan Zweig made the arrangements for its publication. [2] Baroness Dr. Emmi Weber, later Mrs. Erich Stoerck.

Dr. Stefan Zweig
Palermo, Villa Igiea, Sicily
November 4, 1913
Baden near Vienna, Mozartgasse

My dear:

Now you are in the deep south. Lucky sheet of paper to travel the same route as you. I see you in the garden of your villa high above a sea much, much bluer than my stationery.

I still do not dare write a long letter, lest I be involved again in the emotional crises I've been through. There have been some new deeply disturbing ones.

How glad I should be to hear about your beautiful trip! Hope you share Goethe's delight in Palermo.

My work is progressing. I enclose a sample poem.—Am so grateful to you for this job.[1] Of course I don't know how it will turn out. The language of the original is anything rather than merely pretty. The book deals with facts and so does not allow of free translation. Besides, I am a beginner.

Wrote Verhaeren and hope he doesn't mind my informal manner and my mediocre French. As long as the children are small, I can't perfect myself in anything. Time is lacking and the needed quiet.

Farewell my dear. Write me all about your raptures. I need your gladness.

Devotedly yours, Fri

1 The first of four translations: *Verlaine's Last Days* by Cazals.

November 8, 1913

Many thanks, my dear, for your greetings from afar. No matter what the day brings forth, I always greet you in my thoughts. But I get lost, peering into the unknown, which is a wall, shutting me off, beautiful but impenetrable. Yesterday I had a wonderful day in Vienna. I visited the wife of my dead friend. She feels closer to him when I am with her. And that makes me ashamed.—The death of this extraordinary man has been a wondrous revelation. For now I know that out of my life he built his own anew, and that people are now getting together to go on with that which he was moved to do through me. Isn't that glorious? It seems as if I had only met him just now for the first time. For now I believe I can bring out the good in men through my faith in love.

My dear, I wrote you about the *Wind-swept Wheatfields*.[1] Hope it will appear in the *Wiener Tagblatt*.[2] Also I wanted to tell you that the lecture on ancient poetry will be delivered on December 27, in the Urania.[3] Shall we go to it together?

Have I thanked you already for your greetings from Bozen? Hope that the ladies whom you gadded around with have added another pleasant memory to those you already had of Meran.

Farewell and do be gay and happy for me too.

Fr. M.

1 A volume of Verhaeren's poems.   2 Vienna newspaper.   3 People's University in Vienna.

Baden, November 19, 1913

My dear, my dear:

Your letter was so precious—yet didn't astonish me in the least. I've always known, nor ever doubted, that you had in you creative genius, that miraculous endowment. Yes, to hearken to one's own experience, to hearken to oneself echoing and re-echoing through one's moments of solitude—that is perhaps the sweetest mystery of all. And thanks a thousand times for telling me about those hours. You have no idea how happy it made me. And, my dear, many thanks for the ocean of honey. Alix wants to write you herself. So beautiful to think of orange blossoms, sun and bees, and yourself. The honey is smooth and good. The children lick it up blissfully. Their little tongues may have a sort of inkling of the miracle that produced it, far away in the southlands.

Yesterday I was in Vienna. First I did some things for my mother. Then went to the old gentleman's [1] lecture on his favorite hero, Prince Eugen.[2] All kinds of Countesses and Princesses attended, accompanied by their sons—and even one of the Emperor's granddaughters with a typical Habsburg face was there. The lecture was quite stimulating. Many acquaintances whom I hadn't seen since going out of circulation and who acted as if I were some sort of little freak. After dining with friends, I joined the younger crowd and finished the evening in a bar. . . .

At home I found your honey, the merry children, my work. So I am very happy. And you, dearest? Do you find Rome beautiful? I want you to be joyful and may your joy merge with all the beauty you see around you. I can't tell you how much I am looking forward to you. Finished Verlaine except for the last thirty pages, the Argot Couplets, which I can't do and the two wicked ones you promised to translate for me. Perhaps it'll interest you to know that Schmittbonn [3] is moving to Baden.

Again my devoted thanks for everything!

Yours, Fri

P.S. (on lined paper) Many thanks. Alix and Susi.

¹ My father-in-law and friend, Privy Councillor von Winternitz, of the Press Bureau of the Foreign Office, was a journalist, and functioned in various literary and social capacities.   ² Prince Eugen of Savoy, Austrian General in the wars against Turkey.   ³ German author and poet.

Dr. Stefan Zweig
Vienna, VIII, Kochgasse 8
Baden near Vienna
December 6, 1913

You write, today, I should feel securer in my relationship to you. Don't you see, my one and only beloved, that I am making a superhuman effort—to keep myself *above* your life, not to intrude myself on you—because I love you too much. I would implore you, on my very knees, to understand me. To be sure of you—would be paradise! The mere thought of it makes me tremble with joy. I am like this because I am a coward, dearest. I would die were I to lose you, and so I do what the miner does, who, aware of the dangers he must face, commends his soul to God every time he goes down into the pit. I have told you these ultimate things, so that you will not make your feelings the measure of mine and so that you may stay happy and free. For you are so much to me, and everything you give me is so much. And I'll strive with all my might so to refine my emotion that you will always be giving to me—never taking from me.

Be gently and devotedly embraced by your

Fri.

December 1913

My dear:

I'm so happy to have you with me on Sunday. Maybe you can stay overnight, so that the children can see you in the morning. Or come early, before they go to bed. They are looking forward to your visit. If Schmittbonn wants to meet me, I shall be delighted to receive him.

Fri.

Baden, Christmas, 1913

My dear:

How nice to have someone here ¹ who is of your household and serves you so faithfully. That makes me feel some-

43

how reassured. The landscape and the familiar things about the house make me feel very much at home, especially when I look at your lovely but much too costly presents. I have just been to see about your room.[2]

Heartfelt thanks once more from the children and myself—also for Joseph's fine help.

Farewell and come soon. The air is marvelous, the whole countryside glittering with snow.

Your lamb sends you a kiss.

You can have a meal here any time without letting me know beforehand. The pantry is well stocked. Have called off all other guests because of Alix' sickness.

[1] Stefan Zweig had sent his valet, Joseph, to deliver the presents and to help in the house. [2] He always occupied the same room when in Baden.

1 9 1 4

My dear:

Today I was deeply stirred by a passage in *Les Amies*.[1] It probes much deeper into the problems of women's emancipation than all the usual babble on this subject: "It is the great misfortune of present-day women that they are too free, and not free enough. If they were freer, they would want some ties, finding in them security and charm. If less free, they would become resigned to bonds they know they couldn't break, and thus they would suffer less. But the worst of all is to have ties that do not really bind, and duties that may be cast aside."

[1] Novel by Romain Rolland.

Dr. Stefan Zweig
Berlin, Hotel Fuerstenhof
Potsdamerplatz
January 26, 1914

I was delighted by your card today. It sounded as if you were in good spirits. After all, it must be gratifying to hear your words spoken in a foreign city, even if not spoken and acted entirely to your liking. The people of Mannheim were satisfied, I am sure. And the public of Hamburg too.

The evening with the Schmittbonns was charming. They invited me to visit them in Murnau. Perhaps you and I can go there together. Greet my dear room in the "Fuerstenhof" and jot down the number of your present one. I'd like to have it if I should come to Berlin.

Yours, Fr. M.

Vienna, March 18, 1914

My dear:

Am only a few houses away from you and shall stay here overnight, since the old gentleman [1] has gone to Baden with the children. Forgive me for taking up your time. But I may not be able to see you alone before you leave and I want to tell you about various things before you go. You mustn't believe I am sad. If I seem so sometimes, my nerves are to blame —not me. I am ever your lamb that wants to be glad when she is with you. And don't worry about any difficulties I may have to face while you are away. I've done my best to get all my affairs in order before you leave. Everything has been taken care of, including financial matters.—I don't want you to feel that you are under any sort of compulsion. Stay free and detached, the way you think you should be. I have faith in you, but ask nothing of you. By now I've gotten free of my old ties completely, because I want to be clean and unblemished in your eyes and my own too, and because you wished it. It was the first thing you asked of me, and I had been waiting for you to ask something of me for a long time. But it was inevitable, in any case. Only you made the struggle within me and the final decision easier. For that I thank you, come what may.

Farewell, little brother, and stay fond of your

Lamb

[1] The nickname of Privy Councillor von Winternitz whose apartment was on the same street as Stefan Zweig's.

Dr. Stefan Zweig
Paris, Hotel Beaujolais
Rue de Beaujolais
March 22, 1914

My dear:

Your card put me in a good humor. I sensed how eager you were to be with your esteemed friend.[1] I hope you had a happy reunion with him and with Paris and with the woman who is your friend and with everything you love there. I do sincerely wish it. If you hadn't had the travel jitters, you would have noticed what a brave lamb I was when we were saying goodbye.

Are you working? I am looking forward to seeing the finished *Dostoievski*.—Today I received my first proofs [2] and have already sent them back. Also the article on Romain Rolland is done.—Have you read Bahr's [3] feuilleton on Mahler? [4] It's based on *Jean Christophe* and a kind of hodgepodge. Bahr's exaggerated subjectivity always annoys me a little. One shouldn't undress oneself in a newspaper article as one would in a book. Yet his subjectivity achieves effects not found in the work of anyone else.

Affectionately your lamb

[1] Verhaeren who used to spend the winter in St. Cloud.   [2] To my novel *The Call of the Homeland*.   [3] Hermann Bahr, Austrian writer.
[4] Gustav Mahler, famous conductor and composer.

My dear:

Just received your letter and am answering it right away. Now I have something to be happy about despite my anguish at being separated from you: your cheerful letters. I hate Vienna because it obscures your really open happy nature, which makes your letters from abroad so joyous and radiant. How I wish I could be a witness at first hand of this kind of happy mood, although your letters are so kind, so alive, and so much *yourself*, my dear!

I feel pretty well. I did manage to sleep the past few nights. My nerves were calmer. Yesterday I received the final papers all ready for my signature.

Affectionate greetings from a heart rejoicing in your joy.

Yours, Friderike

Baden, April 1, 1914
My dear:

Am writing at my most beautiful window flooded with sunshine; the sun is already quite warm with a touch of May zephyrs in it.—My dear, I am so joyful, so happy—I am not afraid to say it—happy to my very finger tips. Early this morning, after a good rest, I saw the jays and little hawks balancing on their favorite trees in my neighbor's garden. Then they soared up towards the morning sun, as light as my heart. And I sent them all to you, these buoyant, strong birds flying through the clear morning air, to bring you my greetings.

Found your letter on my return from Vienna yesterday afternoon. It crowned my joy at having attained freedom. Can't say definitely whether I am coming to Paris. In my present happy, radiant mood I might enjoy it as never before.

Victor Fleischer called up and we spent an hour together. I am so glad that this dear fellow is your friend. Please write him soon. He is too comical when he insists: "You exaggerate my interest in Dr. Zweig" and then listens with "ten ears" to everything I tell him about you. He clipped the page for me on which my book with your preface was announced, out of the *Bookdealers' Journal*.

Thank you for the much too complimentary things you said about me. I can best thank you, my dear, by promising never to profane the tiny flame within me. Then, maybe, some day it will grow stronger and justify the kindly indulgence you show for my work. Now only my heart can thank you.

F.M.

Baden, April 9, 1914

My dear:

Am full of bliss in spite of bodily aches and perhaps doubly so, because I have come to understand that they have nothing to do with happiness or unhappiness. There's one passage in your letter I'd like to kiss. Where you write about wanting to lie in the grass and hum like a bee. Dearest, I hear you humming and the sweet sound of it makes all the music of the spheres seem just cheap honky tonk by comparison. On Tuesday you'll get a letter or wire asking you to reserve a room for Thursday or informing you that I am not well enough to travel. But I am still hoping for the best.

Never imagine I would assault, even in thoughts, the secret citadel of your being. I belong to you, way up a hundred thousand feet above the earth.

Yesterday I finished dictating my story *White Crocus*.

47

Am afraid as yet to show it to you. Thanks for the good selection of books.

Am so glad that you see Rilke [1] so often. He means very much to me.

Now I send you all my good wishes for your journeyings. When you see an Easter lamb, think of your own, happy lamb. I kiss you affectionately.

Fr. M.

[1] Rainer Maria Rilke, the famous poet.

April 11

My dear, good darling!

Today I thought I saw you walking just ahead of me, in your usual brisk way. Your head was inclined a bit, as it always is when you consider a new idea. You seemed nearer to me than you had ever been before, while away, during your trips abroad. I can understand now how those that are far away can be conjured up. I understand the little Maid of Lourdes and Jeanne d'Arc—all that is supernatural. Often I seem to be separated from the miraculous only by a thin wall.

It is beautiful outdoors, the maple trees are in blossom. It will be wonderful to travel with the fullness of spring about me. But without the children, spring is not quite so vivid. I am so happy that I can leave my little ones behind in a flowery meadow where they will find new marvels every day.

I'll wire only in case I can't come. If you shouldn't be able to come to the station, I'll drive to your hotel and find out the address of mine. I visited with Mr. von M. for a quarter of an hour and shall meet Miss Eugenie at half-past four. M. had been away and returned for a few hours just to see me. I was flattered—I wouldn't be a woman if I hadn't been. He brought some poems by Ady (who will be visiting him in the next days), extremely strange, savage things; their fervor can be compared only with Rimbaud's.[1] But there's also a touch of Lenau. For instance, a hymn to the Hungarian plain: "I make deep obeissance to the sacred soil." And then he puts his ear to the ground to listen to the sleeping soul of the earth, to learn whether the fertile seed is stirring, whether flowers are about to come forth. Mr. von M. says that Ady was Hungary's greatest poet, but absolutely untranslatable. Even the Hungarians didn't understand him, because they didn't understand themselves.

I embrace you

F.M.

1 Arthur Rimbaud, French poet.

April 16

My dear:

I find such contentment in the thought that my joy has leaped across to you, my joy of which a good share has stayed behind in me too, though I must fight for it against my various aches and pains.

And your letters, my dear! I read them again and again with such keen pleasure! I almost regret that I shall miss them when I come to Paris. Or will you keep on with them just the same in case we can't see each other often? Perhaps you'll have the urge to work that last week, and I wouldn't want to interrupt you. I should be so happy if something beautiful and vital were coming to flower in you again, like your Schneeberg story [1] or your Dostoievski. Those are things I can't ever forget. I understand how spring makes you feel that all this and art in general are unalive. But what you create is not apart from nature. It is nature's most melodious and most richly flowering manifestation; a nature which only an eye touched with grace, and the heart's fantasy, both of which are yours, can make manifest. My dear, I believe you don't know your own shortcomings, what in you is unfruitful. If you knew you would wrestle with it—if that were possible without pulling out good roots with the bad. Great men are allowed to have shortcomings; good machines consume their own waste products. But they need a great deal of fuel to give them power. Even their thirst signifies fruitfulness.

My dear, be joyful and light of heart a little also for your

Fri

1 "Moonlight Street" (in the volume *Conflicts*).

My dearest and best:

Oh, I could beat myself. But I had no idea my aches would keep you from enjoying something you wanted to do. I am not used to such thoughtfulness. How good, good, good you are!—I had no choice but to write the truth or nothing at all. The pain is gone, only I feel weak from this miserable dieting. As soon as I can eat nourishing food, I'll be all right. I promise not to come to Paris unless I feel up to it. I expect to wire tomorrow that I'll arrive on Thursday and accept your kind offer to reserve a room for me in a hotel near yours. I don't want to be under the same roof with you because of this woman friend of yours. The slightest look askance cast in my direction would hurt me.—Since I must stop over in St. Poelten [1] to see the notary, I can't be in Paris before Thursday night. I'll catch the express train after finishing my business.

I'd be happy if my letter of yesterday had induced you not to give up your Easter jaunt.

Schuster and Loeffler [2] are as charming as ever. They sent so many samples of bindings that it's hard to choose between them. The old gentleman is very happy. He read the book again and was once more moved to tears by the ending. And he thought my new novella my best. I am glad that I have made him happy. He talks a lot about my trip.

Many kisses from your Lamb

[1] A small town near Vienna where the divorce papers had been filed to avoid publicity. [2] Publishers who were going to bring out my novel *Call of the Homeland.*

My dear:

I enjoyed the letter you wrote after you awoke from being spellbound by the church choir [1] and had returned to Paris.—My dear, I'll arrive the same day you get this letter. I'll have to straighten out my things today, but will look rather moth-eaten anyway, because I couldn't bother about clothes these past few days. But you'll overlook it, won't you? I am not going to speak of my happiness. Perhaps my indisposition just smothered it a bit, down to a sort of inner glow. Au revoir and many kisses from your far-off

Lamb

[1] In the Cathedral of Chartres.

Hotel Beaujolais
Vue sur les Jardins de Port-Royal
15, Rue de Beaujolais
April, 1914

My dear:

Just returned to the hotel and find your letter. I hope you'll have good news from your woman friend.

I'll be delighted to visit your friends Thursday.[1] Please accept the invitation for me.

At the moment, I am half dead after shopping and trying on my new things. I'll go back to the hotel in the evening and leave a message telling you where you can meet me. My dear, I've bought you the butterfly you liked.[2]

Affectionately yours,

Friderike

[1] Mr. and Mrs. Grautoff, translators of Romain Rolland's works. I met the latter a few days later at the Hotel Beaujolais. [2] A Brazilian butterfly under glass used by Stefan as an ash tray for many years.

Hotel Beaujolais

Dear Stefan:

I have four complimentary tickets for *Psyche.* Would you like to go tomorrow?

Just received the *Fremdenblatt* with my feuilleton on Romain Rolland.

Greetings, Fr. M.

(A few days later Stefan and I returned together to Vienna)

Dr. Stefan Zweig
Ostende, Kursaal poste restante
Sanitarium Tobelbad near Graz
June 1914

My dear:

Am writing in a hurry to thank you for the letter from Middelkerke. The trip was very hot. Up to now there hasn't been a quiet moment. I'll wait for one before writing at length. Wire your address after leaving Ostende. Am still very tired. So you must forgive me for not answering at once, your suggestions about the trip.[1]

Affectionately yours,

Fri

[1] We had planned to meet in Zurich and travel together through Italy.

My dear, good darling:

Am taking advantage of my first hour of leisure to write you. Fortunately the heavy cloud of weariness is lifting a bit. I realize I may have a relapse but the fear of a relentless something weighing down upon me is gone. It's too bad I can't get as much done as formerly—especially now when I have to face the daily round of life all alone, at a time when I need more than ever before to keep my strength intact. Of course, I still have strength within me. I'm sure of that. But I am spiritually and physically dispossessed, evicted, as it were, from the peace and quiet I should have for my work. Life demands too much of me. A woman is confronted by so many tasks. You feel it would be frivolous to value art above nature. Similarly, it seems ridiculous for me to sit down to work when children need tender nurture, a chaotic household must be put in order and beloved friends [1] need comfort and alleviation of their anxieties. Yesterday I received a nice card from Strunz. [2] Whenever he likes a place especially, he sends me greetings from it. All he knows of me is my work. My book has been passed from hand to hand here. The people dining at the tables near the one at which I am sitting talk about it without knowing that I am the author.—Now I want to answer the things you brought up in your letter. Don't be afraid that I won't be able to bear with your little nervous crises. And don't bring up anything .that happened in Paris. Neither of us wants to think of that any more. But, my dear, don't expect something different from me now. Perhaps you think I am not sufficiently dedicated, that I cherish the landscape only as a framework. Don't be angry with me, if I look forward not only to you and the landscape, but also to you and tranquility. I am not in the least fearful lest you shouldn't be able to satisfy your craving for solitude when you are with me, for I am often withdrawn into myself, aloof, taciturn, too. My dear, here I go on at a great rate, yet secretly am all atremble lest the trip fall through. I offer up daily prayers to God asking that I have a chance to be exposed to your spells of "depression." [3] There's just one thing I do expect of you, my little brother. While you are with me, you'll have to get to work. I wouldn't pride myself on distracting you from work that will eventually be a source of enjoyment to so many people. This is undoubtedly true in your case, although doubtful in mine. The hours when I sat next to you and watched your pen racing across the paper with lightning speed are just as unforgettable as our nights.

My dear, I kiss you gently. Yours,

F.

1 My friends, the Stoercks, were superintending the Sanatorium Tobelbad where my children were to remain during the trip I had planned with Stefan. The two friends had become involved in grave conflicts. 2 Dr. Franz Strunz, Professor of the History of Natural Sciences. 3 Stefan Zweig had warned me in a letter of his spells of depression which often assumed dangerous proportions.

Sanitarium Tobelbad near Graz
My dear:
Talk of a general mobilization frightens me to death.— Be good to me. In times like these we must feel more keenly than in ordinary times how much we mean to each other. I am thinking anxiously of Felix,[1] of all human beings. It is terrible to sit here so completely helpless.

Lovingly yours,

Fri

1 My former husband who had joined the armed forces as a Captain.

Monsieur Stefan Zweig
Coq-sur-Mer, Ostende
Hotel Bellevue
My dear:
If I am not mistaken, I wrote a silly, hysterical letter yesterday. No wonder, for everybody here is excited, patients as well as physicians. I hate all these busybodies strutting around because there's a war on, instead of being more reserved and kindlier. Every puffed-up fool indulges in orgies of pomposity and makes himself important, because something evil is happening or at least threatens to. And despite everything, no one is really profoundly moved. You are, of that I am sure. I, for my part, also, although I must confess, not so much by patriotism as by common humanity. At such a moment, it were hypocrisy to utter words of sympathy for *only one* part of mankind. My feelings go out to all and *cannot* be localized.

53

Am sending two clippings to let you know how the news was received in Vienna and Berlin. Latest reports speak of a revolution in Serbia.

Farewell, little brother.

Fri.

Tobelbad, July 1914

Dear Stefan:

Now I almost believe you didn't receive my letters. The wire was sent to "Lecop, Hotel Bellevue" (instead of Le Coq). My dear, I feel my heart palpitating incessantly. What a terrible time, with danger hovering over so many thousands of hearts. It is disgusting to find people so indifferent. Thirty of the guests here have left, and many of the staff. According to the latest wires from Vienna, the situation is less acute in spite of the mobilization.

My dear, you gave me an awful fright when you said there was some question now about our trip. If you were here yourself, you'd only get angry at the general indifference. I don't like being here at all.—If you really intend to give up our trip, wire immediately.

Just imagine, last night despite the declaration of war, there was a dance at which the Prince Eugen-and Rakoczy Marches were played. An entrancing soubrette from Budapest, whose husband had been called up, holding a tear-drenched handkerchief in her hand—danced a tango.

I shouldn't be at all disappointed if we met somewhere in Austria and just stayed there. All I want is you and good country air, although I had looked forward so much to the trip as you had pictured it to me.

F.

Dr. Stefan Zweig
Vienna, VIII, Kochgasse 8

Every day, every hour, brings changes. Your wire reached me on my way to Graz where I went with Alix to meet Felix. He will go on to Goerz tomorrow night, wears a uniform bringing his weight up to 86 kilo and is in excellent spirits. He said Vienna was very quiet. But in Graz the excitement in the streets was infectious. People shouted enthusiastically and hailed the soldiers as they marched by.

54

And you? You wouldn't stay abroad, of course. I shall be more tranquil, knowing you near. Who knows whether you could have done any traveling at all in the immediate future? Have you any idea when we can leave? Won't the situation clear up soon?

My darling, even if the danger of war brought it about, I am nevertheless happy to know you are nearby.

Fri.

Tobelbad, August 1

My dear:

Am too sad to comment on the caustic tone of your letter. Do you really believe I wanted to go on a pleasure jaunt when human blood was being shed? I was still hoping it wouldn't come to that. How could I have endured many things that have happened to me in my life, had my optimism not stood me in good stead.

The flu, or rather an angina epidemic has broken out here among the few guests who have stayed on. It is terrible to be here, for the pharmacy can't keep up with the emergency.

Love me still; these are sad days.

All the news we get is belated. That's the reason why I didn't know about the most recent developments and wrote things you thought were so frivolous. Now my pitiless imagination makes me aware of all the horror—also that you could doubt me at a time like this.

Hope your brother won't have to worry too much. If you need help getting things shipped, communicate with my brothers in the Railroad Ministry.

I would to heaven I knew where to go. No news from Felix.

Fri.

Graz-Baden
August 4

Writing on the train. Will be in Vienna between half-past nine and ten. I'll phone from the Café Eiles or leave a message there to let you know whether I can meet you.

Affectionately Fri.

(This was our first meeting after the outbreak of war. I had hurried to Vienna because of an alarming letter in which Stefan informed me that he intended to enlist as a private and go to Galicia. He had grown a beard, which symbolized his distressed state of mind.)

Baden, August, 1914

My dear Stefan:

Many thanks for placing the poem.[1] Also I was glad to have your letter.

I am quite sure you won't be called up for the time being. Only the first group of reservists (up to 37) of the local corps have as yet been called up.

Kissing your dear gypsy tinker's face, I am faithfully

Yours, Fri

[1] An appeal to the mothers, published in the *Neue Freie Presse*.

Baden, August 17, 1914

My dear:

I received an eight page special delivery letter today from Frau von Molo. Her four brothers have volunteered, and her husband has been stricken with the prevalent neurosis, begotten of having nothing to do. She asks me to have Chl. back his petition to the War Press Bureau. I don't believe I could help her. But, since she wants so much to talk things over with me, I'll come in on Wednesday. Perhaps you'll go with me to the Molos on Thursday. In times like these, we should try to help one another as much as possible.

Farewell "little father." It was so wonderful to have you so near. I am well.

Affectionately, Fri

My dear:

I want to say good night before drowsiness makes my lids still heavier. I say it every evening with my lips pressed to your watch (the one night it was at the watchmaker's my hand felt so lonesome).

My days are happy. I am almost ashamed to admit it. But probably others do the same as I: fill their days with things that seem important. I manage to do all the daily chores with very little outside help, and without sacrificing any of my own work. Today I wrote fourteen pages of my new novel. I've always felt I could lead a decent kind of life if only I had untrammeled independence, and I only need to be sure of the rightness of my decisions, and serenity of soul, to be myself, and not a nerve-wracked creature tempest-tossed by every little painful impression.

I walk about the house and am conscious of your presence everywhere, your presence that has endeared it to me. Who knows, perhaps I couldn't have borne up under the loss of happiness those perished days [1] would have meant to me, if it weren't for your visits which have cheered me up so wonderfully. The nights, though, are lonely. I often ask myself why this should be my destined lot.

F.

[1] Referring to the journey we had to give up.

September, 1914

My little brother:

You can't imagine how happy I am with my four children.[1] They are so affectionate. When I come to visit you on Thursday, I'll be running over with children's kisses. I'll pass them on to you, dearest, and should like to do so this very minute.

Just got through bathing them. How happy they are in their sweet nakedness! And how much we love them! Oh, to think that those poor fellows out there—I can't get them out of my mind—have mothers who knew them just like this, little and helpless, and petted and cuddled them too. To know what misery may befall mankind! But also, what good fortune! Another reason why we should clasp our children to our hearts, inasmuch as we know them destined in their lifetime to joy and sorrow.

Dearest, every kiss I give you is also a prayer.

Next week will see many departures. My mother and sister and little nephew leave on Friday, the Stoerck children soon afterwards. Felix, who is to arrive on Saturday, will leave again on Sunday. But by then I hope to be busy with food distribution in Vienna.

Your feuilletons and articles (the first excepted) were

57

highlights of my reading. Also Hofmannsthal pleased me. He always works in precious metals which gives a certain value even to trashy content. But it's dangerous to imitate him in brass. My dear, will the lamb see you Thursday?

Devotedly yours,

F.M.

1 The children of our friend Dr. Erich Stoerk were staying with me for a few days.

Baden near Vienna
October 24

The light of your benevolence reaches me by proxy, through your friend. Just think: Miss Eugenie wrote again, to say how sorry she was we were so far away from each other. To offset this, she proposes to establish a sort of linguistic propinquity. She suggests that in our letters we address each other with the familiar "thou." For all of which I have you to thank.

I'll be in Vienna at half-past seven. Although I've been listed for night duty at the District Commander's Head-quarters, I don't think they'll need me there this week. Went to the hospital and brought the soldiers a bottle of champagne I had been hoarding. They were immensely pleased. Only trained nurses are allowed to take care of the wounded. It is disgusting that, during the first days, the whole population of Baden rushed in to look at them. Even when they arrive at night, thousands of people gape at them. The poor fellows make fun of all the silly ado.

Yesterday the old gentleman dropped in at noon and told me a lot of things the newspapers suppress.

Felix will come from Marburg on Saturday, just for the day. Since it's not impossible that his regiment will be sent north, I am glad that the children and I too can see him without going to Marburg. My dear, I thank God every hour that you are near me, and in gratitude for this blessing, will multiply whatever good I can do, a hundredfold.

Farewell, dearest. Affectionately yours,

Lamb

My best and dearest:

I thank you a thousand times for having come to see me yesterday. You don't realize how happy it made me.

I asked the old gentleman [1] to come over today. He said that, according to the new regulations, only every tenth man would be drafted. It might be possible for you to get into the Sanitary Corps if you had a little pull. Hope I don't bore you with these things, but I want to let you know that a certain lady, whose brother is in the War Ministry, offered to help me if I wanted anything. Should I make use of this channel? If you agree, I'd find out first whether this brother, whose rank I don't know, is in Vienna. If he is, an interview could be arranged which would tell you how to go about choosing a branch of the service for which your profession fits you. I, for my part, am not at all anxious and hope that everything will shape up in the best way for my good, beloved shepherd.

Kissing you very tenderly, I am your

"Sheep-Lamb"

[1] My former father-in-law, Privy Councillor von Winternitz.

My dear:

Miss Schr. just told me she was sending an orderly to Traiskirchen.[1] The officer in charge will have an answer for her by tomorrow morning at eight. (A high-ranking military personage has agreed to everything but only if there is an opening.) The officer said they would welcome you with *open arms* and be happy to have a man of your caliber among them. You would be a real treasure-trove for those youngsters. Evidently you made quite a hit there, my dear little brother.

I'll phone tomorrow as soon as I hear something.

Affectionately your

Lamb

[1] Refers to the possibility of teaching at the military school in Traiskirchen near Vienna.

December 30, 1914

My dear:

I greet you on the last day of the year. How difficult it is to keep away from sentimental retrospects! But all I want to do is to kiss you in my thoughts and add the fervent wish: that your buoyant spirit may not be overcast during the coming year by anxious hours or by being hurt by friends. My sweet darling, I wish you all the happiness you can honestly enjoy. And among many other wishes the greatest: getting a lot of good work done. You didn't understand when I told you that would help me, too. Sometimes you are so far away—but I hold you close to my heart through your work. Your work builds golden bridges from you to my heart. It gives me a home in the clouds and in your heart, too—in your faithless, faithful heart. This isn't the sort of literary adulation you dislike so much (I am less uncritical than you think). Your poem "The Cripple" I found almost bad.—No, what I mean is, a common homeland in which we can keep faith with each other forever. The war hasn't changed us. We always had the same love of humanity and justice.

1 9 1 5

The war went on. I had caught an infection while nursing typhoid cases in Baden. And, since a Headquarters Command had been established in this small town, it became increasingly difficult to live there and travel back and forth to Vienna. In order to have the children nearer to their grandfather and be closer to my mother and Stefan, I took a temporary apartment in Vienna. Stefan Zweig was serving in the War Archives as contributor to a literary magazine, *The Danube Land*. Many Austrian writers, such as Franz Karl Ginzkey, Franz Th. Csokor, Paul Stefan, Alfred Polgar, and later also Rainer Maria Rilke were his colleagues at headquarters in the office at the Vienna Stiftskaserne. For the first time since his schooldays, Stefan Zweig was no longer master of his time and found it hard to go on with his own work. Often he wanted me to sit next to him and make him stick to his writing. But at times he lost all desire to stick to it.

March 8, 1915
Vienna, Langegasse

My dear:

Thanks for the sad news—for, unfortunately, I am not sure I can come tomorrow between four and seven. Josef [1] always vanishes without waiting for an answer. He seems to assume that all the arrangements you suggest are final and any objections on my part, of no importance. I know, of course, that you are always in a hurry when giving him your orders in the morning. Please do go on with your work without me. It hurts me more than you think that you might consider your work unimportant. You can always have peace and quiet, undisturbed by any intrusion, from outside, if you want it. How glad I would have been to see a part of the *Dostoievski* finished. Also your poem will suffer. Its quality of supplication and its warmth will grow cold unless you sink yourself in it completely. My dear child, enjoy yourself as much as you like. But despite your Archives, the day is long enough. Only you must never forget that there is but one unpardonable sin: to be lukewarm in your work.—Forgive me for writing so frankly. I love you and kiss you and want the best for you.

Fri.

1 Stefan Zweig's valet Josef, who served him for many years. He was drafted even though he was an older man and the father of a family.

Vienna, March 1915

Isn't it strange that I sit down to write you now when I was as tongue-tied as a schoolgirl and almost unable to talk to you when your living image popped up so suddenly in the dark street? You live so near, and yet—everything that happened seemed a sort of fairy tale.

Ought I to talk to you like this just now? Can you feel it—be touched by it? My dearest, I know how nerve-ends can be worn bloody through constant fretting against whatever fetters. But I want you to be so great that you will be able to interpose a barbed-wire fence of self-control between your nerve-ends and the world. Oh, if it were only true that you actually managed to get to work yesterday! You seemed in such a hurry. Of course, I am ready to believe you would be in more of a hurry to get to work if you felt the urge, than to some woman or other. But, somehow, you seemed embarrassed, and I was too. But why? Does something like suspicion (not distrust or ill-will) suddenly spring up between us, because of the way we are living, away from each other, and among strangers? I wish I could make you see how little I value everything else in my life, and how you are all in all to me. I know your weak-

61

nesses and sometimes hate them, because you acknowledge them so freely and think that makes them quite excusable. I can't ignore your faults; I realize that you have a tendency to cultivate them, and make much of them—yet I, a woman, and a weak one at that, think this kind of "patting yourself on the back" smacks too much of the feminine. Darling, don't be angry. My admiration for so much in you is sky-high. I am on my knees to what is incomparable in the soul of you. Within you is a radiant light, human, crystalline, unique. Who knows when and how it will burst through the slag, and shine forth a glorious brightness! How I want to give you the peace and quiet you need for the splendid project you have planned! Oh! If only you'd begin it! Who knows, it might accumulate such an impetus of its own, that it would sweep everything before it. Such things happen. Perhaps the first words will kindle a fire within you. I beg you: *try* everything. Please, please, don't imagine I wouldn't be willing to give up seeing you, if you wanted to lock your door. Don't ward off, be obstinate about what is possible, even miracles. You are a free man and shouldn't become fossilized by: "It's impossible," or "I can't work in Austria," and so forth. Stay at home for three or four days, or get sick leave and go some place, shut yourself up in a room. Don't you see that what you could accomplish in a few days would justify a thousand times over a little dishonesty like that? Or try going to the country after office hours, maybe to Rodaun. If you got a place located somewhere between two good inns, like Stelzer's and the Red Haystack, you'd have the whole evening, stay overnight and so you would have quite a few hours to yourself. If this worked out satisfactorily, you could do it again often. At any rate, try it! My dear, I send my greetings and am a thousand times yours.

F.M.

My dear:
     I read, and then played some Beethoven sonatas. But Mr. von M. came and brought me down to earth. Then a messenger from the old gentleman brought the *Journal de Genève* with a long article by Romain Rolland "Le meurtre des élites." It will interest you very much. Maybe I can bring it tonight to the little café, though the paper shouldn't be

passed on to anyone else.—Read one of Balzac's stories that I want to discuss with you. I am working on the stories for prisoners. You promised to contribute something.

Kisses from

F.

(Though not engaged in active service, Stefan Zweig suffered so terribly because of the war and everything connected with it that he was unable to concentrate on his work. Thus it was my endeavor to lead him back to his writing, which always alleviated his spells of moodiness. Finally I wrote to Stefan's great friend, Romain Rolland, who was also well disposed towards me. The following letter was written in answer to mine, in which I had described Stefan's condition.)

Madame Friderike Maria von Winternitz
c/o Privy Councillor von Winternitz
Foreign Office, Vienna, Ballhausplatz

Red Cross Committee, Geneva
International Agency for War Prisoners
Beauséjour, Geneva-Champel
Inter Arma Caritas [1]
Geneva, Easter Monday, 1915

Dear Madame:

I am troubled by the thought that you haven't received my letter. Your kindness has touched me very deeply.

You may be sure that I understand and share your sorrow as well as that of my dear Stefan Zweig. I have passed through months of agony when it seemed impossible to breathe. —But now I have regained my peace of mind and balance. Be the days through which we are passing ever so tragic, I can see now that those that went before were even worse. For then the atmosphere around us was stifling, surcharged with egotism, nationalist pride and hatred and with murderous electricity. So Thor's hammer fell with lightning hissing among the peoples locked in combat, and that cleared the air. Formerly we were too apathetic, we had accustomed ourselves too easily to the torpor that precedes the storm. Now we have awakened! And I feel my spirit all at once free, my mind clear of all the prejudices and compromises that used to confuse it and which it accepted less from conviction than from a sort of lethargy, and a subconscious fear of making decisions. The

63

frightful crisis compels each one of us to search his conscience, probe deep into his soul, and take sides. I am convinced that Europe's conscience will in the end, like the rainbow after the storm-clouds in *Rheingold*,[2] shine forth out of this melee of European nations; and we who feel this conscience already stirring within us cannot utter a word, have a thought, that does not glow at least a little with this inner radiance. We clasp hands across frontiers and know we are brothers. Brothers like those who followed the Christ and were made one in Him through their common love. (Yesterday a German lady passing through Geneva gave me, as a souvenir of our conversation, a Bible in which the verses 47-50 in the twelfth chapter of Matthew were underlined. And how true they are!)

This is a difficult hour, but great too, and our task glorious. We will be envied our sufferings. These are moments in mankind's history when even tears may be fruitful. It is good work we are doing. As always, the world will be renewed through suffering.

Please tell Stefan Zweig how I treasure his letters. With cordial and devoted greetings, dear Madame, yours,

Romain Rolland

Recently I saw Anette Kolb.[3] (She wasn't the one who gave me the Bible.) The war has hit her hard too—perhaps harder than the rest of us because she is Franco-German and, therefore, is torn both ways. She is very fine, loyal and good. I hope you will meet her sometime ånd have her tell you many things about which I cannot write.

[1] Motto of the International Agency. [2] Refers to Richard Wagner's *Rheingold*. [3] Author of many novels and essays.

(The Bible passage mentioned in Rolland's letter was the following: "Then one said unto him, Behold, thy mother and thy brethren stand without, desiring to speak with thee. But he answered and said unto him that told him, Who is my mother? And who are my brethren? And he stretched forth his hand toward his disciples and said, Behold my mother and my brethren! For whosoever shall do the will of my Father which is in Heaven, the same is my brother, and sister, and mother."

A few weeks later I was successful in inducing Stefan to return to his work. We spent a few days in the mountains.)

My dear, my dear, my dear:

I am well and thank you again from my whole heart. Sometimes I am stirred to my very depths by the bliss of these past days. Hope they'll remain dear to you too. I found the children in the best of health and the old gentleman as kind as ever. Everyone helped look after the children; Erich [1] for instance, came in the morning before going to the hospital. He returned today, believing that I was still away, and told us so many things about the Gstettenhof.[2] There is also other good news, excepting about Ernst Lissauer.[3]

Hope you arrived safely, got your mail, and so forth. L. writes that his wife has left him and psychiatrists say she has become insane.

Victor Fleischer [4] may come to see me Friday evening.

In any case, I shall call you up within the next days. For, naturally, I miss you very, very much and want to hear your voice. . . . Thanks again, my dear, from your

F.M.

[1] Dr. Erich Stoerck.   [2] A place near Maria Zell where we had spent a few days.   [3] German author, who had written the *Song of Hate* against England.   [4] Author, publisher, close friend of Stefan Zweig.

My sweet darling:

I must use the time at my disposal to write you, for next week you'll be gone. It seems a long time since I wrote you a real letter. And I want to tell you you shouldn't imagine that your show of affection yesterday wouldn't have been welcome. If I was a bit standoffish that was because the house across the street seemed to be gaping at me with a hundred eyes.—Do you want me to be different? Leave me as I am; don't lay violent hands on this quality in me. Perhaps, my darling, if it were taken from me and you missed it you might, now and again, feel a sudden chill, and when you were dizzy, bewildered, your hand, now and again, might reach out in vain for something to hold on to, if even for a moment only, and your work might suffer from it.

You wrote: "Be with me again, soon," writing in white-hot intoxication of work. I loved that more than anything else in your letters.

65

Never tell me anything about people who don't belong to my and your *beautiful* world. *Let us live, once for all, like two poets.*

I promise you to be less selfish about your little pastimes. But it offends me when they get too close to me.—I am thankful that you have peace and quiet and that I needn't worry about you.

I kiss you gently. Your

Lamb

Sanitarium Parsch
near Salzburg
August 18 [1]
Rain on Japanese lanterns
Fizzled out fire works
Festive Banquet with fear
of festive speeches.

My dear:

If someone dear to you should ever be seriously ill, you must let me go to him. I am beginning to believe that a new strength has come to life in me.—There is a lady here who had been confined to her room for a long time, could not take any food except milk and was suffering from various ailments; medical treatment for one of these makes treatment of the others impossible. Ladies who had known her when she was still up and about with the other guests, told me about her. She had heard about me too, and so I went to see her yesterday. Here was a bit of isolated invalid-life amidst the Sanitarium's incessant bustle. A splendid woman, who never once mentioned her sufferings. But, as I was told by dear, wise, old Mrs. Franzos, the patient had cried bitterly just before I came in. Just think of it, my dear: your usually tiresome and taciturn sheep became garrulous. I thought up all sorts of amusing things to talk about. The invalid forgot her troubles and sparkled with merriment. And after I left, her friend, waiting outside, who had been with her during her moments of despair, hugged me. Now I know what it is, my dear. I wasn't really feeling very gay. But when I am with someone who is sick I am immediately dominated by a stronger inner excitement that transforms me completely and makes me identify myself with the poor invalid and sense his needs. When it is all over,

I feel as though I had lived through a tremendous experience.

Yes, you sent a message by Josef saying you were dictating while ill and stretched out on a couch. My dear, how are you getting along now that you are freer? If I could only see your dear face for a moment.

Affectionate greetings from your

Fri

P.S.: Just received your good letter. Many thanks. I am so happy because you seem to be happy.

Shall remain here until the Doctor has made his diagnosis. Imagine, all the beautiful Lafcadio Hearn translations were made by a lady (Mrs. Franzos) who is taking the cure here. She is Ellen Key's friend and translator. A splendid woman!

1 August 18 was the Emperor's birthday, which used to be celebrated throughout Austria.

Sanitarium Parsch near Salzburg

Dear Stefan:

Thanks for your letter. Don't think I am restless. I can take it all in my stride, even get some work done, while they bang out popular songs on the piano and women jabber for hours about their clothes and the latest fashions in nightgowns. And, in spite of the bacteria, I am in good spirits. Why should those little pests stick to me forever and why should just they be true to me? The new medicine did me a lot of good. I seem to be perfectly well at the moment. Had planned to stop over in Gmunden. The weather here is very humid. I don't want to spend so much money and get no benefit from it.

My dear, after Tuesday I can meet you whenever you wish. Shall wait for your message and not disturb you with any of my own.

Affectionately

F.M.

Sanitarium Parsch near Salzburg
August 1915

My dear:

My stay here is drawing to a close. I had a good time in spite of the rain, rain, always rain.—A few people here will miss me. I am sorry about that. This or that old woman will sit all alone at her table and weep four or five more tears than she otherwise would have done for her son out there in the fighting. I feel like describing life in the Sanitarium. Suddenly people show up who had been confined to their rooms for weeks, sit down at the piano and play with such artistry that one wonders why they aren't famous. Others one sees only from afar, as it were, through the veil of their illness, lying in the rest hall. And then one day a car drives up, something is carried down the stairs on a stretcher and stowed away and then disappears into another life; one doesn't know whether it will be a life of better health or perhaps entirely hopeless. Then the petty intrigues of the hysterical cases. And so on.

My dear:

I spent a glorious hour yesterday with Privy Councillor Lammasch [1] which may give decisive direction to many, many other hours of my life. I am still so entirely taken up with it that I can't write about it yet. I shall bring along some of his works, which you will find are really worthy of your attention and seem to have been written expressly for you. If you could only go to see him. (It made him so happy that I knew Rolland.) Foerster [2] visited him recently. There's so much I must tell you. A childlike and devout letter from Strunz [3] fitted well into this hour's afterglow. Yesterday I received a reassuring letter from Ernst Lissauer [4] which I want to show you and Professor Strunz.

Just now someone is playing divinely solemn, beautiful music. If you could only hear it. Imagine, I was enough of a lunatic to think: "perhaps he will come!"

Farewell, my dear, be tenderly embraced by your

Lamb

1 Privy Councillor Lammasch, Professor of International Law and eminent pacifist. Was one of Emperor Charles' advisers and Minister in his last cabinet. 2 Professor Friedrich Foerster, leading pacifist and author of many works on ethics. 3 Professor Strunz, Professor of the History of Natural Science and Director of the Vienna Urania. I was his protégé. 4 Ernst Lissauer, who had written the *Song of Hate* against England, had been converted by Rosa Mayreder and myself, and was now opposed to war. Later he disavowed his Song of Hate.

My dear:

Probably my greetings from the Koenigsee will arrive later than my letter mailed in Austria.—Berchtesgaden has all the charm of the Austrian mountains, but is built in the German-Munich style. There are a lot of well-dressed people, almost exclusively Germans. It's all very lovely. Trains and boats leaving on time, despite crowds of people. The lake is entrancingly beautiful. The day was radiant, the sun shining down on the snow of the glaciers. Now I must tell you why I stopped over here. I felt that there was going to be some good weather and wanted to enjoy it. When my little cure was done with, I bade the Sanitarium a friendly farewell. Here in the inn I have a nice room for two crowns a day.

Tomorrow I'll send you a feuilleton I managed to write yesterday at a single session, although only just escaped from the Sanitarium, but happy because of the doctor's favorable diagnosis.

Goodnight, my dear. I daren't even think that had I left sooner, I might by now have been looking upon your dear, good face.

With many kisses, your

Lamb

Hinterleitner Inn
Parsch near Salzburg

My dear:

Yesterday I read your friendly letter over and over again. Forgot to tell you that I am looking forward to your essay.[1] There's something else I must say, my dear man. I admit that I was irritated, but not *irritable*. Nobody could accuse me of that except a certain unsentimental gentleman who thinks because of the war he must change his naturally silken-soft skin into a rhinoceros's hide. Now don't tell me that neither you nor anyone else, "thank heaven," can shed his skin. Now if Wilson, "thank heaven" can't shed his skin, there'll be war with America. But who knows whether there would have been any war at all if people could have shed their skins. I am always ready to shed mine, if it will do any good. Is one's skin so important after all? Of course, I am in love with yours, no matter what kind of skin it is, and certainly don't want to watch you while you shed it. You say I am too easy-going, forebearing; that this is my cardinal sin. I am really very strait-laced. But I always understand what people should be forgiven for. And weren't there reasons enough for your spells of moodiness—reasons I have always understood? For your moodiness is always on the outside, as it were, superficial. And then I am doubly happy when you recapture your normal serenity, for then I know all is well with you. Your theory that your good humor is nothing but make-believe never sounded very convincing to me.

I feel the beauty yonder, out of doors, so intensely. In the evening, people sing as they come down from the mountains. Everybody is happy because the rainy season is over. Yesterday it was as if a new light had been thrown upon my conception of life, when I read this marvelous poem by Hebbel: [2]

> *The thought made me tremble and I sprang up*
> *And clasped life to me,*
> *And in white-heat of living*
> *Furiously fought through to God and Nature.*
>
> *Death, return often and touch me lightly*
> *When I go soft in my soul,*
> *That I may win myself back,*
> *Remembering Thee.*

Thanks for everything and a thousand greetings

Fri.

[1] Reference to a trip to Galicia undertaken by Stefan Zweig on official duty. The essay described the devastation wrought by the war and possibilities of rehabilitation.   [2] Friedrich Hebbel, famous German playwright and poet.

Parsch, August 30

My dear:

I sensed immediately that your letter was written in the forest and was happy for you and me too. How nice of you to let me select the letters.[1]

Thank you, my dear, for having made my stay here beautiful with your letters, and so brought comfort to my

70

melancholy hours, and even cheer.—I hope to phone you Thursday. In a few days it will be three years since I longed just as much for Vienna as now, so that I might see you.

Affectionately your faithful

F.M.

1 A selection of Lenau's letters was to be published by the Insel Verlag.

(Stefan's great friend Romain Rolland had put me in touch with other pacifists working in neutral Switzerland for the International Red Cross. The correspondence that follows resulted from these new contacts.)

International Women's Committee
For Permanent Peace
French Section
Breitlauen, September 16, 1915

Madame:

I have heard from Monsieur Romain Rolland that you were interested in the question of pacifism.

I am eager to find out how the women of Austria view these problems and what action they are planning. I am taking advantage of a trip to Switzerland to communicate with persons of all nationalities who, in spite of the present great difficulties, work for the realization of pacifist ideals. I want to find out what is being done in each country and am ready to keep you informed about what we are doing in France.

We are convinced that the cause will benefit very much if we can keep each other informed about our various activities.

Thanking you in advance, I am most sincerely yours,

Susanne Duchaine
Secretary of the French Section
of the International P.P.P. Committee

(The letter's envelope was stamped: Opened by the State Police)

My answer:

Mademoiselle:

The exchange of information has already produced results. The Austrian section is about to begin its work. It will be organized next week, and I shall keep you informed about what we are doing. Following the Hague Conference, a well-attended meeting was held. Furthermore, a Hungarian woman by the name of Madame Schwimmer has been traveling about with a Dutch colleague. Like Miss Jane Addams, the two ladies were well received by Cabinet Ministers and several Sovereigns. The General Association of Austrian Women is trying to initiate a lecture series for the discussion of various proposals. Also the Viennese review, *Women of Today* carries reports of our work in every issue and publishes appeals for peace. This magazine has given publicity to the founding of our section.

I would be happy to keep you informed of whatever effective action is taken. I hope we can keep in touch with each other. Thanking you in advance, I am yours most sincerely

Friderike M. von Winternitz

(The following letter from Romain Rolland, in which he thanked me for a feuilleton I had written, is of a later date, but shall be inserted at this point.)

International Red Cross Committee
International Agency for War Prisoners
Inter Arma Caritas
Geneva, January 31, 1916

Dear Madame:

I was deeply moved by your article and your wire. Our small group of friends is one of the few stars still shining in the night. May it never be obscured! May it continue to give forth its pale, trembling light until the time has come when it shall merge with the new day.

Your grateful and respectful

Romain Rolland

1 9 1 6

We were seldom separated during 1916. That year and the next, we occupied, from spring until late in the fall, adjoining garden pavilions in Kalksburg near Rodaun. Every day, after his work at the War Archives was over, Stefan would concentrate on his play *Jeremiah,* a Song of Songs to peace produced in the midst of war. When the play was finished, he presented me with the complete, artistically bound manuscript written by him in longhand without a single mistake. On the first page was a sonnet dedicating the work to me. This is the first stanza:

> *Whilst all the land was ringed with bristling arms*
> *And flames laid waste our world,*
> *All that was left me was a little garden*
> *And thou within it, my beloved, my comrade.*

Jeremiah was passed by the Censor and accepted for performance in Zuerich. We now went ahead with our project for a short trip to Switzerland.

1 9 1 7

In December 1917 we went to Zuerich and also visited Romain Rolland at the lake of Geneva. It was a marvelous feeling to be in a country not involved in war, and this feeling made it extremely difficult for Stefan to return after his leave had expired. So I went back to Vienna by myself and persuaded the Editor-in-Chief of the *Neue Freie Presse,* a daily for which Stefan Zweig had worked since his highschool days, to procure his contributor's discharge from military service. The price Stefan had to pay for his freedom was an article to be sent in by him every month. My message telling him about this arrangement was answered in the following wire:

Will accept arrangement with *Neue Presse;* am staying here in any case and am expecting you soon.

Zweig

A second wire followed:

Remaining here until permission for entry given; will call for you at Buchs, as soon as informed arrival.

Zweig

At the same time the following letter was sent:

My dear:

Many thanks for your good news. I am delighted at the extension and do hope you'll be coming soon. You will surely bring Susi along with you; she will like it here. Further details I will no doubt have from you either by wire or letter.

Now I want to get at my own work. Up till now everything has gone into essays, translations, waiting and watching.

Another thing: if you know which the right manuscript is, bring along the *Dostoievski* for me. It is in a blue cardboard portfolio, each chapter in a separate folder with its title, and the first drafts are still there with them. But only if it is no trouble for you. Then I could finish that job in good and definitive fashion.

Mrs. Albert [1] is *very* poorly. An operation apparently can't be avoided, and it seems, will be a life-and-death business. Today I wrote Rilke. I have made the acquaintance here of a lot of people, almost too many. Painters, poets, all sorts. My portrait is being done. Also there is a lot for you to do. The translation of a book which ought to keep you busy for your entire stay, is practically assured. And would be a good occupation for you.

Many thanks for the trouble you've been to. Let's hope it will be a success! But I am content with everything. And I'm in good spirits. Everything seems to be working out right. Our exchange has leaped upward mightily. The crown is at more than 50.

Affectionately yours,

Stefan

1 The artist, Lou Albert, a friend of Rilke; she and Rilke had frequently visited us in Kalksburg.

1 9 1 8

Stefan had called for my daughter, Susi, and me at the frontier, and then we went for a rest of a few weeks to Engadine, then again spent some time at the historic Hotel Schwert at Zuerich while Susi stayed at a children's boarding school. Then pretty soon we moved to Rüschlikon, into Hotel Belvoir which looked down upon the lake from a considerable height, and which became our headquarters. Here we had Romain Rolland as our guest for a few days. Hermann Hesse also visited us, and later, Frans Masereel, who came over from Geneva. And many others. In June Stefan visited the Swiss writer, Carl Seelig, in Lucerne, and then went on to Wengen.

Picture postcard with postmark 7/6/18.

My Dear F.:

Made it up here in one pull (but not in a Pullman). Enjoying ourselves thoroughly and also a good menu. Many greetings from my faithful bride, Virginia Brissago,[1] and your

Stefan Zweig

[1] The inevitable big black cigar.

Picture postcard Wengernalp, 7/8/18.

L.F.:

Pilatus was beautiful. Anyway I'm an all-fired good tourist. Today a lovely trip over the Bruenig to Interlaken, from thence to Wengen. No sign of Mrs. Privy Councillor [1] for which I'm grateful. It is too incredibly beautiful—also a heavenly day—the kind you never see except in dreams. Arrived 2 o'clock, took in the view for a quarter of an hour, and then, impelled as well as enraptured by my performance of yesterday, I walked without more ado for four hours over the Wengernalp, Scheidegg, and as far as the Eiger Glacier. It was lovely, not to be described. Now I am on my way back; at 6 o'clock I'll rest up at Wengernalp and hope to be in Wengen again by 7 o'clock, after consuming three sandwiches here. The old fool in me comes to life as soon as I am alone— luckily the foolishness paid off. Tomorrow I'm going to Interlaken; Wednesday I'll arrive by the last train in Rüschlikon and hope you'll be waiting for me. Oh! You must come here without fail!

Affectionately,

Stefan

[1] Mrs. Bertha Zuckerkandl, daughter of the newspaper publisher and politician Szeps, who was a trusted advisor of Crown Prince Rudolph; after the death of her husband, Professor of anatomy, she was generally known as Mrs. Privy Councillor. She was an internationally recognized art critic and presided over a *salon* in Vienna. Her sister was the sister-in-law of Clemenceau. Through this connection Mrs. Privy Councillor was able, while in Switzerland, to influence the peace negotiations toward a speedier conclusion. I met her through my father-in-law, von Winternitz, and my acquaintance with her was of long standing; our friendship lasted until her death after the Second World War.

L.F.:

Despite the missing Mrs. Privy Councillor, I stayed over here a whole day, and wouldn't leave at all if I didn't have to get back; it is so supernaturally beautiful here. The air has the same clarity as at St. Moritz. Wonderful alpine flowers and an endless number of walks. I intend to walk down to Lauterbrunnen and then will travel on. I simply can't get enough of traipsing around. The old Adam is stirring in me again. But he salutes Mrs. Eve herewith.

Affectionately,

Stefan

Spietz, 7/9/18

Dear F.:

I've had such wonderful luck: (A) with the weather, which is simply fantastic; (B) with the business of the visits. The fact that I didn't meet Mrs. Privy Councillor gave me that unforgettable trip to the Eiger Glacier and the descent, the following day, to Lauterbrunnen. Again, the fact that the Cassirers [1] were away for the day, gave me a chance for a wonderful swim in the warm lake and a quiet evening. By Wednesday evening, I'll be back home! Just think, in Salzburg there have been frightful floods, trains aren't running on some sections of the line.

Affectionately yours,

Stefan

[1] Bruno Cassirer and his wife, the actress, Tilla Durieux.

(After a long battle with the Austrian passport bureau we managed finally to get my daughter, 'Lix, to Switzerland. However, our governess, who had been the family factotum for years, couldn't get a permit to stay in Switzerland. I engaged someone else to help out and the children were settled near Weesen, at Amden, in the mountains, not far from Rüschlikon, and I traveled back and forth during the summer months between the two places. The following, undated letters were written by Stefan during the months of July and August. Most of those written at this time were not saved.)

Dear Fri.:

I am sending you, herewith, a special delivery letter and with it my warmest greetings. This place has emptied out since you left and I return to work, my head lowered like an ox pulling a plough. For really my urge to work has taken unto itself wings. I am not going to Zuerich today, not till tomorrow, and after that probably not again for some time. You needn't worry.[1] Rejoice in your play.

Stefan

P.S. There is an item in today's *Neue Freie Presse* about the arrest of a "Krowoten" [Croat] who sold a loaf of bread for 200 crowns.

[1] The reason for my worrying was the epidemic of so-called Spanish Grippe in Zuerich.

Dear Fri.:

I hope you arrived safely and found Susi in good spirits, and that my grouchiness has been forgotten. It was only the sort of prophetic *Katzenjammer* I always get when I have a presentiment that I must face an unpleasant fact—I have been suspecting right along that my August-September plans won't work out, and that I won't get the job finished, and above all, that I won't be able to make that longed-for trip. Don't be angry with me! I was terribly upset about it myself.

Write soon and come, as soon as you feel more tranquil, to your

Stefzi [1]

[1] Nickname which my children gave him.

(In French)

L.F.:

I was very sorry about your sharp letter. But we are all wrought up; how can we stay calm in the midst of this insanity. I am very tired, I no longer have the will for any sort of a change whatsoever, I even doubt whether I shall

have the energy for a trip to Tessin. A horrible feeling of
the uselessness of anything anyone could do, an impotence
for happiness, all this weighs on me and I try to drown it
in work. I've been writing letters for four hours this morning,
and postcards. Tomorrow I'm going to Zuerich to visit Hohenlohe.[1]—You know, don't you, I don't want to tie you to myself,
I am such a poor companion, impossible to comfort me, full
of evil humors, whereas the children enjoy having you with
them. For the moment I am at a crisis—it will pass, but I
don't want anybody to get infected by it, through me; I am
not isolating myself for the mere pleasure of it (I haven't
any pleasure in anything now at all), but because I am considerate of the peace of mind of others. Yet you reproach me
because of a tiny "hurrah" which was only ironical at best.
I am coming soon.

1 Duke Hohenlohe, an invalid. Occasionally Stefan visited him.

My dear:
  I haven't as much to tell you from here as you have to
tell me from your end. Because I don't know anything. I
haven't had any mail from Austria for some days, and I don't
go to Zuerich. The only one of our friends I've seen is
Ehrenstein who was here yesterday evening with Miss Bergner.[1]
Both were awfully sorry you were away. Otherwise, only rest,
work, letters.
  I'm glad things are going so well with you, that you
feel well. But I am entitled to demand another six pounds [2]
of you, now that I am not around to bother you. Please take
care of yourself. The past three days have been most unusual, the heat chalked up a nine years' record for Switzerland
—which might explain your loss of appetite. Or is it perhaps
the absence of this captain? [3] I daren't think that it might
be me.
  Paul Stefan is to arrive tomorrow. That probably will
cost you a letter from me. And a visit. Because I wanted to
be with you Sunday. But it will have to be some other week.
The piece [4] must be finished and this undoubtedly will take
another fourteen days; meanwhile, of course, you'll be here.
  Extraordinary how badly I can write when I am writing to you. My unwillingness to communicate with anybody

turns inwards, I exchange a few words now and then with our neighbor, Mr. d'Obry, read a lot, and am glad to be so isolated. I sense in myself the suspense that grips the whole world; this month and till the end of August must decide whether it is to be war or complete shipwreck; every minute is pregnant with fate. And ours, too, will be decided by the event. Anyone at all sensitive to the general atmosphere of tension must be conscious of this dreadful pressure bearing down on one—now or never is the moment to speak out. But where? But how?

Be happy, my darling! Forgive me if I write so badly! The air all about me is so sultry! Let's hope it will soon be pure and clean again. Give my best to the children!

Affectionately yours,

Stefan

[1] The poet, Albert Ehrenstein and the actress, Elisabeth Bergner.   [2] I had lost weight.   [3] Refers to a war casualty in whose rehabilitation I was interested.   [4] The "piece" he was working at was *The Legend of a Life* whose hero he had given the name of Friedrich Marius.

My dear:

I always write you now in the morning, just before the letter-carrier arrives, so that anything that comes for you can be sent along with him. The manuscript of your novel came. Eventually it could be submitted here, perhaps some excerpts from it. Also I have a laundry ticket for two children's dresses. Shall I fetch them?

The heat has really been fantastic. I won't stir out of Rüschlikon—also there is the grippe, which still continues in Zuerich. Last evening I was at Faesi's;[1] then at midnight we rowed around the lake and that was marvelous.

My darling, my beloved, I can explain about things so badly in a letter. I have my pen too much in my hand. I can scarcely bear to look at a sheet of paper any more. Yesterday I finished the feuilleton and must work at the piece, because Paul Stefan gets here tomorrow and will probably nag at me about *Donauland*.[2] I won't let him push me too hard. On Friday there is to be a performance of *Alt-Wien,* no doubt at the instance of Dr. Bach, who, however, hasn't been to visit me.[3] I won't go if I can help it. Even to look at this sort of prancing around would bore me; I can't get over my indignation because of the thousands and thousands of francs that are wasted on this kind of silly entertainment, while at home the whole population is starving and destitute. This sort of art-profiteering digusts me to the very depths of my soul.

I have heard from Rolland; he doesn't know what is behind the *affaire Gilbeaux* [4] either. Like me he is convinced of his honesty *jusqu'à la preuve du contraire*. He appears to be much taken up with this business. As always, R. is the only human being from whom I receive real letters. Out of Vienna not a sound. I have a feeling that everything there is in stagnation.

I ought to read you a lecture on politics. I believe things are working out *very well,* very well. My optimism will surely prove to have been justified. The Germans have become more conciliatory, and the only thing that could have blocked this rapidly spreading mood, the Offensive, has bogged down completely. Soon the military clique will have sung its last song. Only a last-minute, phenomenal stupidity could prevent an agreement; but I tell you again, everything at this time argues against that.

Goodbye. I have another twenty pages of work, and letters to write.

Affectionately yours,

Stefan

Best to the children, take good care of yourself and come back with a plus of ten kilos.

1 Professor Dr. Robert Faesi who lived on the opposite shore of the lake and for whom Stefan had a high regard. 2 The periodical, *Donauland,* which published the Austrian War Archives with the help of native writers, among them Rilke, Czokor, Polgar and the musicologist, Paul Stefan. 3 Editor of the Vienna *Arbeiter Zeitung* and director of the Austrian Propaganda Bureau. 4 Henri Gilbeaux, the French poet, who had translated Zweig's poems into French and, because of his friendship for Russia, was condemned to death *in absentia* in France, but later pardoned.

My dear:
I've already written you once today and am dead-weary of writing, but your letter must be answered for the

sake of complete frankness between us. Nothing must be passed over in silence between you and me. Your last letters were so sweet and warm and beautiful—but they hurt me nonetheless.

They are really an indictment of me, without your being aware of it. I thought you were living up there with the children in complete freedom, and did a little work now and then. And you write me that you're pinned down to the typewriter, and that excursions are a thing of the past. And how do you think I feel? Like the wicked jailer who whips you on to work, who, in his greed and money-madness, steals away your peace of mind.

I am truly conscious of my innocence. I warned you, I begged you to take a look at the book, to find out whether the translation was usable. Nonetheless, although I feel I'm guiltless, this kills my pleasure in knowing that you are up yonder. I haven't any more pleasure in it, only a *troubled conscience*. And meanwhile you go on torturing yourself! But I've told you: *There is no sense to a sacrifice after you come to feel that it is a sacrifice.*

Perhaps your lack of confidence in me is infectious; in your wonderful letters I can see only those particular passages, but they spoil my whole day—I beg of you, I adjure you, in the name of our fine friendship, *get away from that typewriter right away*. Miss Henning will type everything, you will make corrections, and I'll do the revising. This job will be a joy to me if I know you aren't sitting at that typewriter any longer. I promise you as a reward, that I'll blow in the three hundred franc fee on loose women, as soon as I have the time.

You write your own piece! It spoils the little pleasure I still have thinking of you, at daybreak, and telling myself that you are happy. I grow melancholy because it's been my doing that you have been so upset. *Please, if you love me,* get away from that typewriter, write your own piece. If you won't give way on this point, *I shall be angry, really angry.*

Affectionately,

Stefan

81

Could you, out of your fantasy, write a review of Rheinhart's [1]
Garden of Paradise for the *Donauland?*

1 The Swiss poet Hans Reinhart.

My dear:

I'm writing you despite the fact that I feel inclined to
be lazy, because this air wraps one about in such beautiful
warmth that one wants to stretch out one's legs and just con-
template the smoke—oh, excuse me, I didn't want to give
that away. Well, at this precise moment I haven't a Virginia
in my hand, but as its substitute, a pen-holder! [1] There is
nothing worth retailing to you. Because it's so warm I don't
even go to the postoffice, am reading all sorts of books—including some erotic memoirs our good d'Obry [2] lent me; they
date from the time of the French Revolution. Also newspapers, but these latter without any appetite or interest. The
revision of my piece, done in red ink, is finished. It has actually
nothing to do with Expressionism or Modernism, seems to
be not especially new or unusual, but clear in its humanity
and somehow well-rounded. I am glad to work on it now.
As soon as it is done I'll reward myself with a visit to you,
but that is undoubtedly a full fourteen days off as yet. One
or another feuilleton for the *Presse* looms over me ominously
—actually I wanted to write it today. Perhaps the needed
energy will come with the coolness of evening. Because I
really make this a test of my strength, this twaddle that I
turn out only half willingly.[3] In one of the books that I have
the author says that Rousseau wasn't any good unless he wrote
with feeling. And as far as the *N. Fr. Presse* is concerned,
I suspect that I think too much about my readers.

Tomorrow evening I'm going over to Faesi's. Aside
from that, the good loneliness. Zuerich is only an unattractive
thought. Just now, on a warm evening like this, it is so beautiful, enveloped in its lilac veil, and with rose-colored clouds
over its hilltops, that I haven't any desire to see it by day-
light. I enjoy your meadows with you! Take care of yourself,
darling! Get a respite from our psychological and pedagogical
discussions, be happy and lighthearted. Love to the children.

Affectionately,

Stefan

1 This was a reference to oft-repeated warnings I voiced to the effect that smoking strong Tessin cigars might prove harmful.   2 Our neighbor in the Hotel Belvoir, an interesting man, a member of the Danish nobility. He had for a long time done research in the Belgian Congo on the expeditions of Livingston and Stanley. He had no children of his own and fell in love with my little Susi, who often came from the Institut in Zuerich to visit us. Twenty years later he looked Susi and me up in Paris, and offered to adopt her so that, with Danish citizenship, things might be made easier for her.   3 Nevertheless there were some little masterpieces among these feuilletons.

Dear Fri.:

I am sending you the essay; hope it meets with your approval. Strange: Miss Widman, our neighbor, and another young lady were here today, to bring you a bouquet. Now they want to send it on to you. Why? How so? I haven't the faintest notion. Today I am to have a talk with Dr. Bach who has forgiven me my remarks about propaganda. He told me that the *Wiener Reichspost* 1 recently attacked my *Jeremiah,* which is now regarded in certain circles as *the* play. *Tant mieux.*

Another wonderful letter from Rolland! Gilbeaux threatens a hunger strike unless he is cleared. The whole business really only amounts to a sort of preventive arrest.

And now my very best! As for me, I don't seem to be able to write and make sense. I must first get through with all this work. I haven't yet decided what to christen the piece. *The Great Shadow* would be good, except that Duhamel's piece which has some similarity in one scene, is entitled: *Dans l'ombre des Statues.* I shall doubtless hit on something. Take care of yourself, darling. And farewell. I hope to visit you by the end of the week.

Affectionately yours,

Stefzi

1 Daily with antisemitic tendencies.

At the postoffice.
Thanks for your sweet phone call. I was, as always, a bit confused at the telephone. Don't be angry. I can use a secretary only when the piece is ready, and even if I work at white heat, that won't be before the end of the month—I hope.

Then everything will be easier and clearer; perhaps then I can come to Amden for two days. But I must roll this boulder off my chest; even now my brain and hands are aching with the effort I'm making to roll it off. Anyway, I haven't changed it much, only made it more concentrated.

From Vienna practically no letters! I am feeling well: I work, but I'm scarcely living just now. Perhaps things will be better after the *Dostoievski*. I long so for freedom from worry—if only a short reprieve, but at any rate, freedom. The first thing I'll work at after the piece is finished, will be the *Rousseau*. I am hoping that newspapers will be getting here soon again. I am *very* happy at the prospect of having you again with me.

Stefan

My dear:

Thanks for your sweet letter. I implore you again, don't torment yourself: what I need first and foremost is a hundred pages of the *Emile;* that will be something to send Kiepenheuer anyway.

Yesterday Mrs. Privy Councillor called up from Wengen. She is about the only one of all our "friends" who think of us even when they don't want anything (of course, also Felix Braun). But just now, when the mails are delayed for weeks at a time, and I sit waiting for news about my piece, I get nothing but requests asking me to do reviews of books. Sometimes I think I see a certain contempt in this and then I have to be on my guard lest I fall into a general contempt of mankind.

My dear, don't be angry with me. I am just now oppressed by a fearful bitterness anent the time: never was there an era as insane as ours, with the slaughter going on and on. The German defeat was a good thing and served to break Ludendorff's power, but now this unheard-of joy that sweeps America! They have tasted blood. And now *they* want the same sort of victory that the Germans wanted only two weeks ago, the great, decisive victory, with their adversaries beaten to their knees. Truth to tell, we are all criminals if we remain silent, and perhaps it will be imperative to speak up. Moreover, those things in the *Fr.W* [1] *have attracted atten-*

tion in Bern and have been much discussed. I scarcely think the gentlemen will make a move, however—I feel the urge to speak up just once, to cry out. In any event, day after tomorrow at latest, we'll see the world's end. Paul Stefan tells me about the misery that grips Vienna, at the same time that T. writes me he is going to Karlsbad for four weeks, then to Gastein. Some people have "peace" all the time. But not much longer! I believe that the hour of decision is about to strike for each one of us.

As usual, you've had bad luck with your affairs. Just at present it takes three weeks or more for the mail from Vienna to get here. There no longer is any regular means of communication. And on top of everything else, comes the fall of the Cabinet, the drop in the rate of exchange, utter confusion and insanity.

When will we see each other again? I think Paul Stefan is leaving next Saturday. You will have more news before then. I haven't been to Zuerich for days. I have no desire to go there. And besides, there may be some danger.[2]

How mistaken you are if you think I waste my time in frivolity! I am big with awareness of the world—I have no pleasure in anything at all. And work like a criminal condemned to hard labor. In the next day or so I shall drink a few glasses of wine with Paul Stefan—he says it is good medicine. I hear it is pretty generally indulged in in Vienna, in spite of the prevalent high prices, as the only thread to cling to, while one is suspended over the abyss.

Affectionately, my darling, that hast wings within thyself, and the children!

Your

Stefan

I hope Susi is feeling better.

[1] The review *Friedenswarte,* organ of theoretical pacificism.   [2] Spanish grippe was still widespread.

Dear F.:

I have corrected twenty additional pages of *Rousseau* with a great effort, or rather have re-written them almost completely. The number of essential corrections made me realize what you have accomplished in the fifty pages you have corrected and which are still here. Please tell me what I should do? Send the book and work up to you? If I must plough through the whole of it myself, it will take me eight days for that alone. And I have to write a feuilleton, wanted to do the *Dostoievski,* because Kippenberg [1] is coming in eight days, and then I would have the chance to let him take the manuscript along with him. I don't know which way to turn, with this press of work, otherwise I would have taken it all on myself.

I had a word with Mrs. Privy Councillor while on the run between Kessler [2] and Fried.[3] She sends you a thousand greetings. It was infernally hot; enough to make one collapse. Wiesner [4] is in Pontresina, she told me, and a lot more. I enclose some letters for you.

Please do write soon and let me know how you all are, and if and when you are coming. I must know your plans, so that I can make mine to accord with them and wind up this accursed *Rousseau.* I hope you find a reasonable resolution of your inner conflict which I entirely understand, a resolution that will let you attain tranquility at least. Many greetings,

Your

Stefan

*Postscript:—*Evening!—I have ploughed through another thirty pages and hope, by working at top speed, to have everything done by day after tomorrow. Your part I'll edit later. So don't worry. But it is a bitter pill for me to swallow right now, because, due to the heat, I'm not up to my usual working form and am already yearning for a rest. Oh! the bondage of these feuilletons, all these stupid hack jobs that keep me for months on end from my real job, of turning out a poetic work. That is why, and only why, I am so harassed, unreasonable, and so quarrelsome; my whole yearning is to be once more so tranquil within myself, so composed, that I could write a poem. But that will probably never happen. And at the same time, in the political sphere, an infinity of horror confronts us, endless, pathless, and at the end, catastrophe! What frightful days!

Please, in any event, write me the name of the woman secretary; I have a few merely manual things to be done, the seven copies of the piece, some corrections to be transferred to the second copy of *Dostoievski*. So terribly much is pouring in at once, because I want to give the manuscript to Kippenberg to take along, since I don't care to send it by mail, and I must get through with the *Rousseau*. I shall also write Dr. Rieger [5] who may help me.

[1] Professor Anton Kippenberg, director of Inselverlag.   [2] Count Kessler. [3] The composer and conductor, Oscar Fried; both were on a diplomatic mission for Germany.   [4] Baron Wiesner, head of the Section of the Press, at the Ballplatz (Foreign office), Vienna.   [5] Erwin Rieger, in later years a good friend, the excellent Austrian poet, critic and translator, and Stefan Zweig's biographer. Rieger belonged to a family whose members were of the officer class, but took a job as apprentice to a pharmacist in Zuerich in order to leave Austria during the war.

L.F.:

Here the receipt of Elisabeth v.W. documents, also the receipt for the 7 Fr. 50 which I had accepted for you and which I intend to spend on light women. In addition, the corrections of the *Switzerland* which I attended to immediately.

The Gilbeaux business seems not too bad for him (morally speaking). He is accused of having aided the "Revolution in Russia." Who hasn't? All the statesmen of the Entente —and anyway that happened over a year ago. I am convinced it is just a French plot. Debrit [1] is advocating his cause in a big way. It is to be hoped that all of us will help him.

I'll keep you in touch, as soon as I know more.

Here things are quiet. I chatter a bit with that pretty girl from the Gymnasium in La Chaux-des-Fonde—happy, unfeeling Switzerland—where young boys and girls study together. Under such working conditions I would have flunked out every year. I have taken care of everything and done everything needful in Zuerich. My article on the Vienna Exposition finally appeared, after the event.

I hope you are all right. I am glad to get news from you. Love to the children and yourself.

Your

Stefan

[1] Publisher of a pacifist newspaper in Geneva.

Postcard, 8/12/18
L.F.:

Austrian border closed. Bahr is leaving Salzburg; will become director of the Burg Theater.—*Neue Züricher Zeitung* is publishing a third piece about my article. It seems to have caused a big sensation.

Affectionately, Stefzi

Postcard, 8/13/18

Darling:

Only the good news that G. was set free on Monday; as we suspected, the case collapsed for lack of proof. I am very glad.

There was a *sublime* feuilleton in the *Berliner Tageblatt* by Leonhard.[1] So wise, so lucid, so humanly gay and masterful: I went to three shops trying to buy it for you, unfortunately in vain. I have attended to the flowers.

Affectionately, Stefan

1 Leonhard Adelt, who was assigned to the Press Bureau in Austria and was a war correspondent.

My dear:

The reviews haven't come in yet; on the other hand a letter from Leonhard did. Professor Weilen,[1] a dear friend, was killed by a fall while mountain climbing in Austria. When are you coming? *Please let me know in time.*

Affectionately, Stefan

1 Professor at the University of Vienna, publicist, editor of the papers of Crown Prince Rudolph.

I stayed overnight at Faesi's; I couldn't get back across the lake. I absolutely can't write any more; my essay has started a flood of letters, among them a very nice one from Prince Hohenlohe, inviting me to visit him. But how I hate ink and pen. Forgive me, I can't write letters just now, but I'm coming soon.

Affectionately, Stefan

88

L.F.:

Mrs. Privy Councillor just telephoned that she is traveling by way of Zuerich; I am going down there now and will spend an hour with her. She was terribly sorry to have missed you, she would so much have liked to talk with you. But I didn't want to phone you to come down from Amden to Weesen [1] in this fearful heat just for five minutes with her.

[1] To meet the train on which our friend was traveling to Austria.

(In the beginning of September I returned to Rüshlikon, while my daughters stayed with a family in Zuerich under the supervision of a young Zuerich lady and attended an excellent school. Since Miss Schinz had an uncle in Nyon on Lake Geneva where he was superintendent of schools, we decided later to send the little group there, so that the children might, for a time at least, have a chance to learn French.)

1 9 1 9

(To Lugano)

Dear F.:

You won't be angry will you if I tell you that I was tremendously pleased *not* to find you here on my return. The day up in the mountains was so unsurpassed in its beauty and I was happy to know you were in such heavenly country. Please don't stint yourself in anything; the best things left us will be our memories, and not banknotes. Eat well, go on excursions, don't worry, stay as long as your heart desires. Conditions in Austria improve from day to day, the trains are still running, although somewhat infrequently, nevertheless things are getting back almost to normal. Please let friend Rieger cheer you up and you cheer him up too and be assured it's perfectly alright. I send you my most devoted greetings.

Your faithful Stefzi

(To Nyon)

It's a happy coincidence that we always telephone each other at the same time. But you seem to me to be a bit disappointed because I still stay on here. But, my dear, it is very quiet here, I am in the midst of my work, get my mail regularly, am tranquil, because I can be reached in case of emergency, and am glad at last to be at peace again. In my room it is, as they say in Berlin, "Budelwarm" (warm and cosy as a dog-kennel). Babettl, moreover, just as if she knew exactly what I wanted, puts a warming pan in my bed every evening. In short, my dear, it would be foolish for me to make an abrupt change for no good reason since things are just right for work and research. I hope shortly to be able to send you parts of the Rolland book to copy.

The reform in the divorce laws [1] has been held up arbitrarily by the Christian Socialists, but has not been abandoned. I have given my mother notice in writing of my intentions. Alfred has also talked with her. You have, apparently, absorbed somewhat of my humor and coloration and so are also taking a rather dark view of things. I am not as bad as you imagine. And I love you very much, even if I stay away for several weeks in order to go on with my work.

Please don't forget to telegraph Rolland tomorrow. Also, surely you should dedicate your book to him. There's not another human being who deserves our gratitude more than he.

I am looking forward to being with our friends. But at the moment I'm afraid to interrupt my work. What I'd like best would be to get it pretty much finished in one big push. I am fearful of *Dostoievski's* fate.[2]

Goodbye, best to the children.

Altogether yours,

Stefzi

It would be unpardonable for you to leave Lake Geneva before the middle of March. Every day now means something gained by the children and by all of us. Who knows what awaits us in the future?—Rieger sends his very best. We took a long walk together.

[1] This refers to the legal dispensation to divorced catholics, on which depended the possibility of my getting married again in Austria.   [2] Delay in completing his work.

Dear F.:

I have just received the enclosed letter from my mother, from which you will see that, without saying a word to you, I have acted entirely accordingly to your wishes and that, on her part, as I foresaw, she will interpose no obstacles. Of course, I had to send in the bitter Salzburg pill [1] today. It is time to make an end of all this secrecy.

I don't see any objection, now, to your writing my mother a longer letter; that is what you always wanted to do (date it from Rüshlikon and don't be any stupider than you usually are). It goes without saying, do it only if you feel so inclined. And don't muddle it up with your money obsession. [2] The preliminary peace will be signed by March. That will be the signal for me to return home. And then will come another kind of peace, the inner peace.

Affectionately yours,

Stefzi

Greet *les enfants* for me. Do they talk a little already? (French.) You know the address, Vienna, Garnisongasse 10.

[1] Change of residence to Salzburg.   [2] Refers to my conviction that I should pay my own way.

HIS MOTHER'S LETTERS

Vienna 1/23/19

My beloved Stefferl:

The content of your dear letter was a great surprise, although we had been informed by reliable sources of a very close friendship with the lady in question. But now we find ourselves confronted by facts. I hope that you, as a mature and serious man, have examined such an important step from every angle and made a choice worthy of you. As we have heard, the lady is endowed with superior intelligence and a gentle nature. These are qualities that may be of benefit to your own character. You know, my dear son, that I love my children with my whole heart and was always deeply concerned about your and your brother's future. Thus you will understand how much I am affected by your decision. There are many problems to be discussed, more than there is space for in a letter. All that will have to wait till we can talk together face to face. My eager wish to have a daughter now has been fulfilled. And so we greet your bride-to-be most cordially. I shall be delighted to press her to my mother's heart. May the future bring you all the happiness for which we have been praying. My beloved son, remember me to your future bride whose personal acquaintance I want to make as soon as possible. Thanking you for the marvelous chocolate, I am your loving

Mama

February, 1919

Dear Frau Friderike:

Your sweet letter has moved me deeply; the more so, as the sentiments you expressed are the same as mine. Though I cannot write as beautifully as you do, I can say wholeheartedly that Stefan's decision to found a family has made me extremely happy. It was our constant, even if heretofore unfulfilled wish to have a daughter. And now we can look forward to an event that we consider a highly fortunate one. Your letter expresses so much warmth of feeling, such a tenderness and, what pleases me most, so much touching solicitude for our beloved Stefan, that it seems to guarantee a happy marriage of the kind devoutly hoped for by loving parents.

A clever woman like yourself will have realized that Stefan needs to be treated with extreme gentleness. He is good-hearted, his way of thinking noble. During the past years he, like everyone else, has suffered a good deal, and become very unsettled. But I am quite sure that a tranquil and well-ordered family life can restore his balance.

I long for the moment when I can meet you in person, embrace you and become your loving mother. My husband joins me in sending the most cordial greetings.

Affectionately yours,

Ida Zweig

(From Rüshlikon to Nyon)

Dear Fritzi:

Many thanks for your letter to my mother which will make her very happy. Salzburg will be a bitter pill for her to swallow.[1] Alfred writes me my parents had planned to let us have a large apartment in their house. But just now Vienna is impossible for me. Though I hope to be able to get over that hurdle too.

Things seem to be going badly in Vienna. A. writes that Dr. Schenk's house was burglarized yesterday and all the gold he uses for his dental work was stolen. I am really impatient, despite all this, to get back to my regular routine and to my own things. We shall have to remain abroad at least another six to eight weeks, which I dislike every day more and more, although I am getting along excellently in Belvoir.

Don't be angry with me if I advise you to stay on in N. with the children. I am leading a quiet and very contented life. It would be madness for you to undertake the long journey now. I am coming to you in any event, in the near future. You know that I am always in a much better mood after these absences; let's allow ourselves the fun of looking forward to being together again.

The business with Ch. touches me very closely, above all because of R.[2] The unhappy man is always involved in other people's troubles. How great are the demands upon his benevolence!

Now goodbye, don't worry about me, everything is in good shape.

Affectionately yours,

Stefan

Best to the children.

[1] Stefan had, two years before this, already bought our future house at Kapuzinerberg, which I hoped we would occupy only during the six warmer months, because I would have liked to be near my mother and have the children near their father and grandfather. The house had to be remodelled to make it habitable in winter and that proved to be a very difficult job. I had to get the alterations made during the next few months, but even afterward, for the next few years, we had a lot of trouble because of them.   [2] Romain Rolland.

(*From Rüshlikon to Nyon*)

Dear Fritzi:

I was very sorry that you were so upset, but gradually more and more will be unloaded on your shoulders, and it is a mistake for you to take these small matters so hard. I hope the interesting people you met in Bern have diverted you.

The enclosed card from your sister-in-law is not calculated to make you happy either. But perhaps it will re-enforce my appeal to you to fold your tents in Nyon as soon as possible! We shouldn't stay separated any longer than is necessary at this time, and the twelve hours that separate us are just too much. We'll have lots of running around to do about getting passports, permission for Fräulein, the moving, packing. I'd like to get on with my work. Fräulein can help you with a lot of things in Zuerich; you should husband your strength. Just because nothing can be decided upon in advance, one has to be prepared to move quickly; the delay of a day in the arrival of a letter may have serious consequences. This proves that I am right in believing that in these catastrophic times we should stay together in or near Zuerich, our heavy luggage should be ready to be sent off on a moment's notice, so if anything unforeseen comes up, we could make an immediate decision. If worst comes to worst, you'll have to go ahead with Rieger; I certainly won't burden you with commissions and responsibilities. I won't be able to figure things out to the exact day and hour. This terrible cold spell can surely not last, in a few days winter will be over; don't take this decision of ours too hard, everything will come out all right. We are fighting the great fight for the great peace, each in his own way, but in the last analysis, we are fighting for each other. Think everything over quietly, don't take trivia too seriously, always think that this is our final and most difficult hour which we shall get through unscathed.

Affectionately,

Stefan

Give my best to Fräulein Schinz and the children.

(Stefan was now terribly impatient to return to Austria, where chaos and near-famine still reigned. Believing that my Viennese housekeeper would be indispensable in helping us move and unpack, we brought the Swiss governess with us to Salzburg. There were five of us—our friend Rieger traveled with us—on the train, in windowless cars, and we arrived during the night at Salzburg. Because we were residents of Vienna and not of the Crownland of Salzburg and since every Crownland, owing to the food short-

94

age, forbade the entry of non-residents, we had to battle for permission to live there, and this made a lot of trouble for me, due to the fact that I didn't as yet bear Stefan's name and couldn't, therefore, claim to be a resident through ownership of a house. And no sooner were we settled in a hotel than the young Swiss girl fell ill with an attack of appendicitis. The hotel doctor who smelt Swiss valuta (Francs meant a fortune compared with the Austrian crown) had her taken to his home while I was away and insisted on operating on her. We succeeded in getting her reliable medical attention and then sent her back to Zuerich. Meanwhile Stefan had gone to Vienna.)

(*To Salzburg, Hotel Nelboech*)

Wels, March 29/19.

Dear F.:

I'm writing this on the train. I left because there's no train on Sunday and I couldn't have gotten at my things until Tuesday and in the meantime would have been bursting with impatience. It will be much simpler for me to return to Salzburg after I've disposed of the *most* urgent matters in Vienna. Perhaps next week, when more trains will be running.

As to various matters, only this: (1) Don't try to economize on food. (2) Get somebody to help you in case L.[1] keeps on being useless. (3) Hire a lawyer in case the affair seems to be going badly. (4) Hand over the trunks, duly insured, to an expressman. (5) Order everything that we agreed upon. The house ought to be in good condition and should be quite liveable in all seasons. We can either enjoy it ourselves or sell it or rent it to someone. Please phone immediately if you need me. I won't even consider the worst that can happen, that you won't be allowed to stay; we'll put up a good fight; eventually I'll make this whole business public. Should you, however, have to leave, there is nothing left but Vienna. There we'll do our best to get hold of the Salzburg house.

The trip is working out well, Attnang was a hideous sight; the people were bellowing like a herd of steer as they stormed the restaurant and literally trampled on each other to get a scrap of black-pudding sausage. A fearful thing to behold, foreshadowing worse to come.

My dear, don't be angry because I went to Vienna. But you know that I've been en route for a week and can't go on, because I'm so impatient; I have actually an infinity of things to do here that *can't be put off*. I know how strong you are, you will be able to win through; don't economize, but above all, do arrange matters so you needn't worry about the children.[2] As long as they have enough to eat, that is the most important thing—bringing them up, caring for their spiritual welfare, education, these are all secondary. The one important thing is to give them an orderly regime, no matter what kind, it doesn't matter whether it is a little better or worse. But there must be order.[3]

Affectionately,

Stefan

[1] Loni, the Swiss girl who was practically kidnapped. [2] He meant placing them under trustworthy supervision. [3] The Salzburg Provincial government didn't give me a temporary permit to stay until some time later.

(Vienna, April, 1919. From his apartment, VIII Kochgasse 8.)

L.F.:

I'm writing you a few lines per Lisi.[1] The mail is horrible, likewise the telephone.—To date not a penstroke on *Rolland*.[2] Worked on letters, sold some of my books [3] for 1200 crowns—errands and worries, and in between from early till late at night, the telephone. But I am cheerful and calm. Mrs. Privy Councillor hardly recognized me. At home they stuff me full of food and pamper me. My parents look forward to your coming with the most affectionate anticipation. You'll be given a whole miscellany of furnishings, curtains, linen, dinner services; my good mother is really touching, my father very old and in a mental decline.—Actually, everything that you hear about Vienna is exaggerated; true, very expensive, but despite the fact that Bolshevism is so nearby, pretty jolly. *Jeremiah* is to be put on in May. I have little interest in it, or the lecture.

Let me know when you are coming, if you want to stay at my place, whether I'm to send you money. And if you come soon, don't worry too much about the children, they'll get along fine even without you. And we must plan to inaugurate some sort of orderly regime. Good Mrs. Mandl [4] would like to visit us on her vacation (therefore not at my expense); it would be invaluable for me to have this able woman put my papers in order and carry the Rolland-Dostoievski business through to the end. Darling, think how wonderful that would be for Stefan Pascha. These first months are most important, getting the cart hitched up, after that it will run along of its own accord. I believe you won't object to this.—As for packing the things at my place, I'll harness up those old troopers, Josef and Mrs. Mandl, so you will be relieved of that job. I found a treasure at my parents': an ancient, iron travel-chest belonging to my Italian grandfather, just what I dreamed of for my manuscripts. It has been standing there in the attic for twenty years and I never even noticed it. Also, I am receiving cash, some 20 to 30 [5] which in any case will cover the most pressing expenses. So everything goes along in good order and indifferent well, unless Communism arrives the day after tomorrow. Come as soon as possible, we are all looking forward to your arrival.

Affectionately your Stefzi

Eat as much as you all can! Wire me so that I can meet you.

[1] Our family factotum, Elise Exner, who came to Salzburg and moved into the house on Kapuzinerberg, which was by now partly habitable, with the children.　[2] The biography of Rolland which had already been begun in Switzerland.　[3] Books in his library which at that time already comprised several thousand volumes.　[4] His Viennese secretary, a woman of unusual ability.　[5] 20-30,000 Crowns.

(After a short stay in Vienna we returned to Salzburg and entered upon our twenty-five-year sojourn at Kapuzinerberg.)

I insert here a letter from Stefan's father:

Vienna, May 2, 1919,
Garnisonsgasse 10

Dearest Fritzi:

We only just received your card of April 29 which announced your safe arrival. We were and are continually with both of you in our thoughts; we are anxious to know whether the furniture truck arrived with its contents intact and in good condition. Now you are faced with a difficult and troublesome task, for I know from experience what it means to move into a new place, especially when the circumstances are so complicated.

The dreaded first of May went off yesterday quite peacefully; to a certain extent this was due to the fact that the weather was so miserable, and was quite the reverse of propitious for big crowds in the streets.

Send us some good news soon. With affectionate greetings from—as I hope—your soon to be, Papa.

(Vienna, probably in the beginning of June 1919, to Salzburg, at Kapuzinerberg.)

Dear Fritzi:

Many thanks for the package which was very welcome. Here in Vienna Bolshevism seems irresistible. The situation becomes more acute from day to day. I meet a lot of people here, was with Professor Ferrière [1] yesterday at Frau Rundt's, tomorrow at Mrs. Privy Councillor Zuckerkandl's—was at the Volkstheater, at Heller's, Tal's, saw Benno Geiger [2] who has come back from Italy with a load of loot. My parents often speak of you and always most affectionately; they would like to go to Gastein. I'd much prefer not to have them leave at all before the situation clears up somewhat; for the time being it's best for old people like them who can move about only with difficulty, to stay where they are and not to wear themselves out or be worried. Marienbad is out of the question because they couldn't survive the chicanery at the frontier. I send you my most affectionate greetings.

Your Stefan

Take care of yourself.
Your novel is already at the bindery!

1 Professor Ferrière of Geneva, friend of Romain Rolland and President of the International Red Cross.   2 The poet, art historian and art dealer.

(Letter from Salzburg to Dr. Stefan Zweig, Vienna, IX, Garnisonsgasse.)

6/6/19

My dear:

Hope you aren't having too bad a time. Also hope this will be the last bout. Stay as calm as possible and don't wear yourself out tilting at irrelevant fear-born phantoms. Reality is hard enough. But don't persuade yourself, my darling, that you have less strength to cope with it than other people. Never forget that the world whose child you are is indestructible! I have just read some of *Thersites* again. I could weep when I see how you cut it. I bewail every word.

Worked on *Chresta*. I managed to get the phone installed the same day I applied for it. You can hear it ringing out in the garden and all over the house . . .

Affectionate greetings to your dear parents and Alfred, whom I wish the best of luck. I embrace you and am your

Mumu

(From his parents' home in Garnisonsgasse.)

Vienna, 9/26/19

Dear Fritzi:

After an interminable trip arrived home in the dark at 11:30. The journey is absolutely impossible for a woman carrying handbags, especially in the absolute darkness of the third class.[1] The discomfort is out of all proportion. I am still quite exhausted from it today. Today I shall start on the thousand errands I have to do. Just now I'm going to the Ministry.[2]

Affectionately yours,

Stefan

Write me your mother's exact address; I've lost the house number.

[1] I wanted to be in Vienna for the opening of *Jeremiah*.   [2] To expedite the permission for our marriage.

Vienna, 9/26/19

Dear Fritzi:

I was at the ministry today, had the (not as yet approved) document looked up, demanded to see the Commissioner—Trentini[1] greeted me cordially. Naturally, everybody being on vacation, not the least idea where the document was—am desperate; eight days ago the matter could have been managed easily. Now, because of this new regulation, it must, at least *pro forma,* be referred for "investigation" back to Salzburg. They promised to do that *today as an urgent matter.*

I haven't been to the Volkstheater yet today. The city is quite cheerful, well fed, you can get anything you want, sausages in the shops, chocolate, etc., but very dear. No sign of collapse. Everything as usual with us.

Affectionately, Stefan

Trentini told me he had read your book with great interest.

1 Mr. von Trentini, an excellent poet and writer, was a top official in the Ministry of the Interior.

L.F.:

Here everything is quite fine, but I'm altogether superfluous, the opening of *Jeremiah* is not to be until the 9th of October, for they had squeezed in a Suderman première for October 4th. For the time being I am not attending rehearsals; the whole affair has disgusted me because of these endless postponements. Nothing of mine ever goes off easily and smoothly. I am glad that everything is in good shape at the house and I wish I were back again; babbled about Salzburg with Buschbeck [1] yesterday.

My best, Stefan

1 The poet, Erhard Buschbeck, a native of Salzburg, later director of the Burgtheater in Vienna.

Salzburg, September 26/19

Dear Stefan:

Hope you are quite rested up from your trip, and found your dear parents and Alfred in good health and not unduly depressed.

Here, golden tranquility, warm and clear like summer. The mail that comes for you consists of the following items: the Vienna Peace Society reminds you of your really uncalled-for promise, that is, they allege you promised last spring to give them the net proceeds of *Jeremiah*. I would certainly advise you to do nothing of the kind, since the Society doesn't get anything at all done. You might send them a little something. I can't imagine that you really promised the net proceeds *en bloc*. You know how difficult such an extravagance will make things for you, and how much you dislike writing feuilletons and how much more important it is to help individuals rather than societies.

D'Obry asks whether you want to send any messages to Paris. He is leaving on Monday and will go on to Belgium. The house repairs will be finished by the middle of next week.

Many greetings to your parents and Alfred. To you, my dear, I wish all the best and as few aggravations as possible and whatever will make your heart glad.

Friderike

P.S. Did you get Rolland's letter that I forwarded?

Vienna, 10/2/19

Dear Fritzi:

Thanks a lot for your dear news—I can't write you today in much detail, the whole house is devastated by paper-hangers. There isn't a single place where I can write. *Jeremiah* is a tremendous humbug, they haven't yet, even today, Thursday, had a single rehearsal on the stage, because they pushed Suderman in ahead and the première is to take place in a week. I was at the old gentleman's [1] yesterday.

Affectionately, St.

[1] My former father-in-law, Privy Counsellor von Winternitz.

L.F.:

10/2/19

I'm writing a second card. I have just learned that the trains won't be running on Sunday; I'm leaving, therefore, without fail, early Saturday the 12th, so as not to lose a day, although I am lecturing the previous evening at the Grillparzer Society. Today, unfortunately, I missed your phone call: I am delighted that your troubles are at an end, that now we'll be able to live in peace and quiet at Salzburg. I wouldn't bother the old gentleman about our affair; if they don't grant us what they have granted 80,000 others within four weeks,[1] I'll make the whole business public and then these gentlemen will find out a thing or two. I am not at all inclined, in this world of pettifoggery [2] to take anything from these toplofty bureaucrats. I want to get things moving as fast as possible.

The Volkstheater business is nauseating; they intend to put on the play next week, only for one performance. Nevertheless, the tickets for the opening were sold out in a half hour. Oh, I loathe all business matters to the point of suffocation, yet you have to dive headforemost into them in these frightful times. I should have preferred having proofs of the *Three Masters,* which no doubt came in two sets, all together. Please send them to me as well as anything else of importance; a day's delay won't matter. I certainly want to have a look at a book as important as this one before it is brought out; this isn't merely a new edition, like *Thersites.*

Affectionately, Stefan

1 Delay of the marriage license.   2 The Social Democratic Party demanded that permission to remarry be given parties to a Catholic marriage that had been dissolved by divorce, while the Christian Socialist Party sabotaged the whole matter. When the Commissioner or Provincial Governor was a Christian Socialist, while the Vice-Governor was a Social Democrat, there developed a lot of bargaining between them, *pro* and *contra.*

(First trip to Germany after the war.)

(Picture postcard with view of the Munich Registry Bureau.)

October 1919, Munich, Free State of Bavaria

L.F.:

Arrived safely, will be leaving in three hours, meanwhile am loafing, writing this at a café.—I find Munich uncongenial, at the same time everything is very expensive for us. A piece of chocolate, six marks, and the prices in the café are much higher than at home, reckoning in crowns, everything about four times as much.—Take care of yourself, I'm doing the same, am pleased by the extreme order and cleanliness of everything, looked at from the outside anyway, and am curious to have a look at the inside of things. Regards to the children.

Your encore fidèle Stefan

(In French)

Please buy some Christmas presents, for me, perhaps some shoes.

P.S. My travel literature consists of the timetables of the German Reich. I study them for hours on end. Believe me, in me the world has lost a hotel *portier.*

Dear Fritzi:

Report written in haste. During the trip from Munich (third class)—naturally no sleep, but had a seat. Arrived at five o'clock in the morning. I could get accommodations only in a pretty low-grade hotel, but you have to be glad to have even such. Then to Kippenberg's.[1] We didn't talk about the *Haupt Geschäft*; we are saving that up for this evening, to be discussed with a select group of people. But as to other matters, magnificent agreement. He takes over "Den Zwang."[2] *Jeremiah* will be brought out after Christmas in an edition of 7,000 copies (which means 20,000 in all). A new edition of *Fruehe Kraenze,* and we are still negotiating about *Komoedianten.* They are also going to do *Verlaine.* This publishing house is prospering fabulously; wants to bring out everything in new editions and print additional copies of everything. K. and I get along very well together. He is a man with a broad outlook—at the moment he is trying to get F. (this is confidential) a large advance. Then we had a wonderful meal. K. paid fifty marks for both of us, the equivalent of two hundred fifty crowns. So you see we are still living in the Land of Cockaigne. I'll be lecturing next Sunday in Berlin (matinee in the Tribune Theater) and Wednesday in Hamburg, then Saturday and Sunday in Kiel. I'm very well taken care of, and will bring you some marks (I hope). Perhaps we can meet in Munich.

So much for business matters. I have sensed a lot of things, especially the infinite disgust in Germany for this impotent government. People, particularly in Bavaria, openly demand the return of the Monarchy, not in our timorous fashion, but in railroad compartments every expression of this sort evokes general shouts of approval. At the same time you have plenty of everything, the shops are crowded with goods, every kind of delicacy can be had, naturally fantastically expensive; workmen chain-smoke cigars at a mark apiece. Yet even here there is a hidden threat of bankruptcy hovering on the horizon. Please buy everything you can—from leather shorts to children's umbrellas—everything is ridiculously cheap in comparison with here. Do it soon, so that you can be free to devote yourself, without interruption, to your own work.

Best to the children!

Affectionately, your completely sleepsated

Stefzi

P.S. I still have to read through all the *Dostoievski* proofs.

1 Professor Anton Kippenberg head of Inselverlag, an eminent Goethe connoisseur and collector of Goethe manuscripts. He and Stefan used to talk in a sort of code language derived from Goethe's works. "Haupt Geschäft" is taken from *The Conversations with Eckermann* and refers to the project which Stefan had planned and which was very dear to him. The series was finally published with the title: *Bibliotheca Mundi* (World Library), and consisted of a collection of world-renowned works and anthologies of every age, in their respective languages, and, in format, was a wonderful example of book designing. 2 The one-act play, *Der Verwandelte Komödiant*. The greatest German actors were eager to play the title role in this play.

(Postcard on the same day.)

L.F.

I'm afraid I'm the victim of some sort of stupidity: I don't find the transition passages anywhere in the *Dostoievski* proofs and am afraid that the section "Realism and Phantasy" has been left out altogether. Please look up the other manuscript and see whether it is included in it and then telegraph me to Hamburg if necessary. It's dreadful to have to read proofs for this kind of book while traveling; a curse must have been called down on it. I hope I'll be able to hold up the final proofs till I'm back in Salzburg again and can finally go over the whole thing. I'll be with Kippenberg tonight; he still seems to have doubts. Forgive me for being so much the traveling salesman; I am busy all day long and haven't slept a minute.

Affectionately, Stefzi

Salzburg, October 1
Addressed to Leipzig

My dear:

Thanks for the wire which arrived at lunch time. It was a poor substitute for not coming to lunch. I believe you will continue to enjoy the good order that prevails in Germany. The people there are efficient. Today a lot of Bavarians lined up in front of the shops, in spite of the rain, to buy everything in sight. I have followed your advice and bought as much as possible, even Christmas presents.—The mail is unexciting. A wire from Ch. about Nicolai.[1] But you had better not meddle in international affairs. It eats up your time and makes contemplation of poetic work to which you could devote yourself now, after finishing the book on Rolland, difficult. How I am looking forward to your doing just that! Then all the things you glorified in your beautiful dedicatory poem [2] will come true. I am giving up the French course [3] so as to have time to put your things in order and do my own work, and manage the household and take care of the children. Only be good and kind to me, dear Mr. Mumu!—Borngraeber writes that he wants one of your books. What German publisher doesn't? Yet I'd suggest giving a few things, like *Episode on Lac Leman* to agents, just as you did with the *Errant Trees*. Am curious whether you'll reach an agreement with Professor K. with regard to the project. Renan's *Souvenir d'enfances* would be suitable, if you need something of more recent date. Also an illustrated edition of *Corinne* would be nice. And the *Journal de Baskirtschef*. My dear, I was just thinking of the tearoom in Leipzig where you showed me the Goethe poem you had bought.

Affectionate greetings and don't forget your

Mumu

[1] Leading pacifist. [2] Refers to the dedication of *Jeremiah,* in which Stefan called me the guardian of his work. [3] Courses given by Salzburg writers—Bahr, Stefan, Rieger and several priests—for a so-called County Educational Institution (Adult Education).

Postcard, Leipzig, 10/20/19

L.F.:

Such a lively day, I couldn't even begin to tell all about it in a letter. To begin with, in this barracks of a hotel where I'm living, my shoes, which I'd given the drunken bellhop, disappeared. The police became involved, and this very moment the shoes, just "by chance," showed up in the bedroom next door. Then conferences about the "Haupt Geschäft." Everything has been settled except the financial details, but in any event, it is infinitely easier to work with K. than with other publishers. It was my fault that my books didn't go better:

now they will advertise, etc., etc. In dealing with such a gigantic concern you have to look out for yourself because no one else will do it for you. (Do the same at S.F.[1]) I hope, on my return from Kiel to sign the final contract. *Verlaine* is to be included. —I am lecturing next Sunday in Berlin, Wednesday Hamburg, Sunday Kiel. Then I'm coming back.

Affectionately, Stefan

[1] S. Fischer, Publishing House which brought out my novel.

Tuesday, to Berlin

Dear Stefferl:

Am copying Rolland's letter for you.

Also received excerpts from the Desbordes-Valmore book, probably for the *Literary Echo*. I'll correct the proofs and send them off. My dear, there's so much work to be done. The time will pass quickly while you are gone. Rieger arrived last night after missing his train. He lost a hatbox and a book about Offenbach he needed for his work and for which he had paid 1000 crowns. He felt quite at home with Blei and Guetersloh [1]—I am after him to finish the *Cressida* [2]—My mother wrote that one of our relatives heard Luitpold Stern lecture in the People's House; it seems he praised my book extravagantly and people are flocking to buy it. The poor thing has made friends in Innsbruck too. I mention this merely because I can't make myself believe that I can be the object of all these ovations.—If you should see Greiner and the Molos in Berlin, please remember me to them. And, in Hamburg, give my best to Miss Silten—you will meet her for the first time there—and especially to your friend Dr. Ami Kaemmerer. Perhaps you'll see Miss von Frobel too. And now goodbye, my dear. Yours,

Mumu

[1] Authors.   [2] The translation of Suarès' *Cressida*.

Leipzig, 10/22/19

L.F.:

At last, at noon, Wednesday, I have a chance to write you, two hours before traveling on to Berlin. I had an endless lot of things to talk over with Kippenberg, was with him at

106

noon and in the evening. The most important part of the business is as good as settled. The first sixteen volumes agreed upon. The main outlines are all right. It will be a beautiful project—of course, the first volumes won't be ready until Christmas, 1920, everything takes so long. *Thersites* hasn't even been printed yet. *Fruehe Kraenze* and *Desbordes* are being set up now; there are unforeseeable difficulties. *Jeremiah* hasn't sold too well, 3,000 copies still on hand, because Kippenberg won't deliver to Austria any more without guarantees. There is a general fear that Austria will go into bankruptcy and even if I lose by it, I can't say that he is not within his rights.

Overall impressions of Germany: Feeling of attraction and repulsion stronger than ever. Marvelous industriousness: at Insel everybody works from 8 o'clock until 8 o'clock in the evening, and they work incredibly hard. I'll have a lot to tell you about that. On the other hand, boundless arrogance—dissatisfaction with the government indescribable—I haven't talked to a single person who doesn't yearn for the monarchy or a dictatorship—Jew-baiting has increased to the point of frenzy (pamphlets in every toilet, on every table, in the trains no other conversation), hatred of the French likewise. You can buy anything. The shops are overflowing with foodstuffs like in a fairyland. I have never seen anything like it even in Switzerland. So everything is lovely but insanely expensive, especially for us. At noon today in a little restaurant I paid ten marks for a meat course, two marks for vegetables, two for pastry, also there was a fourteen mark minimum, which meant seventy-five crowns. The same for everything else. In this barracks of a hotel where I am staying, I pay six marks, that is to say thirty-five crowns, for a disgraceful hole in the wall. Of course I always dine here as K's guest. What I'll spend in Hamburg and Berlin where, because of telephoning and visitors, I shall have to live in good hotels, I don't even want to translate into our currency. Just now I am working on the *Biblioteca Mundi* (that's the title of this child of our fancy) and this job will net so much that hereafter I'll be able to bring you along with me if you are good. Kippenberg would very much like to make your acquaintance. They are really fine people.

I am staying at the Palace Hotel in Hamburg from Monday till Friday, then Kiel; by Monday or Tuesday in Leipzig again, and from there probably right back to Salzburg. Perhaps we could meet in Munich, in case you feel so disposed. I should be there by the fifth or sixth of November.—I didn't find any letters or telegrams from you. I'm not at all tired, on the contrary, unusually brisk, although I sleep but little and must keep alert so as not to forget anything. It was a great joy *not* to have any mail. That gave me a wonderful sensation of being unencumbered. So, tonight, Berlin. God knows whether I'll find accommodations. I'll try the Fuerstenhof anyway. Probably I'll lecture at the "Tribune" in the forenoon, although I learn the director has quit.

My best to you all and many greetings from

your Stefzi

Salzburg, Friday, 10/23

My dear Stefferl:

I received the wire announcing your arrival in Leipzig but didn't get the letter and card mailed from there on Monday until five o'clock today, Friday. Evidently I am still in love with you; for I bumbled around like an idiot and, contrary to my usual custom, I couldn't get any work done because I was so worried. How in the world can a letter take five days to travel from Leipzig to Salzburg? Can you understand it? I looked through the manuscript in the red folder right away and am listing the chapters: Harmony; Faces; Architecture and Passion. The headings are: Limitations; Dostoievski's characters; Anguished Searching for God; Consciousness of his Fate. Found almost no division into chapters in all your Dostoievski manuscripts and the other material. (Strange, how I am always moved by these manuscripts of yours in which your thoughts, written in varicolored inks and pencils, sprawl every which way, out to very edges of the paper and into every corner. They reminded me of your first letters.) But I remember the title you wanted and believe I copied it out. If I have forgotten to do this I'll be terribly upset.

Of course I am waiting anxiously for your report on Prof. K. Am delighted about all the reprints. People attending recent performances of *Jeremiah* told me how much it was applauded.—I have a summons from the police to appear tomorrow; it is about our marriage. You can imagine how much I want to go. Everybody will understand my phobia of government bureaus. It is high time that this matter were decided, one way or the other.

Yesterday I tried to end my French course. But my students refused to hear of Rieger as a substitute and threatened to drop out altogether if I withdrew. My three pretty girl pupils almost wept and the militiaman protested. So I promised to give one lesson a week, and everybody was happy. At home everything is cozy and pleasant. Rieger diligently at work translating *Cressida*. Of course I'd like to know what you are lecturing about in Berlin and Kiel as well as your other doings —except the woman affairs. By the time you come home, you'll have forgotten most of that anyway. There's so much more I should tell you. It would be marvelous if we could meet in Munich. Leonhard [1] is probably at Walchensee. Susi fell down the dark stairs. And so goodbye.

F.

[1] Leonhard Adelt, who represented the *Berlin Tageblatt* in Munich.

Dear Fr.:

I arrived safely here in Berlin. At last found quarters in an old hotel, the Westend. I went at once to Greiner who hadn't as yet read your piece, but will read it between now and Sunday. Tomorrow I am having a conference with the lawyer about *Jeremiah,* have to go to the Lessing Theater and the Deutsche Theater. The big distances become a torture if you aren't really familiar with the transit system. Otherwise everything here is quite pleasant, absolutely no change from peace times except in the prices. Don't worry, I am getting along fine. Now I rather regret the lectures with which I have loaded down my schedule. I was sorry not to hear from you, except the telegrams. Many affectionate greetings to all of you.

Stefzi

I do all my writing during mealtimes and would rather send you something out of the menu than this hastily-grilled postcard.

L.F.:

Your worry-telegram received today. How glad I would have been to telegraph you oftener, but it is a physical impossibility. You waste endless time here because of the distances, especially if you get onto the wrong tram. Add to this, tedious negotiations: I'll get something out of *Jeremiah* and without any lawsuit, on the other hand the chances for *Legend* in the Lessing Theater are bad. The actresses haven't any real inclination for it. Today I had to go to the *Berliner Tageblatt* which had sent me a special delivery asking me to come. Wolff wanted to invite me to his house. But I'm too tired. Tomorrow, Sunday, I'm to deliver the lecture. The theater (it is very small) is sold out. But I haven't had time as yet to unpack the manuscript. I spoke by telephone to Servaes, Stucken; I won't receive any visitors. I am not letting Molo, Lissauer, Rathenau know I'm here. I don't know whether it is that I'm just too provincial, or whether it is the first sign of old age, or the reduced standard of living: by evening I am really tired out by all this rushing about, telephoning, waiting, talking. So I'll just forfeit my theater tickets. I'm not a bit interested. Meanwhile I shall lose one or two days because here too the trains don't run on Sunday. Perhaps I'll beg off Kiel. From a professional point of view I'm making a big mistake not to settle down quietly for eight days in Berlin. I could accomplish a lot here, but I haven't had any letter from you as yet today, and even if a chap feels physically well, nevertheless he may be uneasy if he doesn't get any news. Germany and Austria are worlds apart. The latter, as a matter of fact, doesn't exist any more. Vienna is a ghost city. Oh, I have so much to tell you, but I have to write, eating my meals, and even they must be swallowed as quickly as possible. Best to all of yours—

Saturday

L.F.:

I had a phone call from Ch.; he'll be at the lecture tomorrow. Indeed, strange shapes are bobbing up out of all the crannies of the past. The lecture, with no additional advertisement, has been sold out days in advance. If I hadn't so amiably agreed to the Tribune for 200 marks, I could have engaged the Sachs Concert Bureau which once made me an offer, and then I might have earned 1500 to 2000 marks. But I don't care for these concert tours, am glad of this more intimate circle. I am meeting lots of people, on the street, everywhere, meet acquaintances from all over. After all, we are in an important center here. I believe I'll come here every year now for eight to fourteen days, and then escape, horrified because I find humanity utterly loathesome, but it makes one feel good now and then to have every hour crammed full.

I can't leave for Hamburg till early Monday, can be in Munich at the earliest Wednesday, probably only by Thursday, where I'd be glad to meet you.

Affectionately, Stefzi

Dear Fri.:

The lecture on Rolland was a big success, any number of people must have been turned away, so they are asking me to repeat the lecture, at twice the fee, next Sunday, but I am not doing it (that would be just like a concert singer). The Staatstheater (formerly the Royal Theater) asked for a special matinée.—I'll have to talk that over with them, cancel the Kiel engagement, in order, perhaps, to get *Jeremiah* put on. Regards from Greiner, Chapiro, Servaes (who has started reading your novel), E. H. Jacob. It was a fine success, altogether clean-cut: a number of ghosts from the haunts you don't like to see me in, bobbed up to recall the past; I find that through the decades a friendly memory of me has survived. I am leaving for Hamburg tomorrow. Please don't worry; since I left, except for your fear-filled telegrams, I haven't had a line from home and yet am not at all worried. Don't forget, postal connections are altogether impossible nowadays. I expect to be in Munich next week and meanwhile send you my most affectionate regards.

Your St.

Kapuzinerberg, Salzburg, 10/27/19

Dear Stefan:

Today a veil of snow descended over everything! The snowfall lasted a few hours. But the trees haven't turned yellow as yet. Yesterday the gardener and I went to Nonnthal, where

I bought one peach, one cherry, and one apricot tree to give us some return from our property. And, for my own special pleasure, a few flowering shrubs. I'd like to have a wilderness of many-colored plants, such as one sees in pictures of English estates. Then I propose to grow chrysanthemums and with the gardener's help plant fifteen current and gooseberry bushes which do very well in this soil.—You'll be pleased with a letter from Paul Morisse, editor of the *Mercure de France* and the *Cahiers Idealistes*. He got your address from Balzagette, assures you of his friendship, and would like to come to Germany with his second wife (the first died in Vienna in 1915). What he has in mind is a position with some publishing firm such as Kurt Wolff, as Director of foreign editions. Evidently he doesn't like it in France any more. Today I corrected half of *Cressida*. I found the beginning too literal and made several changes. Every day something or other prevents me from sorting out your manuscripts. Today's *Abendpost* had an odd review of my book by a Dr. B.A., who seems to have no idea what kind of a person I am. Parts of the review pleased me very much, just because it started out in a rather prejudiced way. I live by myself and enjoy the house tremendously . . . And you are having so many new adventures again! I'll become so dull and desolate and live exclusively in a dream world if I am left behind at home all the time.

Ask for Felix Braun's *Novalis* at the Insel, he sent it to me and it has made a deep impression on me. Also the book on the *Life of the Saints*.

Monday, (Berlin)

Dear F.:

I am leaving for Hamburg in an hour. I would like to be rid of Kiel, because the Staatstheater is interested in *Jeremiah*, and it would help a lot if I were here to push the matter. So I shall perhaps come back here again. The big success of the Rolland lecture is beginning to be reflected in the newspapers; *Vorwaerts, Boersencourier* have articles about it. *B. T.* (*Berliner Tageblatt*) will probably do likewise tomorrow. Max Rheinhart sent word he had wanted to see me, and asked me to dine with him when I come back. Theodore Wolff [1] invited me too; on the other hand, I haven't looked up Rathenau,

Cassirer yet. I am getting extravagant and take autos; it's the only way to get the better of Berlin's great distances. I hope to have news from you in Hamburg. There too I shall probably be in the middle of a whirlpool, just like here.

Affectionately, Stefzi

[1] Celebrated editor of the *Berliner Tageblatt*.

(Postcard, Hamburg)

Dear F.:

The lecture was fine and wonderfully well attended and effective, even though one sensed that some of the people resisted the ideas. Mrs. Dehmel was there too. Friends told me that when I said, in the course of my lecture, that Rolland had appealed to Verhaeren and Hauptmann, who, however, had refused to respond, she said *sotto voce*, "Thank God." My friends are charming, really touchingly considerate, also my old friends Silten, Montor, Wlach are splendid. The most interesting things [1] I'm not allowed to tell; so once more: I shall be at Hotel Leinfelder, Wednesday; if you come too, reserve a room for yourself in advance. We can't miss each other.

Affectionately, Stefan

[1] I preferred not to hear any gossip about his flirtations.

Salzburg, All Saints Day

Dear Stefferl:

Yesterday evening I received your wire telling me what you want done. It's a good thing that you really need my help once in a while. After you get back home you should see to it that Felix Bloch receives the copies of *Jeremiah* he needs. I rejoice in your great success. Leonhard was kind and thoughtful enough to send me the *Berliner Tageblatt*'s fine review. Copied out a long Rolland letter for you. Arcos [1] is anxious to find out whether I have a publisher for his stories. He had in mind someone like Kurt Wolff, Insel or Seelig. I believe my trip to Munich will fall through. Hope you are coming soon. I promise you good food. If you should see Leonhard in Munich, greet him cordially for me and tell him I have been wanting very much to see him again. Come soon—am looking forward to having you back. Yours,

Fri

P.S. Another summons about the permission for our marriage. Felix Braun has dedicated his novel to me.

1 René Arcos, French writer.

Palace Hotel, Hamburg 10/29

My dear:

At last I am getting to write you, to which a decent hotel has contributed considerably. I must regretfully admit that while traveling any attempt to economize is just a waste of nervous energy. But now: I've altered my plans, have given the Kiel people an ultimatum: the lecture to be on Friday, otherwise I'll cancel it, because I have to be in Berlin Monday. There is still so much to confer about, the Staatstheater is interested in *Jeremiah*. Also we now want to have a new acting version printed, also a matinée in the Staatstheater is to be discussed. The really sensational success of my lecture has stirred up a bit of commotion all around—also Rheinhart invited me for dinner Monday, but I won't go. There is too much to do. I see now that I can accomplish more in a single trip to Germany than by a hundred letters, and at the same time the material gains are sevenfold. But I must have more confidence in myself—which, unfortunately, I haven't got, and am drawn out of myself too little. I could easily get *Jeremiah* put on at the Schauspielhaus where they are all for me. What is holding me back is that I haven't a corrected copy. Everything leads me to the conclusion that I must build up my life more on mobility and economy of my strength than on money. If I weren't the slave of my correspondence and my own disorderliness, I could accomplish much more than heretofore.

Here in Hamburg the people are charming to me, with the particular type of delicacy that makes one feel so good. I saw all my old friends at the theater, spent some most pleasant hours with Kaemmerer.

I am skipping the pages in the chapter you forbid me to write you about! Let *Cressida* be. Why didn't you write and tell me what you wrote Ruetten and L. You haven't had, if you'll pardon me, enough experience in this matter of correspondence. Apparently I've got to do more traveling to train you through actual experience to become a perfect forwarder and handler of mail. Otherwise everything appears to be in excellent shape. I am curious for a glimpse of Salzburg once more; the "inner me" has forgotten it altogether: while on a trip I suddenly shed all my ties, I feel entirely carefree—detached and free. You can't understand that, because you always feel lonely and deserted or not altogether complete within yourself. How powerful and pure and without any spiritual infidelity is this feeling within me! Perhaps you would not envy me because of it (it isn't a feminine phenonemon) but there is that in it that is wonderfully uplifting and stimulating. Entire years suddenly come back to one out of the past: nothing is lost, everything still full of beginning and seduction.

Best to you, with greetings to all,

From Stefzi

Wednesday

My dear:

We are having our first snowfall here. The landscape is indescribably beautiful, trees still in leaf though laden down with snow. I am only afraid that my plants will suffer. How happy you will be when you look out of your windows in the morning and see the snow-covered trees outlined against the blue sky, with mountains like glaciers in the background and the house so comfortably warm! Yesterday I was so exhilarated by the fresh air that I sawed and split wood downstairs in the woodshed. It was marvelous. Susi and Lisi tobogganed fanatically all the way from the hammock posts down to the gate, until it was too dark.—My work is progressing, although I can feel how every word struggles not to be born. It's pure physical agony that finally culminates in a great *élan,* which then engulfs the agony and all.

Hope things are going well. I keep busy—but only *en dépit de.* Shall do better as time goes on.

Affectionately yours,

Friderike

In December 1919 the Ministry of the Interior wired that the marriage license had been granted. Consequently Stefan went to Vienna in January to have the marriage ceremony performed at the Vienna City Hall. I had chosen our friend Felix Braun to serve as my proxy. Others present were the witnesses and Stefan's mother. Afterwards mother and son phoned their congratulations to Salzburg. The following letter is the first written by Friderike Maria *Zweig* to her lawfully wedded husband:

1 9 2 0

Salzburg, 1/30/1920
(Addressed to Vienna)

My dear:

How did you spend the wedding night? Steffi, it just occurs to me that I should have written to your parents. But you'll understand why I can't do it. I don't feel the slightest change. The reason is that you have cured me of my sentimentality. Were it still on tap, I would write you a letter you could frame. I have a dim notion of what I'd say to you in it— but, as I said before, there's no chance of my doing it now. And, my darling, I say my prayers even when you are with me.

Yesterday Miss von Lammasch came to thank you for the article [1] in the *Berliner Tageblatt*. She brought me a photo, unfortunately a bad one, of her father whom we held in highest esteem. He dictated a letter inviting you to visit him just before his death.

Leonhard sent the *Berliner Tageblatt* with the article about my book.—Now something that will please you: Thomas Mann, whom Eliasberg had told about your collection, sent you "as a token of his high regard for you" the manuscript, in his own handwriting, of his story "The Hungry" published in the volume entitled *Little Mr. Friedemann*. The writing is very clear and characteristic, with a few corrections. I was very happy for you. Then you were informed that a judgment has been entered against the Lessing Theater and they will have to pay you 1000 marks and put on *Legend* in September and October, 1920. Kippenberg wants to know whether they can get *Liluli*.[2] Kiepenheuer would like you to edit a collection of stories (*Tales of World Literature*). Toni [3] returned from his trip, reported that it was all up with Bolshevism in Vienna, but that it was flourishing here and in Upper Austria. But that shouldn't scare you or anyone else.

The railroad shut-down is very annoying. Though I don't begrudge your mother's having you with her, nevertheless I'd like to have you back. Did a lot of work sorting out your letters. Huge batches of them have been weeded out. It's difficult to separate personal letters written on publishers' stationery from business communications. I have to read every word—otherwise more mountains would pile up and the mess be as bad as ever. *You* could tell them apart at a glance. I am rather irked by the letters from women, dating from the time when I assumed you were too much taken up with me to have leisure for this sort of thing. Some of the letters would make you look like quite a Don Juan to our worthy Mrs. M.[4] So you couldn't possibly let her go through the whole correspondence. You have probably forgotten what sort of, and how many wretched letters there are among them. But in time, I'll fix up everything, including the library.

Remember me to your parents. I am afraid you found my dear old mother's house quite dilapidated. Her six children have carried away all the beautiful things she had. But I hope you were sensible of her gentle, simple kindness that seems almost holy to me. Especially her simplicity. Please don't destroy whatever of this same quality of simplicity I may still have in me.

I hope, my darling, you managed to attend to all your business affairs and aren't too worn out, but have been enjoying yourself a bit too. Your correspondence indicates that you are going to Berlin. That's news to me. Now I believe I have reported all the day's happenings. With kisses from your

Mumu

1 Feuilleton commemorating the death of Privy Councillor von Lammasch, pacifist and specialist in international law.   2 Satirical comedy by Romain Rolland.   3 The son of a former gardener's wife, born in the house on the Kapuzinerberg, which he refused to leave. He headed the group of the unemployed, and was a communist.   4 The secretary we had just engaged and who worked for Stefan faithfully for many years.

Vienna, April 12, 1920
Addressed to Stefan in
Salzburg

My dear:
Perhaps this letter will arrive only a short time ahead of me. Saw so many people that I hardly had time to breathe

which isn't to be recommended anyway in this leaden, dust-laden atmosphere. Vienna has changed tremendously since last winter. Anyone asserting that the city is doomed has no eyes in his head. Everything is flourishing again—but the glamor is that of a "Cosmopolitan Set" in its decline.

The women are beautiful, dressed in light and gauzy clothes, with hemline above the knee. Fashion has suddenly decreed that thousands of women should look ten years younger than they really are. They also look as if they were a luxury only sound foreign currency could buy. In the evening, I saw smartly dressed couples strolling about and singing at the top of their voices, unmistakably tipsy, at 200 crowns per. Girls at seventeen get salaries of 1500 crowns. A few people I know have servant girls with infants in arms. Many families have been waiting for months to get servants or apartments.

Your parents are well, Stefferl. Your father and my mother have become fast friends. Papa will be visiting her now and then to have a little chat with her. I'll give you news of our friends when I get back home—some good and some bad. My dear child, let's be glad we are away from all this lunacy. It would take you half a day to get your bearings and get over your amazement.

Yours,

Mumu

(Addressed to Stefan in Vienna)

October 1920

My dear—and—

Although still somewhat giddy after your affectionate leave-taking, I must send off this special delivery letter. Masereel [1] is already in Berlin and will arrive in Munich, October twenty-first. Since I intend to use his woodcuts for my Insel translations, I'd like him to tie up with the Insel people. A charming letter from Hotz and he sent you three little pipes from Marseilles. A card from Kosor about *Three Masters,* most enthusiastic; he evidently has been reading the book with great interest. The proofs of the *Verlaine* introduction came, which I read eagerly. Was amazed at your downright condemnation of Verlaine, the man, which is scarcely calculated to attract the reader. But as regards style, significance of the material, and intensity of feeling, the book is absolutely masterful. Am eager to see the essay on Thomas Mann, for I have never had a clear picture of his spiritual makeup.

Kindest regards to your parents. Be good and kind to them.

Mumu

1 Frans Masereel, Belgian painter.

(Stefan's second trip to Germany in October, 1920)

Addressed c/o Dr. Victor Fleischer
Frankfurt on the Main

My dear Stefferl:

Will these letters reach you in time? All I had from you was the Munich card. Since I didn't get to a café, I didn't have a chance to look up the reviews in the papers.

E. A. Reinhart, Dreimasken Verlag, wants your authorization for a Rolland translation. The only thing I liked in the letter was the fact that he quoted Eliasberg who considers your *Dostoievski* the best work as yet written about the Russian author. Am curious to hear how Germany impresses you. The elections here went off quietly. Some fellow, who also was voting for the first time and was probably just as green as I, laughed at me in the polling place; you would have been amused by it. I walked straight up to the "Urn" an old box with a slot in it, but was informed that one had to disappear first behind a kind of screen and put the ballot ceremoniously in an envelope before handing it to the dried-up old mummy in charge. I believe the latter looked at it anyway. Perhaps he wanted to know whether I had put in a sheet of toilet paper.

Madeleine Rolland wrote on behalf of a Hungarian friend. She and R.R. and the father are all in Lugano.

Susi sends greetings and kisses to "Papscha" as she calls you. Lovingly your

Mumu

Salzburg, October 20

My dear:

Every day is filled to the brim with things to do. In a few days I'll be able to say that the big house with all its rooms as well as the wardrobes, drawers and chests in each room will be in perfect order and immaculately clean. The fireplace wood has been cut and stacked up.—So everything would be fine, except for your worried postcard and the reason for your worry. I called up Vienna immediately, got the connection in five minutes and talked with Mama who was very calm and almost cheerful. Poor Papa had been brought home by a policeman (I don't know whether Papa had fallen down). Mama thought, to use her own words, "it was a wee bit of a stroke." But it doesn't seem so to me, because the maid told me that Papa was just as usual, talking and walking around, only a little weak still. Mama also said he was quite well again. You see, my dear, in the case of old, ailing people such things go on for years. It was the same with my father; only no one knew about it except my brother Arnold and myself. I wouldn't have dreamed of hinting that his condition was serious to my mother or sister. That would have helped neither Papa nor anyone else. All we can do is to be gentle and kind to anyone in this condition and avoid exciting him. It wouldn't do any good for you to hurry back home. Just the contrary! It would only frighten your father—you never were the one to calm him down anyway. Write him and tell him all about your success—that'll please and put new life into him. You don't have to consider me, at all, or worry that I might not be able to get away and come to Munich. If you should feel too upset, or if it should make you feel less so were I to stay in Salzburg as a sort of connecting link (between you and Vienna) send me a wire. Of course, I had been looking forward to the trip. But it is more important for me to know you as serene and cheerful as you can be under the circumstances—I couldn't enjoy Munich if you were restless.—Should I bring along Jouve's Rolland book in case I come to Munich? It is very beautiful, but fortunately quite different from yours, much simpler and more limited, which is due to the fact that the book describes only the war years and consists almost exclusively of conversations (à la Eckermann [1]) and quotations. The book has some very nice descriptions of Rolland's *milieu* and is imbued with a fervent enthusiasm which he tries in vain to curb and keep on a factual level. A certain tendency on the author's part to push himself too much into the foreground and slight others who are also close to Rolland. . . .

Professor Freud sent a long letter. He admires the *Balzac* and the *Dickens,* but doesn't agree with your *Dostoievski,* though he pays tribute to the way you have developed your material. Freud is dead sure that Dostoievski was not an epileptic (all epileptics, he seems to believe, suffer from dementia), but a typical hysteric.

Yesterday Felix Braun dropped in and stayed several hours; very enjoyable. Frans (Masereel) sent his new book, the same old theme: the long sought-for woman who is cast off when desire has been sated. Parts of it are masterful, but it has a tendency to drag, because of the moving-picture (*Histoire Sans Paroles*) technique he uses in telling the story.

Your feuilleton about the 'teenager's diary has come out. Of course, signed with your name. A review by you of that kind in the *Presse* means a day of rejoicing for the "Quai" district.[2] My dear, I wish you would keep away from all that sort of thing. Even if you are idle for days on end, it would not matter, if you were thinking of and concentrating on *your own work*; do give over writing any more *about* this or that.

Please—the time has come, even though your work might be slow in maturing, to have done with biographies and live for yourself—hearken only to yourself, my darling.

I embrace you. Don't worry. There's no reason for it; now and always love your

Mumu

1 Refers to Eckermann's Conversations with Goethe.   2 District in Vienna where many more or less wealthy Jews had their homes, who liked this kind of Freudian book.

(Sent to Leipzig)

October, 1920

My dear:

Have written you six times to Frankfurt. This is my first letter to Leipzig. Am glad you are having such a whirl, but hope it won't tire you out. The mail has brought very little of interest. Books, and more books!

Yesterday we had a ceaseless stream of visitors. First Susi's Catichet [clergyman teacher] who is a perfect darling.

(Everybody loves the child. She also exchanges letters with the Vicar in Switzerland.) In general, there's no lack of internationalism hereabouts. Today I wrote personal letters to five different countries, and Alix [1] gets letters from all sorts of Svens.—Then S. appeared, more hysterical than ever. Suddenly she said she wanted to hurt me in some way, because I was too easy-going and always forgave her for her rude behavior. And that made her feel so ashamed that she felt she had to do something outrageous. What a strange refrain this is, to recur thus in my life, yet it isn't my fault at all. Yours,

M.

[1] My daughter had just come back from Denmark, where, under the auspices of the Quaker Relief Committee, she had spent her vacation with relatives of Georg Brandes.

Hessischer Englischer Hof, Frankfurt am Main
October 17/20

Dear Fritzi:

At last I have a chance to write you more at length. I'm getting along fine, and, strangely enough, the atmosphere of luxury that surrounds me here doesn't harm me as much as it would in Vienna. I am living in unseemly good style and am reminded of your remark that I put on much more side when I'm all by myself, but that was the fault of those two vagabonds.[1] This city is very lovely, full of the most magnificent shops. Leipzig and Munich seem shabby by comparison.

Meanwhile I have developed delusions of grandeur, cancelled Duesseldorf, although I'll have to cover the expenses; I live well and enjoy life. The lecture may not be as successful as the Berlin one, because Schreker is giving a big concert on the same day.—I managed to make very good arrangements with Ruetten and Loening and we came to an excellent understanding. I consider the arrangement good enough to justify your coming to Munich with your shopping bag. I would very much like to meet you there at Leinfelder's. You'd have liked it here, but the trip would have been too much for you and the temptations too tremendous.

I hope to have only good news of you, and am inviting you to Munich far enough in advance, because, since I eat koscher roast goose and live in feudal style here, it isn't likely that I'll bring along very much for you—better buy things yourself. Best to Susi, but only if she feeds my son, Rolfe [2] regularly, and take good care of yourself and don't worry. Come spring we'll make a trip to Italy. I am more than ever determined on it. I've such an appetite for travel that I want to have my fill of it for once. Farewell, I embrace you!

Stefzi

1 His friend Victor Fleischer and another acquaintance had picked out the hotel for him.   2 Our shepherd dog.

Frankfurt, 10/20

L.F.:
I chattered away here until I hadn't anything more to say; it was very pleasant, and it appears to have pleased the people here too. There has been a change in my tour schedule, I still have to go to Stuttgart, but I give myself Duesseldorf to make up for it. I am living in fine style, am afraid, if things go on like this, I'll not bring a thing along with me for you except a kiss. I am glad you aren't here—there are such grand shops, enough to bring on either a heart attack or bankruptcy. The people here are very nice, not at all politically minded. This is a wine country, and they are always much more comfortable than the beer countries. My best to house, children and dog; write or wire care of Insel (Verlag).

Affectionately, St.

I was to have lectured in a dozen more towns, but I refused.

Stuttgart, 10/21

Dear Fritzi:
I was upset by a special delivery letter from Alfred that was forwarded to me here. He tells me that Papa had another spell of weakness, but this time with symptoms of paralysis. Of course I am ready to come back any time—with this sort of distressing news in the background, I can't have a moment's peace or enjoyment. I am well aware why I can't make up my mind to any plans for the future and lightly decide to take a pleasure trip, like other people, to Italy.
I wish all this lecture business were already behind me

and that I were back once more in Salzburg, closer by and more calm. I know now that the real feeling of freedom is gone with such worries prodding one.

Affectionately, Stefan

Dear F.:

I have returned here from Stuttgart, to be closer to the mail. Thank God, no telegram! I cancelled Duesseldorf, and would, furthermore, also get rid of Heidelberg, although in that case everything I've earned will be swallowed up, but the news of the stroke has disturbed me. I am lecturing in Wiesbaden tomorrow; Lissauer will be there. Yesterday in Stuttgart, where there were few people but very pleasant. Mannheim was a success. Thanks for your letters; I am wiring you; do come if you feel you aren't too distracted by worry—I realize that it is bad traveling if one is worried—but if you are free, you will, of course, make me tremendously happy. All my most affectionate,

Your Stefzi

Wiesbaden, 10/23/20

Dear Fritzi:

I was decidedly reassured to find a telegram from you in Frankfurt—I hope things are, temporarily at least, halfway better. No doubt the shock was pretty bad.

I stay in Wiesbaden today, a boring German Montreux —this lecturing has already become wearisome, especially so because, by the cancellation of Duesseldorf (where I had to assume the expenses) the amount of my fees has been materially reduced. But I want gradually to get back to my work, no matter what it costs me.

In Wiesbaden, Mainz, French garrisons—any number of uniformed saunterers with their wives and mistresses. You get to understand German bitterness better when you see this shameful waste, this toy-soldiering. However, I may have a number of French officers at my lecture.—When I was in Stuttgart Wilhelm von Scholz told me that Lissauer was seriously ill, suffering from attacks of colic brought on by gallstones, and is bedridden in Wiesbaden. I paid him a visit at once—he lives with a most extraordinary woman—and found him quite recovered and overjoyed by my visit. His wife is now confined to an insane asylum for good. He has gone through a lot, but works on bravely. He sends you his very best.

There should be a good deal more to tell about Frankfurt and so forth, but I hope to see you soon. I shall be in Munich on the morning of the twenty-ninth, want to be back again on November first. A heap of work is waiting for me. And above all, I'd like to work for a month in complete isolation, entirely at peace, in order to go ahead with my own things and to get the *Clérambeault* behind me.[1]

I hope to find you already in Munich when I get there. —Another thing, buy whatever you can, another terrific wave of increases in the cost of living is due. Goodbye, best to Susi and Rolfe,

Your Stefan

[1] Translation of Romain Rolland's novel.

Heidelberg, 10/25/20

L.F.:

A beautiful autumn day—I no longer know what rain is like—in the Schlosserstrasse in Heidelberg a gentle spreading view of the vineclad hills. Extraordinary resemblance to Salzburg—only there you have an Italian city built into a German landscape, here German architecture set in the midst of the rocky hillocks of a gentle southland. If I didn't have to deliver a lecture this evening my enjoyment of this hour would be quite unalloyed. But today is the last one (not for this time only, but for a long time to come, except for students and young people). The city itself affects me disagreeably on account of the fraternity life; although the term hasn't begun as yet, the place is crawling with caps and becapped militarists. Tomorrow it's to be tiresome Leipzig, then I'll be in Munich as punctual as a concert singer who has sung his last song, and, I hope, bubbling over with variegated impressions. Farewell—forgive me if I haven't sent you any picture postcards showing in pink and red the castle all lit up, with quotations from Scheffel poems. These things are gruesome.

Your Bo

1 9 2 1

As we took the trip to Italy together there is no correspondence about it. The following are postcards and letters from the spring and summer of 1921.

(To Vienna)

L.F.:

Today is Friday and yesterday it was already lovely weather; the garden is beginning to blossom. The wash is hanging up out of doors and is drying properly. Dr. Friedmann delivered your greetings to me. Fuchs (Baron Guido Fuchs) is also here already, besides tourists aplenty. Everything is going well with me, I enjoy the quiet that prevails in the house and go out for walks quite a lot; the mail rarely brings anything of interest; there is a kind of truce within the castle. I hope you'll succeed in inducing my parents to adopt an easier way of life; I know exactly how difficult that will be, but the attempt must none-the-less be made again. Fond greetings to all the members of your family and to our friends.

Affectionately your Stefzi

Wuwu is in good health, I kept him in the house last night, because services are being held every evening in the Capuchin Monastery. (All the chapels were lit up with candles). He would have barked at all the pious people.

(Visit to his mother in Marienbad and his brother, at his father's factory in Reichenberg, Czechoslovakia.)

Marienbad, July 28, 1921

Dear Fritzi:

Traveled in such tropical heat as you can't even imagine, unluckily had a locomotive breakdown en route, so poor Mama had to wait on the station platform two and a half hours, all the time fearful lest there had been an accident. It is magnificently beautiful here, really stylish, not like Reichenhall, but a regular peacetime regime; breakfast here: poppyseed buns, salted breadsticks, delicious coffee and the like, not a bit different from what it was in peacetime. I revert to my original opinion of Marienbad, that it is one of the most beautiful things in the world.

126

So far everything is going off according to schedule. I'll leave for Prague on Saturday, and from there Alfred will take me in his auto to Reichenberg. It is to be hoped the ladies will give you a chance to read this card. I manage to stay well despite the mad rush—except that certain beautiful resolutions are shattered by the heat. You have a firm ally against me in the Good Lord.

Affectionately, Stefan

(Postscript by his mother)

Dear Fritzi:

Am more than satisfied to have my beloved sonny with me. My affectionate regards,

Mama

(The summer school, for which I had made preliminary arrangements and which was to be managed by the English section of the International League for Peace and Freedom, had begun its sessions in Salzburg; this was the first international meeting of the kind since the war. A number of Stefan's French friends took part in the work. Chinese, Indian, Japanese women, mostly students, popped up among native Dirndl costumes and toured the principal sights and attended the festival, together with young people of many other nationalities. The French writer, Pierre Jouve, one of the lecturers, stayed at our house. The following letters refer in part to these matters.)

Dear Stefan:

As usual, lots of mail, but nothing of importance. Corrected the proofs of Johannes Schlaf's badly translated *Confessions* and the Wilde-Zweig Dialogue on *Sadhana*. If you'll allow me to say so, it seems to me as though you sympathized with what the younger of the two had to say, but wanted to indicate that you shared the elder's ethical convictions. Yet you lacked the courage to condemn the former's viciousness. Briefly, the thing isn't treated with the candor to which Wilde is entitled.

Hope you have some pleasant days with Alfred to whom I send kindest regards. I am afraid that the great heat will wear you out, while driving about.

There's much to tell at this end. Mrs. Bahr-Mildenburg [1] has just been here. I had called her up and she came right away. This charming woman promised that she, and possibly also her husband, would attend the opening of the Summer Conference. This afternoon three Japanese and that sweet Chinese girl are coming to visit me. Everything is going along beautifully. I can understand the satisfaction a general or organizer of a great enterprise feels when he sees how smoothly the gigantic apparatus he has built up functions.

To mention something unpleasant: The Housing Bureau has gotten together a big committee and this committee will come next Wednesday to find out whether our house could take in some of the people looking for apartments. I am afraid we shall be confronted with a difficult situation.— You have always refused to worry about this threat.[2] And now I am reluctant to make a decision of which you are sure to disapprove. I suppose the matter could be adjusted by slipping them some money [for the housing fund]. At any rate, the visit of the seven gentlemen tomorrow won't be very enjoyable. They are the type Masereel likes to draw.

Felix Braun is coming on the second. Neither he nor Antoine will be able to find rooms. But it might be a good thing to put Felix and Jouve next to each other. I have always felt that people like Felix miss the finest things in life by isolating themselves behind a wall of nationalist prejudices; one would be doing them a great favor if one could convince them of the error of their ways. More than ever, I feel the joy of discovering myself in the heart of a Chinese or Mexican woman. It seems like a transmigration of souls happening while one is still in this life.

I am very well. Hope you don't have to be rushing about all the time rattling hither and thither in this heat, and have had an agreeable talk with Prof. Kippenberg to whom I send my best regards.

Affectionately yours,

Fr.

[1] Anna Bahr-Mildenburg, famous Wagnerian soprano and wife of the writer Hermann Bahr.   [2] Though we had anticipated the Housing Law by renting out one apartment in our home, there was always danger that the large, historically interesting hall next to Stefan's study might be subdivided into several small apartments. Finally we made a substantial contribution to the Municipal Building Fund, thus saving the hall as well as our imperilled privacy.

Dear Fritzi:

I have just received your second letter regarding matters connected with the house. Of course, I would offer them a release provided they would definitively and finally stop bothering us. Be pretty tough if they try to take a room from us, and say that I'll appeal immediately, because I'd be hampered in my work and as a taxpayer have the right to have my means of earning a living protected.—I'm sorry that you have to take all these things on your shoulders. But I hope this will be the last of it.

Here, in general, hot weather, but I don't feel it when we take these wonderful auto trips. Yesterday we were in Lichtwerda. Tomorrow we'll give the auto a rest and will take a hike up onto the Jeschken. It's mighty convenient to travel by auto, but it somehow makes me feel badly to leave a stinking cloud of dust and people's curses behind us. Somehow I don't care for upperclass humanity, would rather stick to the middleclass.

Tomorrow, Tuesday, I am going by auto to Dresden; in the evening will go on to Leipzig.—I'll stay in Leipzig through Wednesday; Thursday I'll go to Weimar, either with Kippenberg, or alone; can therefore be in Salzburg by six, at the latest by seven or eight. Don't wear yourself out rushing about. Many, many of my best to you and the children, the dog and guests and friends—and save up all your good humor for your

Stefzi

Salzburg, Addressed to Reichenberg

My dear:

Where should I begin with my story?—First of all, you'll see how charmingly I fixed up the new library nook in the hall. It was more work than I expected it would be. The whole hall had to be scrubbed, waxed and sanded—I had to do a part of the job myself. Jouve arrived at six in the morning. He had been unable to find a room in Innsbruck and was so dead tired that he fell asleep immediately. At nine, Rolland's friend Fernand Desprès showed up as his room in the Bristol wasn't ready. I made him take a nap in the garden.

Afterwards a lot of lively conversation. Jouve looks so much better than he did in Florence and talks incessantly. Everyone raving about the house. Jouve is so enthusiastic, I'm afraid he'll make himself ill. Preussler [1] reacted to my wire by coming back from Gastein. The Mayor will extend an official welcome to the Conference members.

No other news that would interest you. It will be a stimulating experience for you, being among all these people. Just think, Rolland himself thought of coming.

Hope you are having a pleasant time. We have made all the corrections.

Greetings to you and Alfred and be affectionately embraced by your

Fr.

[1] The Vice-Governor of Salzburg was present with other functionaries at the opening of the Conference in the large hall of the Mozarteum and greeted the guests.

(Short trip to Switzerland, December 1921
Between Landeck and Feldkirch)

Dear F.:

A very pleasant trip, comfortable seat, diner, wonderfully serene landscape, sun-drenched snow mountains and how different the feeling deep down inside of me from what I felt on those last trips in Switzerland. Do take care of yourself, don't worry about my books, I'm glad that meanwhile my letters and newspapers are taken care of. Don't forget to write Jouve and Arcos, and to thank Mrs. Privy Councillor. I hope to be back by the end of the week, at the latest on Sunday. With all my best,

Your Stefan

Feldkirch

Dear Fritzi:

As usual, my genial countenance was so confidence-inspiring, I didn't have to open up my baggage. And I am overjoyed for I remember the terrible times here during the war years.[1]

Affectionately, Stefzi

[1] Refers to the very disagreeable customs inspections at the frontier.

Dear Fritzi:

Best regards out of Zuerich from me, Faesi, Steinberg, Seelig and all the others. This place is spotless, empty of humanity, stylish, just as expensive as during the war, because the inhabitants don't lower prices and nobody buys anything. It actually makes you dizzy trying to translate one currency into another. My business here is finished. Wednesday I'll be in St. Gall, will hardly be able to leave before Sunday. Weather wonderfully springlike, the lake quite blue, reflecting an April sky, beckoning in friendly wise toward Rüshlikon. If it weren't that things are so expensive, one would like to stay here, or at least make a stop-over. If I manage to wind up everything satisfactorily [1] I hope to return in the best of spirits and find you the same.

Affectionately yours,

Stefan

[1] Matters connected with publication discussed with Carl Seelig.

St. Gall, 12/12

Dear Fritzi:

I was in St. Gall today. Return to Züerich today where I am to meet Schickele, Anette Kolb, Däubler, Kesser, Steinberg, Faesi—the old days appear to be "reborn." As soon as the Seelig business is cleared up I'll be coming back—the earliest date for my departure will be Friday, and in that case I would be in S. Sunday. Best,

Stefzi

(Third lecture tour to Germany, November 1921)

Leipzig, 11/16/21

Dear F.:

Had a good trip, ate in the diner, slept in the sleeping-car, and now in Leipzig—what a prophet is hidden in me—I face the blackest Protestant day of penance. So I ought to do penance too. Insel will probably be closed as well. I hope to get in touch with Mrs. Kippenberg; then I'll breeze along.

Leonhard was at the train, seemed to be in terrible shape. My cough appears to be subsiding, I hope to get rid of it altogether in Saxony. Had a pleasant chat with Hof-

131

mansthal; the fact is that traveling in this fashion is the very opposite of exhausting, a real pleasure. But now I'll do some penance (for you too) and send you my best,

Your faithful Stefan

Best to Metz and the children.

Hotel Prince Friederich Karl, Dorotheenstrasse

Berlin, 11/17/21

Dear Fritzi:

Arrived safely, am staying in this very pleasant Hotel Prince Friederich Karl. Berlin, at first glance, horrible—gray in this wet fog, boiling with activity. This is, of course, merely a first impression. I hope everything is going well at home. I've wasted the last half hour at the telephone—it's just like Vienna, only worse. Affectionately yours,

Stefan

Berlin, 11/18/21

My dear:

So here's a letter! I traveled comfortably, as I wrote you, met friends everywhere, am living very pleasantly in a charming hotel. Oh, if you but knew how warm they keep the place, nothing could stop you from coming here too.—I keep my windows open day and night, that's the way they stoke up.

Berlin *profondément antipatique.* There are cities that can't tolerate standing still.—My God, you should see the luxury in the cafés and beer palaces after seven years, but on the other hand, new night spots don't pop up as fast as they once did. There is something repulsive and rancid in the whole life of this city, but there is more traffic than formerly. And how nauseating the people are—my God, my God!

I went to Camil's [1]—but met only that very nice Hermann Ungar [2] in the Czechoslovak central office. The telephone is absolutely impossible; I tried to talk to several people, but was left exhausted without having reached one of them. The first to give me any news of what is going on was, as always, the busiest of all, Rathenau, who invited me to take tea with him on Sunday. In addition to Camil, I visited several manuscript dealers; in the evening at Sternheim's "Manon Lescaut," and afterward to a grotesque café—sufficient for one afternoon. (I didn't get in till 12:15.) But one absorbs some of the drive of this city subconsciously.

My cough hardly worth mentioning, general condition good. I am determined hereafter as heretofore—now that that day of penance in Leipzig is behind me—to enjoy myself thoroughly. So now I've told you everything. But you are like the lady in the booth next to mine yesterday, who I heard end her telephone conversation with: "Now say something more, my sweet pet"—so then: an affectionate embrace from your as yet faithful

Stefzi

Best to all of you.

1 Camil Hoffmann, boyhood friend of Stefan's, poet and author, at that time head of the press bureau in the Czechoslovak legation and temporarily Chargé d'Affaires in Berlin. During World War II he was deported and killed by the Nazis.   2 The author, who died early in his career.

(In the café of the Central Hotel)

Berlin, November 20

Dear Fritzi:

At last I have a chance to write you and, of all places, in a café. I am in the middle of a whirlpool of people and affairs, and the theater. Yesterday I visited Harden—lengthy and very instructive talks; today two hours with Rathenau, who had just returned from the Reparations Commission: I was really moved because he devoted time to me and told me things without any reservations. On top of which, this noisy, nerve-wracking, strident city which fascinates as much as it repels me.

Oh, who are the people I've already seen: Fischer, Kahane, Handl's wife and daughter, actors, poets, although people are only just beginning to find out that I am here. All this stimulates me and doesn't tire me at all. From Kaemmerer [1] a moving letter; things are going badly for him; perhaps, after all, I'll go down there.

Now something that will amuse you. I have such a strange feeling of hostility toward this city that, despite all the kind attentions I have received, I simply *cannot* do any lecturing here. It disgusts me. Tomorrow I shall have to take on the disagreeable job of trying to cancel the engagement here, and then I shall have to reimburse these people for their losses. This is a piece of extravagance which I choose to indulge in for purely personal reasons. I no longer care to deliver lectures for any but my friends. In any case, the arrangements that were made were rather clumsy—the director himself won't be there.—I have a horror, a horror, of talking to this kind of people. I hope I succeed in getting the lecture cancelled. Please don't laugh at me because the city has affected me in such a weird way, but really I can't force myself; this Prussian efficiency and strenuousness, despite the fact that intellectually I admire it immensely, is soul-shattering. And then, although I have many acquaintainces here, how few *friends*! (Camil is going to Prague for four days, leaving tomorrow.) I think it would be decenter for me to visit my dear, sick friend in Hamburg than to deliver a lecture here for the benefit of a bunch of snobs. I scarcely need an excuse for having come here. I feel that I needed this sort of interlude. But I couldn't breathe and exist here permanently: the intense hustle (including Eros) disgusts me; there is too much oxygen in the air.

Nevertheless, I'm feeling fine, buoyant, young, tireless, brisk, stimulated and gay, even the cough is gradually disappearing. Take care of yourself, I am looking forward with pleasure to Salzburg—these interludes teach one to value peace and tranquility.

Love to you, the children, friends, from

Your Stefan

1 Dr. Ammi Kaemmerer, an old, devoted friend in Hamburg.

Postcard, 11/21/21

Dear Fritzi:

Ernst Weiss just a little while ago witnessed the mess I got into.—I went to give formal notice about cancelling the lecture, ran into the lady secretary, a young woman as pretty as a picture, and all my resolutions ebbed away. I gave in, and will have to "sing." And the prospect gives me

the creeps. A thousand thanks for your letter. You manage
everything wonderfully well.

> Affectionately,
>
> *Your Stefan*

> Affectionate greetings,
>
> *Ernst Weiss*

Dear Fritzi:

After that card from me and Ernst Weiss I receive—it is
good of you—the mail. I was ashamed because I hadn't the
strength of mind to stand by my resolution to cancel the
lecture when I talked with that pretty young girl, who was
really quite frightened. Even Weiss, who realized I was
Baalam uttering a blessing instead of a curse, had to laugh.
But I find it so hard to say no, you know that. Now, let the
evil run its course. Take care of yourself.

> *Affectionately, Stefan*

> Berlin, 11/22/21

Dear Fritzi:

At last a few lines.—I was to visit the Kahanes today,
Wednesday evening, but begged off, so as to have a little
rest and lie abed for eight hours, instead of sleeping merely
a quick five. My lecture, which I wanted to get out of delivering, has become twins: there is to be a great morning meeting
in the Staatstheater (with Durieux, Kortner and Russian
music) for the benefit of the big drive inaugurated by the
Russian Relief for Dostoievski; Karl Krauss was to have
delivered the introductory address, but it turns out can't do
so. When they learned I was here, they begged me urgently
to deliver the speech. You know what an amateur I am at
refusing—I had to consent and now, in addition to everything
else, I have to piece a lecture together in the midst of my other
troubles.

Not only do I have appointments with any number of
people, but every minute I seem to be running across, quite
by chance, Kurt Wolff, Victor Fleischer, Dr. Stiedry, the
director of the Opera, also Busoni; I was at the Heymanns',

and death and the devil knows who else. I've been to the theater; for the most part indecent plays. On Friday I'm going to a "Gala Ball" of an ambiguous sort, with Hermann Ungar—Kippenberg is to arrive from Leipzig on Friday. Let chaos engulf me! At the same time, I feel spiritually refreshed and if only this damnable catarrh would leave me—I devour aspirin every evening and am gradually managing to get the better of it. Then I would do some more gadding about. So today I'll be in bed—or at least I'll try to be—by nine o'clock and will be working at my lecture.

My dear, what a lot of trouble you are having with our establishment. With reference to the capital tax, you will find, unless I am mistaken, a return I have made out in the first drawer of the desk in the library. I am delighted to have your report that our establishment is in such good running order; I am very grateful to you. I am looking forward to the Schmidtbonns with much pleasure.

In general: I feel that these two weeks have been a fine tonic. Unfortunately the trip via Vienna will be a fearful trial. I can't tell you everything in a letter, a lot will still be left to tell.

In the best of humor, but with undiminished tenderness,

Affectionately yours,

Stefan

Best to the children, dog, household and all my best to our friends.

Nov. 25, 1921

Dear Fritzi:

Last night I visited the Fischers [1] and Heymann was there; after a year he has bobbed up again in Berlin. He spoke of you in the most kindly fashion and begged me to give you his best regards, as did Mr. and Mrs. Fischer. The dinner was a regular banquet, Berlin W., with six courses; among the guests were Jessner, the stage-manager, Jacob Wassermann, and later, Rathenau and Kerr. On the whole, quite a success, although I loathe this kind of affair, which, moreover, cost me some eight hours, reckoning the trip there and back.

Today is Friday and I haven't done the lecture for the Staatstheater yet, but now its turn has come. I feel very well here and am altogether in agreement with Hofmannsthal that this is a stimulating climate. Inevitably all racial characteristics derive from the circumambient atmosphere. I also visited Ferruccio Busoni, although with mixed feelings: this remarkable individual is enveloped in a cloud of incense offered up by a female clique, like Liszt in the old days. Also lots of other people, all in a great hurry, rushing by like telegraph poles seen from a train window—oh, this Berlin rush, not only in purely business affairs; you should see the slickness with which erotic appointments are made on the street cars. It's all done zipp-zipp—without preliminaries, just direct approach to the thing itself. It's like on a merry-go-round; you get a lot of fun out of the speed, but also the inclination to vomit.

I'll probably stay here until Monday evening, want to leave Tuesday for Leipzig, Dresden, Wednesday or Thursday in Vienna, Saturday or Sunday want to be in Salzburg. I'm not thinking of lectures in Bruenn, not in my remotest dreams. Please don't be impatient with

Your Stefzi.

1 The publisher, S. Fisher and his reader, Heymann who, independent of Stefan, had both agreed on accepting my novel and then, after the war, had published it.

Salzburg, November 24/1921
My dear Stefferl:

Am sending my congratulations already, today. There isn't anything I can add except my willingness to forego being with you on your birthday. The present, or presents, are waiting for you more patiently than I, who am looking forward to your coming with eager anticipation.

Will you go to Hamburg? If you do, remember me to all your friends.

The evening is full of magic. Shimmering hoarfrost under a clear, starry sky. The mist has melted away.

Rolland sent a dear, closely written card to express

his warm appreciation of the Tolstoi book. He is going to Paris on the twenty-fifth. Yesterday two wonderful things happened. I visited Miss Sirenius' cloisonné workshop and found the things she makes as charming as herself. Then I read a sermon preached by the Pastor of the New York Community Church on the topic: Who is the greatest man of our time? He began with Rolland, whose character he analyzed very well, then he devoted a few words to Smuts, and finally he turned to Ghandi towering above all others. Indeed Ghandi must be a man of unsurpassed greatness. Yesterday I felt an urge to pack up and go to India right off, to kiss the hem of his garment. You must read about him.

Worked all day long on my novel.

Well, my dear, sing beautifully, but not too beautifully—or we'll have letters pouring in about it for the next half year.

Let me press you to my heart, my dear, sweet child, and I send you a thousand good wishes that you may be spared all worries. May God give you vigor, joy and good work. And also a pure heart, the source of all happiness. Farewell, my beloved. I kiss you with my whole heart. Yours,

Mumu

(Postcard)

Berlin, Nov. 26/21

My dear:

Why do you make me two days older than I am, with your congratulations? Isn't forty enough? I'm still having a big vogue here and meet with touching evidence of not being forgotten and there are many newcomers; also no loss of dignity, when yesterday I went bar-hopping with the younger set of the Czechoslovak legation (naturally without the pious Camil) in some quite peculiar bars and cafés. This type of thing in Berlin is something the general public doesn't know about; I shall have a lot to tell you. No, don't make me out older than I am, not by even a single day; every least bit of my youth is precious. This evening I do my "singing" [1] and again tomorrow. I believe it will be more like blowing my nose than talking, because my catarrh has

138

quietly turned into a terrific head cold which I have managed, however, to dry up pretty thoroughly with aspirin.

Your affectionate, not yet forty-year old,

Stefzi

1 He refers to his lecture.

Dear M.:

Many thanks for your premature birthday letter—I am still a well-preserved chap in his thirties, at least for forty-eight hours more. Today's lecture was a grand success, the society has made a profit of 3,000 marks and your Stefzi has received many compliments. Today my song will reëcho through the Staatstheater. The bad part of it all is my gadding about in cafés. I sleep only in the hasty manner of Berlin, but feel ten years younger, as was the case in Italy, where I was also uninterruptedly on the go. I'll telegraph you the date of my departure. I regret to report that I'm not bringing you anything. There is nothing tempting and, least of all, anything that would justify lugging across the whole of Czechoslovakia and Austria. Goodbye. I'll be coming along soon.

Stefzi

11/27/21

Dear Wife:

And now the Dostoievski celebration is over and done with too; it was—I modestly omit mention of yours truly—very fine, especially a Russian actor and a troop of Balalaika players. The Durieux woman tossed off my poem in good, bathetic style. Now all that I have to do is to leave, and I find it hard to make up my mind to it, because I'm so well satisfied and haven't any word from Kippenberg as yet.

Affectionately your

Stefan

I shall be at Hoffmann's for dinner, where I'll have roast goose again (this is a hint to you).

139

Postscript by Dr. Camil Hoffmann:

Stefan's address was a masterful performance and the best of the entire matinée. I am delighted that he is in such excellent form. My sincerest regards.

Camil Hoffmann

Stefan's birthday presents were waiting for him at home. The most elaborate was a large armchair upholstered in a flowered material. For years to come this was Stefan's favorite chair while reading. He preferred it to all the other furniture. It was not taken to London, and the Gestapo stole it, together with many other things that belonged to us. Here I insert the poem I had pinned to the chair and which Stefan found very amusing:

Flower-besprent, wingéd, upholstered in swan's down,
Dear Armchair, thou awaitest thy master.
Like a boy-prince destined to wear a crown,
Thou waitest unconscious of future glories.
Thou wast chosen not merely to give ease to the limbs of my
    beloved;
A higher good fortune awaits thee.
For the eminent head that thy wings will shelter
Holds a poet's treasure, a poet whose heart is aflame with the
    divine fire.
Oh, mayest thou, my dear friend, standing close to the stove's
    comfortable glow,
Give him tranquility to make his dreams—
He who loves peace—come alive in his works striving for peace.
Let Amok be done with! Whisper to him
Thoughts of happier subjects,
Far-reaching thoughts bringing comfort to men in all lands,
Deep thoughts but not terrible thoughts.
And when he leaves thy shelter, may he feel new inspiration,
Feel young as his looks, not weighed down by the weight of his
    honors.
For his youthful appearance hides the burdens the years have
    brought him.
Take thou these honorable burdens and bear them for him
    when they become too heavy.
Dear Armchair, rich and many are the rewards in store for
    thee:
Peering over his shoulder thou wilt see not only the Poet,

But mayest read also the wise, various, old and new books he
    is reading.
Let thy heart rejoice, sheltering in thine arms the master.
Flower-besprent are thy cushions; let's hope they'll outlast
Just thy master's home-coming,
Although present-day stuffs are as shoddy as present-day litera-
    ture.
Then wait as thou art, to embrace my beloved.
If thy gender weren't masculine, I swear I'd be jealous.

1 9 2 2

FIRST TRIP TO FRANCE AFTER THE WAR, IN MARCH 1922

L.F.:
    First greetings from Strasburg. The trip with dear Mrs.
Privy Councillor was fine, the customs inspection at the
French frontier was a foretaste of red tape to come; at the
same time it went swimmingly, but you have to wait and
wait. The good Mrs. Privy Councillor has gone to bed, but
I am sitting down to a rapturous evening repast in which
I have combined some of my favorite dishes that I have been
yearning for for a long time. But now important matters:
send a postcard to Mrs. Privy Councillor right away, care
of Mme. Paul Clemenceau, 12 Avenue Eylau, with the
measurements for the dress. She'll have it made at her dress-
maker's and bring it to you when she returns. Farewell, take
care of yourself, tomorrow I shall be in Paris.

Affectionately, Stefan

           Hotel des Colonies, 27 Rue Paul Lelong, Tuesday
Dear Fritzi:
    This is the first letter: I know you want a report. I
had a very fine trip. We stayed overnight in Strasburg; in
the morning we looked at the beautiful Muenster [Cathedral]
again, then resumed our journey in one of those excellent,
light French passenger coaches, arrived punctual to the
minute. Deprès and Bazal (Leon Bazalgette) were awaiting
me; in a jiffy I was in this very nice hotel, where I have a

pleasant room with a perilously wide bed; then went right out to take a walk with my friends.

Unheard-of luxury, splendor. The streets were never brighter, more radiant, nor good taste so highly developed. Never before have I realized the contrast to our dark, dimly lighted cities. But it is remarkable that I have a feeling deep down inside of me that this world is no concern of mine, doesn't interest me. All these theaters are not giving performances for me—for me nor for my friends here, who haven't set foot in them these many years; all this splendor fails to arouse in me—as it does in most people—a spark of curiosity or eagerness. The jewels are as big as pebbles, but I wouldn't for an instant stoop to pick them up.

This sensation, of not-wanting-to-possess, contributes, of course, a lot to the charm of a sojourn here. An Austrian fashion designer might go crazy here—we have really forgotten everything that is and that was. And not more expensive than at home. But the quality of the food is not to be described. Milk, cheese, vegetables, meat, everything has a deliciousness that we have entirely forgotten existed. I'll have a lot to rave about to you.

My friends, Crucy and Jean R. Bloch, have gone away for a few days. I am to meet all of them at a dinner on the twenty-eighth, which will give them all plenty of time with me and bring them all together. On the twenty-ninth at noon, or the thirtieth, I shall be leaving. Hope you are well; best to all.

Stefzi

Paris, March 21, 1922

Chère F.:

(In French) I have a lot to tell you, but all of it isn't easily put into words. I have had a feeling all day today that I can't express *(from here German)*, a horrible feeling of being an alien; I suddenly sense a thousand signs, both on this side and from yonder, of concentrated hatred. I feel we can never again be altogether gay, or light-hearted anywhere except within our inmost selves. I can't explain how important this return to Paris has been in clarifying my inner consciousness; while I was with Bazal and Deprès, basking in the

warmth of their friendship, I didn't see it so clearly. In the evening I called on Rolland; his sister was there too. He is splendid as always. Unfortunately, he inveigled me into a "movement," a new international club has been founded and he has solemnly invited me to attend the first meeting. But I don't want to go—I want to continue here quite unobstrusively.

March 23, 1922

Dear Fritzi:

I want to write to thank you very much for the way you have wound up the Insel affair and Amsterdam. I am getting along here very well and would feel better except for my accursed lop-sided way of looking at things. When I am here I see things from the French point of view. When you know how people have suffered from the Zeppelins, you can be more understanding; just imagine that in the countryside from Salzburg to Linz not a tree, not a house, were left standing and that everything had been leveled to the ground! Today I spent hours in the Louvre: suppose a bomb had landed here! Oh, why can't one forget, why does everything recall such horrors, much, much worse than in Germany or at home.

On Sunday there will be the *déjeuner* of the International Literary Circle, presided over by Anatole France, in honor of the Galsworthys who have brought the English into the society. To symbolize the international character of the occasion, I have been invited, and the invitation was most cordial. I objected strenuously, which offended Rolland. I don't want to be a "demonstration" of anything. I don't want to be "greeted." But I can't get out of it—a refusal would be an even worse "demonstration," especially painful to my friends. So, whether I like to or not, I will have to join the procession. I did implore them, however, not to have any welcoming speeches. You know how any kind of publicity makes me squirm. Fortunately for me, a number of my friends will be there.

This hotel is charming: unfortunately the owner is coolly, unbendingly polite, like that time in West Switzerland. One is tolerated. I'd like to move over into the Beaujolais, where I could have a small room, but before I could let you know of the change, your letters would have come here. Mail is a fetter. You can only be completely free while traveling if there are no letters. I won't say anything of all this to my friends who imagine everyone loves us Austrians. After all, three years ago a Zeppelin bomb landed in a nearby street and killed ten persons. How could you expect cordiality from these people? We have to do penance for all—and there is a good deal of wickedness one has been guilty of, oneself, though it may stay undisclosed within us. I don't know whether you quite understand what I mean. In a way I am glad to feel this enmity, otherwise I might easily be blinded to the real situation by the affection shown me by my friends. It was right for me to come; I have never felt the need more keenly to go on working toward the goal we believe in. It is necessary, now more than ever.

I spent some time with Zifferer [1] today and Mrs. Privy Councillor came along with me, and with my old friend Crommelynck. We reminisced a lot about our younger days: oh what a delightful hour we spent together! This evening I shall be at Bazal's. [2] In a day or so I'll call again on Rolland who isn't at all well. Jouve and Arcos haven't shown up. Saturday I'll meet Duhamel, in the evening Vildrac, on Sunday there'll be a general farewell supper. I'll be leaving Wednesday or at the latest, Thursday. Send your next letters to Zuerich. It is possible that I'll make an excursion to Chartres. I'm looking forward to the return trip and to my return home. All my best to you, the children and Wuwu.

Stefzi

[1] Dr. Paul Zifferer, Councillor at the Austrian embassy, a fine writer and a reliable friend.   [2] Leon Bazalgette, one of Stefan's oldest friends, author of biographies of Whitman and Thoreau (the latter I translated into German).

3/24/21

(In French)
Chérie:

Unique show in Paris—mi carême in the snow. You can't imagine the exuberant gaiety: hundreds of thousands of people masquerading, dancing in the boulevards, a flood

144

of illumination—I've never before witnessed such a delirium of joy. A vibrancy, everyone aglow with ardor, not to be compared with Berlin where there is nothing but speed and work. I visited Martinet, then was with good papa Arcos. I am very happy about my stay here, nevertheless I couldn't live here, the city is too gay, too luxurious, too triumphant. But I wouldn't want to go on living without seeing it from time to time. Thanks for the card and everything.

St.

(In French)
Chère F.:

Thanks for your news. Here just as cold, but one doesn't notice it. I've been wandering about all day long. Yesterday evening I was at the Moulin Rouge and the Casino —all of it scintillates with fantastic light, full of color and life. But it's enough if I see it once every five years. I have revisited many haunts of my youth. I can return home now.

Stefan

LETTERS TO STEFAN WHILE I WAS AWAY ON A TRIP TO GERMANY IN OCTOBER 1922
(Postcard. In French)

Heidelberg, October 23/22
Chéri:

It's nine o'clock and I am sitting in a small café quite "petit bourgeois" as everything here seems to be. Walked up the main street to the Kornmarkt. The town is dark and looks deserted. Have seen nothing except the silhouette of the church. Am staying at the Darmstädterhof, an old-fashioned, respectable and second-class hotel. My train arrived at nine. Leonhard doesn't look at all well and is very upset about the Munich trial which he thinks imposed an atrociously unjust sentence. I'll remain in Frankfurt till Friday. The trains are not heated. Stuttgart with its new station looks very nice. The townspeople don't seem worried. They talk a lot about money and predict that the inflation will have reached its peak in a few weeks. Hope you are well and have everything you need.

Mumu

My dear:

Thank you for Heidelberg. It was beautiful in various ways. Yesterday evening it seemed to promise very little, quite desolate and pitchdark. But today there was sunshine, the first really radiant sunshine I'd seen for weeks. It brightened a landscape full of varied beauty and pensive magic. Above one of the gates in the castle I read the following words: "Haec est porta Jehovae," [1] and that became the motto of my golden morning. Here you live more history in ten minutes than in ten years of studying at school. And the air, Steffi, the air! Better than on a mountaintop. The hills round about, clothed in their flaming colors, are more beautiful than at home where we have mainly evergreens and fewer leaf-trees. Walked down to the Neckar and naturally had to think of "grazing." [2] The word fits well into this combination of town and country landscape. One of the pictures in the castle caught my eye. Maria Theresa out hunting. The landscape of the painting seemed so familiar. And suddenly the guide said: "Near Salzburg." But it is actually a mosaic of Salzburg landscapes. Had dinner in the station restaurant. In the train, where I was quite alone, I read the Sesenheimer episode [3] in my Goethe book. It is told with enchanting insincerity. It is interesting how Goethe, who is aware of *everything*, yet has an air of not seeing what he wants to omit. This seemingly calculated effect is actually second nature to him and gives an impression of great dignity. Also a great deal of vanity!

Took an open carriage to Fleischers. Medi had come to the station an hour too soon and left again. Discovered my Lenau letters in a bookstore underneath a mountain of other Insel books. Could you ask Insel to provide the "Editor" [4] with a few copies? Haven't seen your *Amok* as yet.

How are you, my dear? How I wish you could enjoy the clear, lovely sun here. Do you miss anything at home? Or do you bear up under it all patiently, feeling you are compensated for everything by my very opportune absence? Have you heard from Bahr? In a local art gallery I found a Signac, very nice water color, a late work. Offered for sale by a private party. Tomorrow I'll find out the price.

Loving thoughts for you and the children. And so many thanks for letting me see all this beauty. Yours,

Mumu

[1] This is the gate of Jehovah.　[2] Refers to an old German folksong. [3] Goethe's story of his and Friderike Brion's loves told in *Truth and Poetry*.　[4] I had edited a selection of Lenau's letters to Sofie von Loewenthal for Insel Verlag.

(Postcard from Stefan sent to Rothenburg, whither I had intended to go.)
Salzburg, 10/27
L.F.:
I am writing this right after receiving your second letter. Everything in fine shape at home, don't hurry about coming back, the weather here is horrible; today cold, wet snow. Don't try to economize on telegrams, because I always want to know where you are so that eventually I can meet you. I imagine you'll be going to Nuernberg (you'll doubtless go to the performances at the Kammerspiele [1] Theater) and finally you'll end up in Munich. I repeat: at home everything is in perfect shape. Have a good time; my very best to you from

Your Stefan

[1] Performance of a Rolland play.

Frankfurt, 10/27
My dear:
Just received your letter and am happy that you are in such good spirits. Also your wire arrived early this morning. Would have bought the Signac [1] if it hadn't cost too much. Fauconnier had told me that these pictures by Signac were in a rather low-price range. It is a friendly picture, the kind of luminous, bright painting we need in our rainy climate.— My dear, Victor [2] isn't at all well. Yet they insist that I stay over Sunday.—Yesterday we heard d'Albert play. Quite impersonal. The Mephisto waltz uncannily grandiose. Today I'll see Schiller's *Demetrius;* watching Medi act will be an education at the same time. Yesterday we took a beautiful walk into the country. Wrote a long letter to Papa. I am continually reminded of Mama here, for Frankfurt is a

town of elegantly-dressed old ladies. All the beautiful villas are full of them.—Kiss the children for me and greetings to all.

Affectionately, Mumu

1 The French Impressionist painter.   2 I was staying at the house of Victor and Medi (Leontine) Fleischer. Stefan's friend Victor was then Director of the Frankfurt Verlagsanstalt; his wife Leontine Sagan was actress and stage-manager. Later she became famous through the film *Girls in Uniform*.

(Postcard written in French)

Monday, Frankfurt

Chéri:

My wire will have preceded this card. Have changed my plans. Shall not go to Rothenburg because the weather isn't good enough any more; I don't want to go all by myself to such a lonely and most poetic place. Besides, I was seized by a thirst for knowledge while looking at the Rhine yesterday. I was in Mainz and saw the Zouaves who were just giving their Sunday concert. It was stunning! Then we took the train to Bacharach. It was unbelievably beautiful: the true Rhine! The houses very ancient. Walked back to Frankfurt, passing all the places where the best Rhine wine is grown. We sampled the different kinds, and I brought a bottle of Rudesheim to Victor, which will be emptied tonight, before I leave for Weimar. Probably shall be in Nuernberg the fourth and should be happy to embrace you there.

A thousand times yours,

Mumu

Weimar, October 30

My dear:

You see what happens when I am on the loose. Now I shall keep whizzing on and on. Yesterday I was still in the Rhine region, but today am in the cozy "Elephant" in a very comfortably heated room with a good bed. Just received a wire from Valerie [1] saying that everything at home was fine. And so I am really gay. My dear, you'll have to compliment me: not a single train missed, traveled in comfort and made all my own hotel reservations. Victor and Medi were lovely and wanted to keep me there. Two wonderful people. Medi is a rare soul. At times we were merry as the Merry Wives of Windsor. Last night I almost ached from laughing so hard. And it was nice to see how everybody loves and respects her. People are raving about you too, my dear. Met the ravishing actress Hilde Wall. Also d'Albert's sixth wife.

It was so beautiful along the Rhine, in Bacharach and Trechtingshausen. What ancient buildings, weird and yet not forbidding. Saturday I spent exploring the old streets. Got to Weimar after a short afternoon's ride that cost 400 Mark (equivalent of one meal). Friedmann [2] is coming over from Leipzig tomorrow or the day after. I'll come back stuffed full of culture. My dear, thanks for letting me have these pleasant, care-free days. I hope you too will be glad to know I've profited by my travels and will return home cleverer than when I left. You must let me tell you all about everything. Please, my dear, come to Nuernberg. I can't wait to clasp you in my arms.

Discovered an actress for *Legend* [3] at Medi's theater. Medi herself could play one of the women.—My dear, I traveled in the company of a laryngologist's wife. She told me how greatly her husband disapproved of overindulgence in smoking. Nicotine poisoning could cause terrible damage, destroy the memory and undermine one's vitality. Don't be angry at me for repeating this warning.

Hope the children are well-behaved. Kiss them for me. Dearest, write soon whether and when (please, please) you are coming to Nuernberg. Be affectionally embraced, my dear man, by your

Mumu

[1] Our Salzburg factotum.   [2] Dr. Wilhelm Friedmann, Professor at the University of Leipzig, an intimate friend of ours, who worked a great deal in Stefan's library. Later hounded to death by the Nazis in France. [3] Stefan's play: *Legend of a Life*.

Weimar, Wednesday

My dear:

Just received your card and the children's letters. Hope you don't mind my going to Weimar. Rothenburg would have been just something to enjoy but here I can enjoy myself and learn at the same time. This makes me happy, especially because it will make me more able to benefit by your great store of knowledge. I sense your presence always in everything I see and experience. The wish to learn has become a veritable passion. I am intoxicated by the idea that, at home, I can find all or at least most of the books I need and that you can answer all my questions. It isn't true that it's more beautiful here at some other season. We are still in the middle of autumn, and the ancient linden trees around Goethe's garden-house have not shed their foliage yet. Today, because the archives were closed, I wandered all through the park. The setting and mood are of late autumn. The bright sun, in a pale blue sky, opposite a large white moon, shines down upon these weirdly beautiful trees interspersed with gleaming columns and memorial tablets. It is a scene as replete with brooding atmosphere as you could wish. Was also in upper Weimar and wanted to visit the Goethe house, but kept strolling around until it got dark. And so I went back to the hotel in the hope of finding letters from you and the children.

Hope to reach you by phone Friday night, but would much much rather put my "sleeves" around you in Nuernberg. It's so much fun to be with you in this town or that for the first time. And there's so much I want to tell you while it's still fresh in my mind.

You don't mention your work in your letters. Today I read in the *Berliner Tageblatt* that the most-read books were those of Hamsun, Wassermann, the Mann brothers, and Stefan Zweig. The *Three Masters* I saw here in the window of a beautiful book store among other wonderful tomes.

This morning I went to the Dowager's Palace. It is entrancing! What a host of new impressions! I feel like burying myself completely in these things and then giving a course on "Weimar in the Time of Goethe." Maybe I'll write it down for the children. Then I went to the Schiller house, but couldn't look at it without bitterness. Especially the list of the friends who were to act as pall-bearers. The following item in the list has been *crossed out:* "Herr Riemer, of Privy Councillor von Goethe's household, will tender his apologies in person." On the desk lay the last page of

Demetrius. Would it have been a good play if Schiller had finished it?

The arrangements for washing oneself and bathing are shockingly primitive. And why has nobody ever paid a proper tribute to the personality of Gölchhausen?[1] Or has someone done so?

The ever cheerful and learned Friedmann has no lectures tomorrow and will be over. Perhaps I'll go to Belvedere; it will be pleasanter to have company on that excursion. Friedmann met Dujardin and is full of enthusiasm about him. Well, my dear, I could go on writing forever. I am very much annoyed because of the letter that went astray.

Embracing you affectionately, yours,

Mumu

[1] Fräulein von Gölchhausen, lady-in-waiting to the Duchess Anna Amalia, Goethe's patroness.

On lined notebook paper

Weimar, October 31

My dear:

The chambermaid, evidently surmising that enough had already been written in Weimar, made off with my letter paper. So you will have to be satisfied to read my ecstasies inscribed on cross-hatched paper. Oh, to see all this with you my darling! I'm having palpitations for very happiness. How am I to get myself calmed down? And, on top of it all I am moving tonight into the most enchanting room with beautiful old furniture.—Well, our dear, faithful Friedmann arrived bright and early. He was in the best of spirits, and so was I. Old friends are so wonderful. The sun came out while we were walking to the garden-house. I gathered a few acorns and chestnuts. Goethe's bed, his traveling bag, his stool at his high desk.—Oh, my dear, how all this thrills me. Then we walked out to Ditfurt; the path we walked on was carpeted with leaves. Have you been there? The castle is enchanting. The charming rooms, the memories, the airiness, and the artful, mellowed wantonness of it! We had a pretty good lunch in Ditfurt and then returned to Weimar, where we went first of all to the best pastry-shop in Middle Germany and then to the Goethe house. At this point, my dear, words fail me. May God grant that, as they slowly come back to me, you'll let me talk. I'd like to stay here for a year, have all of you here with me, and read and study *everything* exhaustively. That's what happens to you if you are seized by a mania like this in your adult years. It possesses you entirely. My dear, the armchair he sat in when he died! And some of the portraits, including that of Zelter [1] are so beautiful! Have you seen the new wing? And the room with the apparatus for his color experiments? I must calm down before I go dotty.

I have to thank you for all this, my dearest. Am keeping a diary of the trip. You must thumb through its pages, for it is yours. Later on I want to show it to the children. May God grant that, some day, I may look at all this with you by my side.

I embrace you. Gratefully yours,

Mumu

[1] Berlin musician and teacher of Felix Mendelssohn.

(In 1922, we traveled together several times. Thus there were fewer letters between us.)

1 9 2 3

POSTCARD AND LETTERS FROM STEFAN SENT TO VIENNA

L.F.:

Many thanks for your postcard. You'll have to explain to my parents that I can't get to writing letters just now: my mail is assuming superdimensional proportions. Here, in the house, everything is in order, Susi is worried about the next few days because she has already squandered this week's time allotted to entertaining her child friends although this is only Tuesday.—I'm working hard, although I'm not under full sail as yet. Today with Schmitz,[1] who is leaving. Take care of yourself and have as good a time as you possibly can.

Affectionately, Stefan

[1] The author, Oscar A. H. Schmitz, who lived in Salzburg.

Everything altogether shipshape at home. But I am bothered about Miss Valerie because she won't stir out of the house or rest up: her fanatic sense of duty is really touching. As to the people hereabout! Robert Neumann who successfully developed the grotesque type of movie has been here. I received word from Fauconnier today telling me he would like to come to Austria in August and do my portrait while he is here. I sent him a cordial invitation to come along after September sixth or before August thirteenth; I wouldn't want to miss having my portrait done by such an excellent artist. Please don't wear yourself out; write me when you expect to be back and meanwhile have as comfortable and luxurious a time as you can. Buy whatever you can get with the money you have. I am fine, and even manage to do some work. Kampen writes to confirm our room reservations. When you phoned early today, I was still sodden with sleep, hence my abruptness without seasoning of sentiment.

Affectionately yours,

Stefan

Dear Fritzi:

Yesterday, Sunday, I profited by the beautiful weather to undertake a tremendous hike (19 kilometers) almost all the way to Lamprechtshausen with Miss Adler; [1] returned by train. Today it's foggy. I have been working without a break and have started a new novel; at the moment I am bursting with new projects.

Susi sees to it that I get properly fed. It's too bad, but I'll have to give her a talking to today.

Friday: her girl friend came; they took a walk in the afternoon. I took them to a café in the evening. Her friend stayed the night.

Saturday afternoon she went out walking with several girl friends. Hertha and Elsie were here for supper; they listened to the radio with Hertha's papa. Elsie stayed here the night.

Sunday morning she went off with some girls; in the afternoon stayed at home with three of them.

Of course, she did none of her shorthand lessons, etc. This will never do.

Give my best to my parents, Alfred, Stefanie, and any friends you may run across (of whom, unfortunately, there aren't many who deserve the name). Have a fine time.

Affectionately, Stefzi

[1] Max Rheinhard's secretary, with whom Herman Bahr and Stefan often went on hikes in the hills around Salzburg.

LETTERS DURING A TRIP TO WESTERLAND, SYLT

Munich, June 20, 1923

Dear Wife:

My hasty best from a café. The first acquaintance I met on the street was Steinhof.[1] Leonhard is very busy, nevertheless I hope to get in touch with him. Trains terribly overcrowded, no porters, hours of waiting to get baggage checked. Berlin-Hamburg train impossible without reserved seats. So no fun; the usual furious rush: nowadays you have to make your arrangements days ahead.

This is written in a great hurry from Munich. Thousand greetings.

I am so harried and confused that I addressed this first to myself.

[1] The artist.

(While passing through Berlin)

Hotel Hapsburger Hof

Dear F.:

Here no friends. I didn't miss anything at Nordsee by stopping over here last Friday. Camil was most cordial, otherwise saw only Henrici[1] who made me a present of some original manuscript catalogues which I'd given up hope of ever getting hold of. Hotel very expensive, 85,000 marks for only a middling sort of room without a telephone. Trains overcrowded. Everybody traveling like mad, because on the first the fares are to be tripled. The people here are awful. Camil feels that this is a sort of nightmare after being in Paris. Today at the barber's I saw a corn-cure. Can you imagine what it is called? "Now get out!" Can such a city exist before the Good Lord, a city that invents such names? On the other hand, the nation buys my books: For *Amok* I received royalty on the twelfth thousand, paid me in Leipzig, so I don't have any trouble with the exchange.

I am hoping to get some good news from you in Westerland and send you my very best with some interspersed kisses.

Stefan

My most affectionate best to the home folks.

1 The artist.

Westerland, Sunday

Dear Fritzi:

I arrived in mild weather. This place is gloriously empty. The ocean is grander than ever. After being here only an hour I began to feel as if I'd been let out of jail. I find a dead calm unbearable even on the Adriatic. In fact, I began to feel fine as soon as I reached Hamburg!

I don't know how long I'll be staying. I think I'll be able to do some reading and some work. Swimming begins today.

I don't know what to advise you to do: North or South? The resorts on the Ost See will be rather crowded; follow your own inclinations. Don't be swayed in what you decide to do by the prospect of my return; don't wait for me.

All my best. I still have lots to tell you, but am keeping it for when we meet again. Best to the children, friends, and with a hearty hug from,

Your St.

Salzburg, June 22,
Addressed to Westerland on Sylt

Dear Stefan:

At last I have managed to escape and get peace and quiet for letter writing. I am glad you have found peace and quiet too. But when you are away people think that our house is entirely at their disposal; any pretense will serve. (Here follows a list of visitors.) Fortunately I can be with you at least in thought: 1 I can follow you across the Wilhelmscanal, past the ancient looking rams and sheep, to the Danish aquarium, where we were once quarantined.—Received answers from Timmersdorf Beach and the Lido. Will write in any case to Dr. Janowitz, where the Bahrs used to live. Please, my dear, take care of yourself and don't do anything foolish, childish or reckless. Don't forget that I am still of this world and have a right to expect you to show something resembling commonsense, even if it's not the real thing. Lovingly yours

F.

1 Recalling our common journey to Sylt the year before.

Dear Stefan:

Rolland writes he'll soon get in touch with you and send the note for Hermann Bahr. Today I talked with an Englishwoman who lives here now but used to see Verhaeren often in England. She told many things that would interest you.

Many greetings,

F.M.

(Letter from Westerland to Salzburg)

Tuesday morning

L.F.:

Just received your letter of Friday. I've quite sunshiny weather here, with a keen, cold wind, just the way I like it, and very few people about. One has to protect one's life. You'll have to admit that I've always warned you not to invite so many people to our house. I know what I'm about when I do my receiving in a café—people don't know when enough is enough and forget that they aren't the only ones to be considered. You'll have to live according to a regime of stern discipline when Rolland [1] comes. Now, as to your plans for the summer: 100 lire for room and board at the Lido amounts to 25 francs. I don't consider that too much, but I'm afraid that in view of the high cost of living there, you will try to economize too much and that will spoil your stay.

I shall probably leave on the seventh, and may make a stop-over at Wuerzburg. I am in fine fettle and enjoy being far away because it amounts to a sort of Being-Alone-With-Myself. I embrace you fondly.

Your Stefan

1 Rolland had written he was coming to pay us a visit.

June 24, 1923

My dear Stefan:

Just received your wire. Am happy at the good news. A few telephone calls came for you. But you are right to refuse to discuss business matters for at least a short two weeks. After all, you have your life's work to defend against intrusion. Believe me, you aren't troubled so much by lack of freedom, although you talk about it a lot, but by a guilty conscience about your artistic accomplishments. It's your conscience that pricks you whenever you turn to business affairs and are preoccupied by them like other people who, however, belong to a different world and can afford to "take it easy." Your world is the world itself. One hour at the seashore will make that clear to you without my having to tell you.

Yesterday I visited Lix.[1] She looks very well and thanks you for your birthday congratulations.—Your mother has invited me to Ischl.

Please don't be foolhardy when you go out swimming. Be fondly embraced, with many kisses by your

Fr.

1 My daughter Alix attended the convent school of St. Zeno near Reichenhall.

June 28

Dear Stefan:

Am hoping to manage your mail so that you won't have to answer any of the letters right away. Replied to a number of them myself in rather "curt and peremptory language." For instance, I hinted to Wiegler that you had a candidate for the job of editing his edition of *Hoelderlin*. Rieger would like to do it. Wrote at length to Balzagette, the Pauls, Arthur Schnitzler. The latter congratulated you on your Rathenau article. I send off eight to ten letters a day. You see, my dear child, it pays to travel without me. Some beautiful books came: Bahr's

157

Self-Portrait, Hauptmann's *Phantom* and the thick volume of
Dehmel letters which interested me a lot, and fascinated me
too. Generally speaking Dehmel emerges from these letters, as
a man of rare purity and humanity. Those to his second wife
were evidently selected *à la* Cosima.[1] These letters should be
read for the light they throw on our poets' attitude towards
war and revolution. In my opinion Hofmannsthal, Mann and
even Hauptmann appear in a much less favorable light than
Dehmel, although the latter put on a uniform. In spite of
everything, one can sense his horror of war. He admonishes his
son, and also his wife, not to consider war as something ro-
mantic or sentimental. The sole exception is his farewell letter
to his stepson before the latter went to his death. Here he signs
himself martially: "Onward! Thy Dehmel."—The letters will
interest you very much. About five of them are addressed to
you, about your *Verlaine* and *Verhaeren,* and one about *Jeremiah.* Dehmel's everlasting fervor which would seem trite in a
man of lesser stature, in him seems something childlike and
very German. At any rate, he was one of the *best* among our
poets.

   And now about you, dear husband? (Not hubby, please.)
Have you found another little giraffe-woman with a billowy
bosom of the Kiel variety? Bring back a photo so I can see the
sort of thing that appeals to you. But, actually, I am more
interested in your thoughts and your work. If you don't want
me to wait here till you get back, we shan't have any unter-
rupted time together until September. *Tu l'as voulu, Georges
Dandin!* [2] I'd be sorry not to behold your cheerful countenance
again before three weeks of Salzburg jitters have left their
mark upon it. Today was divinely beautiful here, the garden
full of roses and, later, in the evening, of fireflies. Bahr is here,
Ginzkey leaves next week, Latzko tomorrow. Am still very
happy about my excursion to Wasserburg. Was away just
twenty-four hours and these twenty-four hours meant more to
me than as many weeks. Leonhard's friendship grows stronger
all the time and I feel it is a blessed thing for me.—Hope to
see you by Sunday evening and then we can talk together all
night long and all through the morning. Have asked Huebner
to reserve a room for me in Warnemuende. On Friday I'll visit

Mama in Ischl. Remember me to Kaemmerers in Hamburg.
I embrace you in anticipation of our reunion. Yours,

F.

1 Refers to the censorship exercised by Cosima Wagner, of all that concerned the Master's first wife and his women friends.   2 Quotation from
a play by Molière.

Dear Fritzi:

We might meet in Salzburg if I arrive on Sunday. If
not, I'll be waiting at the train for you in Munich. I have been
in unbelievably good spirits, due to the fine air, light, ocean,
the blonde girls (one of them a most entrancing creature) and
also the care-free way I've been living. I have gotten along so
well with several of my essays (Masereel, Bahr, Kippenberg,
commemorative pamphlet) that now all I have to do is dictate
them to someone. I am *extremely loath* to leave, but life here
is too easy, too good, too full of all sorts of little things, which
begets frivolity. All in all, a delightful farewell to one's youth.
I hope it won't be the last.

Pack your things in good shape and be ready for

Your Stefzi

Salzburg, June 10/23
To Warnemuende, Ostsee

L.F.:

I trust you arrived safely, have had a swim and rinsed
off the dust of your trip in the sacred ocean, spiritually refreshed by our Munich meeting, and that you enjoyed Susi's
lively company and her astounding chatter. I beg you, have
as good a time as you can—gratify any wish that may pop into
your head, no matter how silly, and so follow my example
when I was in Westerland. Here, at home, everything is in
fine shape, Rolfe is sad because there is no one to throw sticks
for him to fetch.

Most affectionately your St.

(In French)

Chère F.:

I have just this minute received a statement from Insel
that the thirteenth thousand of *Amok* has been sold and that

159

I have been credited with six million.[1] So rest easy and live like a princess. Nothing new. Kisses, love,

Your St.

1 Those were the days of the great inflation when prices rose fantastically. The sensational sums that figure in these letters and the wild currency fluctuations made any sort of reckoning impossible.

Warnemuende, June 11

My dear Hubby (as they say here—or also), *Oh! my little angel:*

I believe I'll stick to little angel; that seems to fit you. We think of you and we overflow with gratitude, for it is so beautiful here. The sea a blessing straight from God (with a capital G.). Hotel Huebner very pleasant; but prices have gone up to 13000 marks per person. Even so, the food isn't very good or very plentiful. Susi was so entranced by the sunset that she embraced me in sheer ecstasy. Hope you lack nothing at home. Wish you were here.

Affectionately yours,

Fri.

P.S. Am glad Lix' expedition turned out so well. Now you can occupy the throne all by yourself. . . . I wrote from Berlin, Neustrelitz and wired date of arrival.

Salzburg, June 20/23

Dear F.:

I just wired Insel to send you three million marks. The flight out of Germany into Austria is growing all the time. People are no longer willing to tolerate the ironical quip of "you Austrians." And so Austria is profiting by a good post-season influx. The quadrupling of railroad fares is a contributing factor. I advise you not to postpone your return trip too long: we have a lot to do before Rolland's visit and a lot to talk over, and will have to lay in considerable supplies. This and necessary changes in our living arrangements will take at least three days. I shall leave to meet Rolland early on the thirtieth.

I forgot to remind you, and am afraid that perhaps you may forget to congratulate Bahr. I had a letter in his honor printed in the *Neue Freie Presse*. Also, the Masereel essay is finished. The beautiful Vasari [1] manuscript arrived safely.

Your devoted St.

Czech crowns are 650,000 per hundred and probably will go even higher in the next few days.

[1] This manuscript was the only one of his whole collection which, if I remember correctly, turned out *not* to be "genuine."

Salzburg, June 23

My dear Wife:

Among news items that might interest you, I have to report that yesterday the little Buchleitner boy who used to visit us so often, fell into the drainage ditch that was opened up ahead of schedule at Franzjosefsbad, and was drowned. Furthermore, Dr. Servaes wrote to say he won't stop over here now, that Latzko has gone to Alassio and Mrs. Metzl to Grado. I don't envy them, because of the heat down there, though we have a fine bit of the tropics right here too. I hope you have been swimming a lot and that it has toughened your skin. Let me know when you are leaving. The crush is terrific, every train from Reichenhall is from one to two, three hours late, and in addition, these everlasting festivals. If you are coming via Leipzig you can get money at Insel, as much as you need. I have just taken ten million, but there are still four there, because they paid me royalties on an additional thousand of the *Drei Meister*—it's astounding how my books go, or rather **run**.

Take good care of yourself and Susi and bring as much of the ocean along with you as you can.

Affectionately, your St.

Yesterday Rolfe kept nudging me and finally dragged me to the chest in the garden room and there he came to a halt and looked at me with a sort of desperate expression. At first I thought his fetch-and-carry stick had gotten under the chest; but on taking a closer look, I saw a hedgehog there which he'd dragged in and which had been clever enough to crawl under the chest where Rolfe couldn't get at it. Rolfe was completely baffled, the more so as we secretly smuggled the hedgehog out from under and let it escape into the woods.

But those miserable cats have already stolen my butter twice and polished off everything that had been put on the table for breakfast.

From Salzburg to Warnemuende
June 23rd

L.F.:

Just received your letter. Now, because a "please" doesn't seem to put an end to your reluctance, I have to take a stronger stand and *order* you not to economize, but to supplement the pension's insufficient stomach-nourishment properly. I want you to enjoy your vacation as much as possible.

Rolland writes he will leave Zuerich on the twenty-eighth, and will be here on the thirtieth. I called him up and advised him to come via Bavaria. I am looking forward eagerly to his visit.

Rolfi in collapse because of his thick fur, is sprawled out on the stone pavement, and keeps looking at me reproachfully as if to say: "Why don't you make it rain?" I don't mind the heat and am generally in good shape. Yesterday I met my fellow grass-widower, Faistauer, the retired church muralist.[1]

I wish you gaiety, adventure, work, good health, and indeed every imaginable good fortune. Please don't be peeved because I don't write oftener, but there is Alfred, Papa, Mama —a whole network of family correspondence. My best to Susi, and tell her I insist on a four-page letter.

Very fondly, your Stefzi

[1] Anton Faistauer painted the frescoes in the village church at Morzg near Salzburg.

(From the train on the way to Vienna)

September 1st/23

L.F.:

By a terrible fatality I forgot the proofs of the poems for which I'd had Meingast get an envelope ready. Please send them on to me *right away*. The poems are *The Artist (Der*

Maler), *The Flier* (*Der Flieger*), *The Emperor* (*Der Kaiser*), *The Penitent* (*Der Beichtiger*), *The Fakir* (*Der Fakir*).

Affectionately, Stefi

Vienna, Sept. 3/23

Dear F.:

Thanks for sending the package so quickly. Here at home Papa quite feeble, moves about with difficulty. A hundred complications.—Everything in a state of chaos. I called on your mother yesterday; she seemed in quite good health, always calm and contented. My best, in haste,

Stefan

September 5th

L.F.:

Thanks for the letter and the proofs. An unfortunate letter from Insel notified me of five billion, which depreciated again right off. I can't be rushing around all day trying to salvage money. It is lamentable to watch million after million go up in smoke.

Affectionately, St.

(On the 7th of October Stefan delivered a lecture in Vienna on the manuscripts in the Vienna National Library.—Friends, too, sent their regards.)

Dear Fri.:

I miss you very much, too.

Affectionately, with kindest regards,

Felix Braun

The lecture was grand. What a pity you aren't here!

Erwin Rieger

I salute you most respectfully.

Dr. Max Pirker

I am longing to see you again and send you sincere greetings.

Faistauer

163

Dear Lady:

I have read the manuscript and found it most interesting. My criticisms, *pro* and *contra* (in general the former greatly outweigh the latter), I hope to deliver in person shortly. Sincerely,

your Franz Th. Czokor

Leo Feld, Franz Spunda—devotedly yours

1 9 2 4

At Christmas my beloved eighty-year-old mother died.

The year 1924 began with Stefan's trip to Paris.

Hotel Beaujolais, Rue Beaujolais,
in the building of the Palais Royal

Dear Fritzi:

Arrived safely—no snow after passing the frontier; the air is mild, wonderful after that terrible freezing weather. At the train, the faithful Balzagette; a splendid room facing the garden at the hotel which has been completely renovated. I am, I regret to say, very much annoyed by one thing. X has wired me that he is arriving on Monday. I haven't the least desire to devote half of eight to ten days acting as a guide for a friend who can only talk German—for once, I want to have ten days altogether to myself. What can I wire him? Dear God, grant me rudeness.

I am writing this in my room before I have even been out in the street.

Affectionately, Stefan

Paris

Dear F.:

I simply can't get to writing letters. For one thing, I have to call on the publishers, then tomorrow I must *dejeuner* with Grasset who is ill; day after tomorrow I'm to be with Stock, in the evening with Jouglet. Preparations for the radio talk (on the fifteenth, at 7:30) to be very short and vague; it will have to be worked over later for the *Nouvelles Litteraires*.

Thursday Frans and the Luchaires, yesterday at Orloff's and Salvador Dali's (a chapter in itself). I've been invited for to-morrow by the Marquise d'Uzès, to get acquainted with the historians.—I begged off, because I'm scared of such "fine" establishments and don't feel at ease in them. Weather de-lightful.

Today I finished all I had to do at the Bibliothèque Nationale. I can or could go on with the work now, but there is such a press of people.

What a comfort Paris is, although everybody keeps com-plaining, but their laments *ne m'effleure pas la peau.*—"I'd be glad to have their worries," would be what any Austrian would tell them with a chuckle. A lady asked me, in all seriousness, whether we were suffering from such a crisis too!

Vale fareque—in simple German, farewell and love me still,

Stefan

Postcard from the Masereels and Stefan: (in French)

Dear friend:

What a pity you aren't with us! When are you coming? I embrace you, also the children who are no doubt growing up fast.

Frans, Pauline, Stefan

Paris, Hotel Beaujolais, 1/30/1924

Dear Fritzi:

Today endless running back and forth, but not a bit tired—except of people just a bit. Today we, René Arcos and I, sat outside at the cafés, wearing only lightweight coats. There isn't any real winter here. I have never been so delighted (to which my hotel contributes a lot) as this time, punctuated, of course, with sentimental moments of deep emotion of which I am almost ashamed. You can't realize what the time I have spent here has meant in my life—liberation from Vienna, espe-cially being a human being again.

I shall probably stay over till Monday. All my best to you and the children.

St.

(Letters postmarked the 28th, and 30th of January, from Paris.)

My dear:

I want to thank you for your sweet second letter. I was at Martinet's today; he appears to have recovered.[1] Also daily posing at Frans' (Masereel) for my portrait. Also Crommellynck, and a necessary visit to Madame Verhaeren. And all the time Paris, divinely radiant, beautiful as never before, a sea of light and color. My dear Fritzi, I really *mean* it when I tell you that I regret every hour that you aren't here with me—this is a God-created contrast to Salzburg and I promise you that next year (if I have some money left which I hope will be the case) we will come here for a fortnight. So then, next year, my dear, sweet girl now living in the middle of hammering [2] while your Stefzi breathes and enjoys the gentle sea-air (with shrimps).— My only purchase consists of a couple of manuscript catalogues, am obsessed by one of Masereel's paintings. They all send you their fondest regards. Give my very best to the children.—You will gather from the fact that I write every day that I am thinking of you.

Fondly yours, Stefzi

1 From a severe illness.   2 At the time a central heating plant was being installed in our house. It proved to be a difficult job.

Dearest Fritzi:

From my delightful room with a view of the garden and the stately portals of the Palais Royal, I am indicting this letter, late in the evening. Have been meeting lots of people. To begin with, Bazal, who is splendid; then I was at Kra's,[1] in the afternoon at the Galerie Billiet to see Masereel's new pictures. You can't imagine how fine his most recent portraits are—all the reproductions of them ought to be burnt up, they are so lifeless and their color so dead. I am completely enraptured and I was passionately set on buying one of the large pictures, but I think it is better after all to have M. paint my portrait. Of course, it takes up a good deal of time, but I enjoy being with this wonderful human being. He isn't as gay as formerly, a certain something—something sinister oppresses him. Then I met Scheyer; dined at Zifferer's. Tomorrow Mrs. Privy Councillor and Fauconnier, and Unruh is coming too.

Ought also to pay Charavay a visit; the day is getting crowded. My greatest delight is to *flaner—bouquiner* [browse among the bookstalls]. Don't like to miss it all because of engagements, dates.

My God, but this city is beautiful! At night incomparably refulgent in the darkness. I inhale the odor of this soft, mild air—and with it my whole youth. Leaning out the window, I reach out to the self of bygone days. Goodbye! It's really too beautiful to think of sleep, here at my window in the Palais Royale, but eventually I shall have to.

Fondly, Stefan

1 S. Kra, a dealer in original manuscripts and an old friend of Stefan's.

Dear Fritzi:

I have seen enough people here to last me eight months! Nevertheless, today I must see Crucy, dine with Fauconnier, afternoon tea at James Joyce's, also must visit Madeleine Marx (now, Paz, her husband's name). Tuesday night, home to you. What terribly noisy days you have been living through, and how happy you will be when the workmen are gone and you have industrious Stefzi the silent, back in the house! I have really benefited by the trip. I hope to meet Andrée Jouve at Jean Richard Bloch's and that will be about all. I am looking forward to getting back to work—without it life hasn't any meaning at all, even when it is as colorful as here in Paris. With love to you and your moppets,

Your Stefzi

Paris, 1/30

L.F.:

I received your Monday letter today, for which my best thanks. I'm terribly pressed on all sides. You will be astonished by the Masereel portrait—it is altogether different from what you expect, very radically unmodern, no color experiments, clear and aboveboard, at the same time shows genius in getting the likeness. It is *superb!*—I pray God will grant us peace and quiet at home this coming year, so that eventually we'll be able to have a fortnight here. The portrait is to go to Vienna to the exhibition. Oh, Masereel is such a true artist. Goodbye, I'll be coming soon.

St.

My dear:

Tomorrow I hope to buy those trifles for you. I am bringing nothing else except my portrait which is to be your property.

Fondly, your Stefzi

Saturday

I'm sorry that there wasn't anything from you today or yesterday. Tomorrow I'm going to Chartres with Frans and Victor. Wednesday night at home, and I'd rather be with you there than merely have news of you. Everything was wonderful and now being at home and at work will be doubly good.

Affectionately,

Your Stefzi

(Letters and excerpts from letters to Abbazia, in March, 1924.)

Dear Fritzi:

I received your rainy-day letters while the sun was shining gloriously here. But it won't be long now before you'll be getting rid of your cough. The main thing is to have a good time and let Susi lie a-bed as long as she wants to. The Kleist [1] manuscript is finished; naturally there will have to be a lot of editing. My mail is gradually getting quite out of hand. Love to Susi and yourself.

St.

[1] One of the essays in the volume, *The Struggle Against the Demon.*

Dear Fritzi:

I am writing you out of the winter of my discontent, like Hamlet, and hope this will find you in the midst of the most beautiful sunshine, and, entirely without any envy on my part, by the blue sea. Here, at home, everything in good shape.

There are terrible disturbances in Vienna, gigantic

losses on the stock exchange, half the city is involved in the débacle; this wanton luxury will be over and done with at least for a few years. Perhaps it was all for the best; the trees had grown too high up into heaven.

Farewell, my child, and once more: you haven't speculated in francs [1] and so can have your heart's desire: excursions, drives, whipped cream and the sun and even a bit of homesickness for

Your Stefzi

I hope you have a room with a view of the sea!

[1] He refers to the scandalous franc speculations which at that time were being aired in the press.

Zuerich, June 17th/24

Arrived safely. You can't imagine how orderly everything is here; one is always impressed by it when one comes back; one forgets the veritable chaos we live in. I intend to go on tomorrow, to Boulogne. I expect to stay there a week. Take good care of yourself; with my affectionate best to you, the children (and Casper-Wuzi [1])

Stefan

[1] Our beloved springer-spaniel, Casper, who at that time was still a puppy and Rolfe, nicknamed Wuzi.

Boulogne-sur-Mer, Hotel Christol & Bristol, July 19th

L.F.:

Here I am and very glad to be here. I have a well-schooled instinct: absolutely no luxury, a rather small bathing beach, unfortunately, but by way of compensation steep dunes with dense green cover; you can lie on them and see England out beyond. A room on the fourth floor overlooking the inner harbor's activities, ships coming and going, and in the distance, the sea; two beds (hélas). Also a fine, lively French provincial town with markets and cafés all peculiarly French in character, which is much more apparent here than in Paris. And to cap it all, very "chic" Paris-Plage only a half hour away. I like to have a city to fall back upon like at Ostend. Westerland is nothing but a resort town built in a void. But here you have continuous coming and going of ships, loading and unloading. The sky shows a fine interplay of clouds and light, but it seems very high up and far away; the wind penetrates into one's very lungs. I hope you will get something of the feel of it out of my letters.

Affectionately yours, and everybody's,

Your St.

(In French)

Chère Amie:

Stefan and I spent a delightful day together here, a most enchanting day. Hope to meet you soon in Paris. Your Stefan is fine.

Frans Masereel

Saturday

Frans left today: We got along famously together. Apparently I am one of the few people who can still evoke a little of his old gaiety and cheerfulness. We went swimming together, ate our meals together—of Pantagruelesque size, wandered around; it was delightful. Now the hour of my withering away has come; I am leaving tomorrow, stop over in Amiens or Rheims. I ought to be safely back in your arms by the thirtieth as per schedule. The sea was frequently pretty rough. I, by contrast, quite unruffled. Deep, black sleep was an unusual experience for me. I have been reading a good deal (chiefly Marcel Proust), did little work. I am hoping to find you in good health and spirits and send my most affectionate greetings on ahead of me.

Stefan

(Picture postcard from Amiens.)

(In French)

I am sending you another postcard from Amiens, *en route* home. The cathedral is even more beautiful than the one at Chartres—I know them all now. *À bientôt,*

Your Stefan

(Meeting with Rolland)

L.F.:

Many thanks! I don't get to do anything because I am so much with Rolland, whose arrival here has remained un-announced for the present: he was very well sheltered from intrusion at Rieger's.[1] We have had a box at the opera every evening and I "Straussed" enthusiastically along with every-one else. We are to be at Freud's on Wednesday, tomorrow my little *dejeuner,*[2] in the evening back home.

Affectionately, Stefzi

[1] Instead of staying at a hotel Rolland lived at the home of our friend Erwin Rieger, the poet and translator.   [2] In *Richard Strauss et Romain Rolland Correspondance, Fragment de Journal* is the following passage by Rolland: May 13/24: Stefan Zweig invited us to lunch with a few Viennese friends at one of the large hotels in the Graben, (Hotel Meissl und Schadn, at the Neue Markt). The luncheon was informal and very friendly; I had Arthur Schnitzler as my neighbor.

(Undated)

Dear Fritzi:

At the moment I am very much confused and very much embarrassed. I have just received the dedication of his new play from Rolland, together with the introduction in which he publicly expresses his gratitude to me for having encour-aged him to go back to his work, his real work. His kindness is so boundless that I am ashamed; he always surpasses all one's dreams and expectations. There never was anybody like him, to have been close to him is reward and good fortune enough for a lifetime.

Fondly yours, Stefzi

1 9 2 5

Freiburg Breisgau, 2/18

(Lecture Tour)

L.F.:

I arrived at three o'clock, took a room in this splendid hotel, then went to sleep. But now I am being led to the scaffold. As I traveled from Appenweiler I got a glimpse of the Strasburg cathedral! It tempted me sorely!

Affectionately, to all of you,

Stefzi

L.F.:

First report by letter. Yesterday evening quite good attendance at the big hall, although the same evening there were two carnival-fêtes, which did some damage. February is a poor month for serious things, because of suchlike. But the audience was grand, really touchingly attentive, not a single fit of coughing. Prof. Wittop and his wife were charming, as was Roniger. Heavenly weather at Freiburg—the cathedral marvelous. I would have liked to go over to Colmar, but rail connections are poor. The people here are very *sympathique*, the hotel is ideal, high class but not ostentatious. You would have liked it! I am not at all tired, am leaving late this evening and will stay overnight at Heidelberg. Tomorrow to Frankfurt, and then will lead an urban existence for a whole week, and hope to get some work done. This Baden region is the best part of Germany. I am lecturing my way from city to city and haven't suffered the least bit from stage-fright (I find it childishly easy to do), and will be working my way step by step homeward. Not a bit nervous, but want to stay anonymous in Fr., give myself a little time for reflection and to collect my thoughts. I hope to have good news from you. Please don't let people wear you out, take a good rest.

Affectionately, Stefzi

I have done my packing in proper style!

Frankfurt, 2/23

Dear Fritzi:

Thanks a lot for your good news. I don't, under any circumstances, want to talk about Rolland [1] in Munich, the atmosphere is too uncongenial there and I have too little inclination for it anyway. I want to return on the eighth, and then, on the fourteenth, we go back again. I don't want to have you at my lecture in any case. [2] I was at Louis Koch's today for lunch—a charming chap. I don't begrudge him his collection. It was a fine meal; Casimir Edschmidt had also been invited. Now one thing more: Did you receive the proofs of *Demon* [*The Struggle Against the Demon*]? If you did, please take care of them. I'd very much like to have that book behind me. I have worked quite hard here. The novel's basic outlines are quite clear by now; meanwhile a second little one is bobbing around in my head. I get more ideas on a trip than at home. Give Susi my heartfelt thanks. Glorious weather. Am in absolutely perfect health.

Your Stefan

1 About Rolland's *Play of Life and Death*, in Erwin Rieger's translation.
2 Stefan always insisted that my being in the audience at his lectures made him self-conscious.

L.F.:

The Rolland was a terrific success. Do show the thing to Martha Walden.[1] With my best from your "oiligen" (humble—that's the way they speak here),

Stefan

1 Our friend, the Dutch actress who was playing at the time in Salzburg as guest artist.

Baden-Baden, 2/28

I am writing from Baden-Baden. Arrived at one-thirty in the afternoon, went out right off for a walk in the misty valley. Really you haven't the least idea of how thoroughly spoiled we are in Salzburg. In comparison these northern landscapes seem banal. Then I paid Schmidbonn a visit and spent a heart-warming hour with him. This evening I do my singing. It is a small hall but attendance promises well, although there is to be an educational lecture [the same evening] and the city has a population of only 20,000. But the consumption of intellectual vittles in these little cities is astonishingly big, and not to be underrated. Tomorrow I proceed to Wiesbaden. I'd like to hire an auto and visit Marbach, Laufen, etc.

I am uneasy about the business of the proofs [1]—I am as much attached to my books as you to your children.

173

I hope to reach you by phone from Nuernberg. I send my sincerest best to the whole establishment.

S.

1 He was afraid that there would be printer's errors, but a phone call to the publishers satisfied him on that score.

Wiesbaden, 3/1/25

L.F.:

The lectures went swimmingly until today when they hit a snag. Father Olden [1] was at the train when I arrived on Saturday and he told me that, because of Ebert's death, the authorities had ordered all performances, etc. cancelled, and that, therefore, I couldn't deliver my lecture, which was disastrous because the hall had been practically sold out. The lecture had to be postponed till Sunday. I am living here in fabulous style in the old, aristocratic Hotel Vier Jahreszeiten. The proprietor considers all the Society's lecturers as his guests, has read all my books. These people in Germany are extraordinary in their respect for literature and art; everyone down to the hotel porter knows who you are. Actually my books sell *very* well, according to all the bookdealers—I am afraid of getting to be a stuffed shirt and the darling of the young maidens. Two ladies have already appeared on the scene and announced they are ready and willing; one of them is a friend of my youth. But I am no lover of warmed-over dishes. Otherwise Wiesbaden very *sympathique*—a city in which you could easily live, because it has a hinterland, Mainz, Frankfurt, the Rhine. Also visited the antiquary, old Levy. I saw a lot of enchanting things at his place. A series of portraits of Lavater, with his own comments on them, ideal for decorating a Biedermeyer room. I am buying only one manuscript. I haven't seen Hermann Kesser as yet.

There is a lot more to tell, amusing bits as well as other things. I am feeling fine, actually refreshed. Spring is in full swing here, crocuses and snow drops—a warm belt of sky right across Germany. I hope you are feeling well and have gotten the better of all the calamities of the household.

Affectionately, Stefan

As to the proofs, everything in good shape. Please do a careful job on the next batch, so that this Alp can finally be lifted off my shoulders: I should have gotten the better of this *Demon* [2] long ago.

1 The father of the two Olden brothers, writers.   2 He refers to the proofs of his book *The Struggle Against the Demon* (Hoelderlin, Kleist, Nietzsche).

(Picture postcard with a view of Schiller's birthplace.)

3/3/1925

My very best from Schiller's birthplace,

Stefan

(Letters written during a trip Stefan took with Romain Rolland through Germany.)

Munich, June, 1925

Dear Fritzi:

I arrived here in good shape and at the moment am busy eating some goose liver [1] with onions and apples, in the Preissing Palais. This morning was at the State Library looking something up; this afternoon I shall visit Bahr and be with Leonhard this evening.

Meanwhile my best to you all,

from your St.

Had a talk with Bahr; he looks much better, and feels in much better health. Adelt is very well. Carossa is away on a trip.

1 His favorite dish.

Leipzig, 6/6/25

Dear Fritzi:

I'm waiting for Rolland. I was at the exhibition here; it was quite good; then visited with Huenich, then with Friedmann, whose article on the *Demon* comes out today and who sends his best; the evening with Ernst Reclam,[1] and now at the station. Everything runs along smoothly. I am hoping that Rolland and I will have a quiet and congenial time together.

I especially look forward to our few days in Weimar. I

don't have to be in Regensburg until the twelfth, so will hardly be home before the fifteenth.

Affectionately, St.

[1] The popular publisher.

L.F.:

We've just been at the Thomanerkirche, R.R. and I, where we listened to a Bach motette. We met your lady friend, Andro,[1] there. Otherwise Leipzig is just Leipzig, and that is about all there is to say about it. This evening *Belshazzar*. Everybody sends regards. I am at work figuring out the time-table, whether I will go with R. to Kassel for the Rembrandts. Most affectionately,

Stefan

[1] The woman writer and music critic, Risa Rie.

Leipzig, 6/7

Dear F.:

Am writing you right away to say that I was glad to get your letter. Please write Freud to communicate with Roniger. Handel's *Belshazzar* incredible, an impression of overwhelming power. I won't see Kippenberg until today. Young Frieden-thal [1] is here too, with whom I've been spending a good deal of time—unbelievably talented. Perhaps we shall go to Kassel. Rolland gave me a copy of the illustrated *Jean Christophe* [2] that he brought along with him. He and his sister are in good health. Goodbye, all my best,

Stefan

[1] Dr. Richard Friedenthal, the gifted poet and writer; between him and Stefan developed a warm friendship; he is now his (Stefan's) literary executor.   [2] With Masereel's illustrations.

Leipzig 6/9

I've had no word from you today. Actually I don't even have time to brush my teeth, not to speak of writing letters. The Handel celebration is wonderful, beyond all imagining, and R.—But you understand.

Everything else goes off according to schedule.

Affectionately, your Stefan

(Card from Weimar showing a picture of Goethe's garden house.)

Dear Fritzi:

No, I can't write. I just don't have a chance to. I am getting along fine, much better than I deserve! Handel festival was heavenly. I've never heard such choruses and organ playing in my whole life. Loafed a lot, have gotten used to not writing and not sleeping.

Affectionately, Stefan

Nos souvenirs affectueux.

Madeleine Rolland, Romain Rolland

6/10

Dear Fritzi:

I am sorry to say Weimar and Rolland are coming to an end today, Wednesday; we have had many grand hours of rest here and congenial conversation; yesterday we went to look at the collection of Nietzsche papers. There we found Mrs. Foerster-Nietzsche who was as pleased as a child by Rolland's visit, and contrary to my expectations, was pathetically grateful about my book.[1] She had sent out hurried word of our visit to a few people belonging to the social upper crust, and there were a couple of ladies there who were really remarkable for their prehistoric *courtoisie* and *noblesse*: sometimes it is really astounding to discover the quality that is hidden away in these small cities. In Leipzig Rolland witnessed the cheerful sight of some 25,000 young men parading: it is well that men of good will should now and then get to know the perils that confront us: he was horrified by the faces of these young goose-steppers, their sullen looks and insolent bearing. I shall stay overnight in Dresden, will be in Reichenberg tomorrow, Saturday in Vienna, and, I hope, back home Sunday. Best to you all,

Stefzi

1 Essay on Nietzsche.

Salzburg, 6/30 to Paris, Hotel Beaujolais

Chère mariée:

Am writing you after receipt of your telegram from Trouville. Alix will write you the more important news items.

Weather continues bad, stayed indoors all day, expect to get on with my work, am always starting something new, instead of finishing the old things.—I am eager to have detailed news from you, above all whether Susi's feverishness, or nettle-rash, has disappeared. Also, I want you to write me in time if you need anything. Most important request: have a good time and please, out of nervousness which you will later regret, don't come rushing back. Here at home everything is in good shape, dogs and cats, Alix, I, all in complete harmony.

Fondly yours, Stefan

To Villiers-sur-Mer (Calvados)
I am still writing you to V. today. Perhaps you can manage to go to Rouen; the cathedral is altogether magnificent. In any case I am relying on your travel technique which you acquired from me. See that you come back in the best of humor. Just think—I had a telegram from Frau Lilien [1] telling me that her husband had died of heart failure (with an unfortunate post-script in which she asks me to write an obituary for the news-papers. This is the kind of commission I heartily dislike). Nevertheless I felt sad and really moved: he was only a few years older than I, and much stronger, a beloved companion of my youth, and it hurts me to have to shift his letters to my "morgue." My very best, and good luck for your other travel projects.

Your Stefan

[1] Wife of the magazine artist and Bible illustrator, Lilien.

L.F.:
I hope your trip to Mont Saint Michel was a success. If you have need of anything let me know in time and don't skimp yourself. It will be a long time before you have a chance to go there again and, anyway, we have to get what there is still left to get out of life: I haven't any faith in the beauty of old age. The notion that poverty is finer than wealth was in-vented for the consolation of the dispossessed. I trust you have better weather than ours here, which would drive me to dis-traction if it weren't for my panacea for all external and in-

ternal causes of melancholy, hard work, which always cheers me up, because at least something gets done. If we had only a little bit of sunshine—to be able to sit on our balcony, go out walking if only once! Then I'd feel cocky again.

Affectionately, Stefan

Did you ask Balzagette when he is bringing out my *Dostoievski?* Today I received two Russian books that were published some time ago, from Insel. *Drei Meister,* already translated, has been banned by the censor because the conception of Dostoievski didn't jibe with Bolshevik ideas. Stupidity assumes a different shape in every country. Here always the same story: "The rain it raineth every day": 50,000 firemen have poured into town, but only to quench their thirst. The city resounds with bellowings and blowing of whistles, alarms and trumpet blasts, despite all of which I have gone on working industriously although not too successfully. I have lots of new ideas, and make long-distance plans; if I were left in peace, this brain box of mine would still function tolerably. Best to Susi—do go swimming a lot, after all there's only one ocean. Alix is leaving on the twentieth to visit her father.

Affectionately, Stefan

(To get away from the Salzburg Festival performances, Stefan left for Zell am See. As usually happened, when he found it difficult to begin a new project, he became moody and fell victim to depression which was always latent in him anyway. The following letter is symptomatic.)

Grand Hotel, Zell am See, August 3rd/25

L.F.:

Thanks a lot for letter and phone call. I am in complete isolation here, more isolated than I've ever been, know nobody either in the hotel or in the village; there are only Germans (from Germany) and Hungarians here—no Viennese—everybody comes from Leipzig or even more Saxonish ports. It doesn't bother me, I work and read a bit, not too much. The novel whose basic outlines I'm filling in, is impossibly difficult, which stimulates me, instead of the contrary, to come to grips with its complications.

There is no real reason for my depressed mood, which isn't due to my work (that goes along tolerably well), nor to nicotine, which, by the way, I have given up for a few days as a try-out. This is a crisis growing out of advancing years, tied up with an uncompromising clarity of insight (not usual at my time of life).—I am not fooling myself with dreams of immortality, know how relative all literature is, don't have any faith in mankind, derive enjoyment from too few things. Sometimes these crises give birth to something worth while, sometimes they simply plunge one deeper into depression, but, of course, it is all a part of the same thing. I have noticed it in Leonhard too, who, however, goes right on fooling himself in the stupidest way.—One should just give up.—We didn't have a great enough measure of joy and youth because of the ten war- and postwar years. And, moreover, the damage to our nervous systems is irreparable, our pessimism has taken root deep down, far below the surface. I expect nothing more from the future; it's a matter of indifference to me whether I sell 10,000 or 150,000 copies. The important thing would be to make a new beginning with something new, a different way of life, to have different ambitions, to have a different relationship to being, to emigrate but not merely in the physical sense of the word. My lecture tour was after all not the wisest thing for me. I undertook it because I was weak, because of Not-Being-Able-To-Say-No and to force myself to be on the go. I should like to make myself become more footloose in the next few years— to travel a lot, short trips, that does us the most good. Take good care of yourself and my very best.

St.

(Postcard from Pfandelscharte)

August 18th/25

Dear F.:

Inspired by a youthful spirit of adventure I climbed (by the lettercarrier's bus) these heights: I have been lying in the grass up here for hours—am just enjoying myself.

Affectionately,

St.

(Trip to Marseilles, where *Volpone* was born.)

Zurich, 11/3

Gruetsi, chaibe Wib (Swiss for: Greetings, dear Wife):

I've seen a lot of beautiful manuscripts, you know, beautiful things, then with Roniger, very pleasant. I visited Zinkernagel [1] today, saw all the Hoelderlin things. Now am leaving for Lyons.

Affectionately, St.

1 Professor Zinkernagel, a specialist on Hoelderlin.

Hotel Beauveau, Marseilles, 11/4

Dear Fritzi:

After my reassuring telegram to you, here is a first news budget: I have discovered the very hotel I was looking for, an old establishment, without a restaurant, the only one that has a view of the harbor (I'll take a snapshot of it for you tomorrow from the window), a spacious room, very good for work. Moreover, Marseilles seems to be just what I need—a lively town. A five-minute tramway ride takes you to the Corniche with its tropical trees and a view of the sea. I prefer it to the resorts, where you meet only tiresome wasters. Wonderful food, and above all, lots of life. And peace in the midst of all the bustle, isolation at the center of movement, that was just what I was looking for. As I write this I take an occasional quick look out of the window. It reminds me of the Alster inner harbor and my Hamburg room, though, of course, there's the climate: the soft, sun-drenched air, shot through with an infinite number of color gradations from gaudy all the way down the scale to mist tones that recall Paris. I intend to stay here for at least eight or ten days; perhaps I'll cross over to those islands (Hyères) to make up for my Balearics-dream. [1] Meanwhile, take care of yourself and best from your devoted who sends you a thousand kisses in French currency—isn't that enough?—well then in Swiss valuta,

Stefzi

1 We visited the Balearic Islands several years later, but Stefan disliked them, because of all the noisy building that was going on so constantly that we left after three days.

(Letter written on the back of the Restaurant Basso's menu, at the Quai des Belges.)

L.F.:

I am using this extraordinary letter paper to prove to you that I have partaken of *bouillabaisse* at its celebrated source. Yesterday was enchanting: I took a quick swim, I couldn't have done without it. The water was so blue, the sun so powerful, I thought it was summer. The city is wonderful, full of life and verve, full of variety, and presents an endless contrast of wealth and poverty. I am reading some good books, eat well, in your honor I devoured a *langouste*. I couldn't wander about the sailors' quarter very much; yesterday evening, while I was strolling through the streets a policeman advised me not to walk there alone: these alleys have so few lights and are as ghostly as they were during the war days. Please take care of yourself.

Affectionately, St.

(Letter from Salzburg to Marseilles)

November 4/25

My dear:

Just received your postcard and wire. Hope everything went off according to schedule. Here is Kra's offer: his prices for the Debussy songs pretty steep, it seems to me, 1250 and 1000 francs, and after all Debussy wasn't very popular as a composer of songs. Orthel offers a few pages of Nestroy's *He Wants to Play Pranks.* Price not specified. One of the Debussy songs *Les Baisers* has lyrics by de Banville and a dedication by D.A. Forget everyday life as much as possible and enjoy what is rare and extraordinary and store it up for the future.

Today seemed like summer. Sat in the garden and finished the first thick volume of *La Pucelle.*[1]

A very enthusiastic young Belgian has written you about *Virata, or the Eyes of the Undying Brother* [2] and tells you that the ruins of Verhaeren's house (which had been bombed during the war [3]) are now all overgrown and quite a poetic wilderness and not at all sad-looking. The boy also sent some nice poems of his own. So life is stirring again out there and new ties are formed.

My dear, all my good wishes go with you. Many, many kisses.

F.

1 Anatole France's voluminous work on *Jeanne d'Arc* which I translated and abridged. It appeared first in 1926 and again in 1946.   2 A story by Stefan Zweig, published in *Passion and Pain*, 1924, Chapman and Hall, London.   3 Caillou-qui-bique, where Stefan had spent many delightful hours.

Dear Child:

A little postal miracle, I received your Munich card today, Tuesday evening. I am leaving tomorrow for Avignon, stay there till noon, will be in Dijon at six o'clock in time for the Gastronomic Fair. If I like it there, and if Frans (Masereel) whom I have been urging to, joins me, I'll stay through Friday night, otherwise by Friday I'll already be in Villeneuve.[1] So I'll visit two more cities without getting tired.

I've reserved a sleeper from Zuerich for the twentieth and, by the morning of the twenty-first I hope to be in Salzburg, all rested up. God, what a relief it is not to have to listen everlastingly to discussions of literary or Jewish topics—to sense the realities of life once more.

I didn't go to Hyères, because the sea is rough—there was an extraordinary mistral with a sparkling sky and the sea a deep blue. I want to vomit when I read the Austrian newspapers: I don't have to go to Hyères to feel sea-sick. So I shall pay another visit to the palace of the Popes in Avignon, will have a look at the antics of the Gastronomic Fair in Dijon, and will wind up in Villeneuve, that haven of solace for restless souls. I haven't brought much of anything back with me. Things here have a strong Linz flavor.[2] The grandest thing here is the filth in the alleys around the harbor; I'd like to describe one of them, where there is a shop housing four cows next door to a cigar store, and children playing in the gutter with their own excrements as playthings, and the dirty wash of some five hundred people flutters from all four stories and blind beggars grope their way among vegetables and mangy cats. This stench is of the Orient; it was no accident that incense was invented there. But these alleys lead directly into the boulevards. Here lack of enterprise mocks the need for demolition. Farewell, be as gay as you may, remember me fondly, pray do, meanwhile on Susi your kisses bestow, be of cheerful mind, but also kind, not jealous, either, of the undersigned,[3] and I salute you in these Arabian Makamen by the familiar name of Muzzi. Amen!

Stefzi

[1] Romain Rolland lived in Villeneuve with his father and sister.   [2] Refers to the Austrian provincial town of Linz.   [3] The original is doggerel too.

L.F.:

Your two letters just arrived and want to thank you for them. Just now we are having a grand military parade: celebration of the anniversary of the Armistice, the only day celebrated in this fashion in France. By the way, how nice the Negroes are in their uniforms, with their big, astonished eyes; they are partly proud, partly they feel strange. What a lot of specimens of the human race are represented here: a bouillabaisse of all races and costumes. I had a letter from Rolland; he wants me to visit him whenever I can. I ought to be in Villeneuve by the evening of the thirteenth—will have more time with Rolland, which would make me happy, although the climate here is incomparable. What radiance! I am going down to the beach, to bask in the sun and enjoy the brightness of the world.

My lambkin, I couldn't send you a wire last Saturday. The Debussy is ridiculously cheap: 200 marks for one of the celebrated songs. Notwithstanding its extreme rarity! I've already written him.

I am glad I didn't go to Paris, because I am really getting a complete rest here and will at Rolland's too. I lie abed late, by the open window, and read; in short I am orientalizing myself completely. But it irks me to see the beautiful white superliners sail away and not be able to sail away on them: sometimes I feel as if the orient were my true home. Give my best to your housekeeper-daughter. I embrace you. Affectionately,

Your Stefzi

L.F.:

Many thanks for your melancholy letter complaining about my correspondence, although you know how fond of it I am myself, nailed down to it as I am all the year round. But I often suffer from similar moods, and am thoroughly familiar with them.—Rolland looks to be in excellent shape, so do Madeleine and Papa, who will be ninety this year but still goes to Territet every morning to fetch the newspaper, and is the sturdiest of them all. I'll have a lot to tell you.—I enjoy these hours greatly: yesterday R. read me passages out of *Voyage Intérieur,* wonderful. One develops an entirely new affection for him. The snapshots weren't too successful; as a matter of fact I had to hurry because I couldn't keep R. standing out in the cold too long.

I leave for Basel Thursday evening, from there to Arlesheim, to Bernoulli's for a look at the Nietzsche manuscripts, at two-thirty to Zuerich, where I meet Faesi, at nine o'clock I hope to meet Mutzi.[1] It would be grand if, meanwhile, the Devil had fetched away all the letters so that I could plunge into work like a tiger, and into your arms like a little lambkin. I probably won't be writing again, since I shall soon, soon be at home.

Affectionately, Stefan

1 Term of endearment for Fr. Z.

1 9 2 6

(Lecture Tour)

Luebeck 1/2, 26

Dear Fritzi:

Out of this city of memories, greetings. I am somehow bewildered by the remarkable success of the tour; yesterday the Kammerspiele Theater was sold out for the first time in years, today everything sold out here and such interest on the part of the general public and newspapers. I find it almost frightening. But now the trip is nearly over; tomorrow the ugly part of it begins, Berlin. At Hamburg every night till 4 A.M. in St. Pauli,[1] unbelievably jolly and amusing.

Affectionately, Stefan

[1] The honky-tonk section of Hamburg.

(A letter from Vienna)

January 26

Dear Nightingale:

How beautifully you sing. It seems as if they would have to build bigger halls for you. Wonder whether the tour will go on like this, so gloriously. Hope you won't be too harassed and that, when you come back you won't shun people for weeks on end and go into hiding. Had a long, pleasant visit with Papa and Mama. They both look well and are in good spirits. Vienna hasn't been so distressing recently. Nobody seems to be hard up. One sees magnificent gowns at balls and in the shop windows, to attract customers. Luxury is more rampant than in Paris where the window displays are less ostentatious.

Hope you found Dr. Ami Kaemmerer in fair shape.

Above all, greet the Hotel for me. *Combien j'ai douce souvenance.* My heart still glows whenever I think of that letter you gave me in the lobby there.

Be embraced, my dear, and may my good wishes be your guardians.

Mumu

(Stefan delivered lectures in a number of cities in honor of Romain Rolland's sixtieth birthday.)

(Postcard from Zuerich)

January 24th/26

My first try at swimming all alone [start of the lecture series] went off excellently, the house was sold out, old friends send regards, Morisse, Beran, Faesi, Steinberg, then visited with Emil Ludwig and Roniger. Everything going along smoothly, this evening Basel, tomorrow Frankfurt. Yesterday I had a phone talk with Rolland.

Affectionately, Stefan

(From Vienna, to Stefan in Berlin)

My dear:

It is a wonderful day for us, but a tiring one no doubt, for you. But it moves me deeply to think of all those people in so many places who are taking part in it today—you in Berlin, Friedmann in Leipzig, broadcasting, Erwin Rieger here, and many others, all sincere of heart; how rare this is on such commemorative occasions. All in his honor. I saw your book next to Rolland's picture and books, in a number of shop windows, where what looked like little altars had been raised in his honor. Felix Braun told me that the *Neue Zuericher Zeitung* praised your lecture [1] very highly.

[1] In honor of Romain Rolland's 6oth birthday, Stefan delivered lectures devoted to his friend, in a number of cities.

(Excerpts from sixteen postcards and letters written during a trip to Switzerland.)

Aug. 8-13, 1926

Dear F.:

I'm well on my way—now in Bern. The cleanliness always astounds one, also the railroad fares. My very best,

Your St.

This time you didn't pack too little, but too much in my luggage, namely, Salzburg rain. I hope it will prove to be, as was the case when we were in Monte Carlo, only a prelude to sunny days. Staying in Zermatt temporarily; tomorrow I shall have a look at Riffelalp and eventually shall rent something. Many best,

St.

Hotel Riffelalp, 8/9

Dear child:

Because I know how impatiently you are waiting for my news, I am writing you right off. Well: I have had my usual notable good luck with the weather: sparkling sunshine, the air unbelievable. The hotel is just my style, very English, a few Basel patricians, absolutely no Germans, located right in the heart of the mountains, across from the Matterhorn, a mere saunter by a good trail right up to the glaciers and eternal snows. It's divine, lovelier than at Wengen, because it is higher up, more open.—You'd be picking Alpine flowers all day long. One has the sensation of having an altogether different pair of lungs here. Give my best to your little ones.

Affectionately,

St.

Dear Wife:

Today, Monday, is so beautiful, radiant, and divine that I've decided to stay another two days. I shall leave Friday; in the evening I'll be at Hotel Byron, but shall stay only through Saturday (I am fearful of intruding too much on Rolland). It simply can't be lovelier anywhere than right here—these hikes at 3,000 meters are heavenly. The only annoyance is this Swiss prudishness. You can't take off your shirt or even collar anywhere. And so we all have lobster faces and are lily-pale from the collar down: it would be wonderful to let the mountain sunshine get at our bodies from top to toe. The trio here is very pleasant; it plays dance music in the evening, but in the afternoon performs the finest compositions in masterly fashion. I can choose whatever I want and have had all the Schubert trios and Beethoven sonatas played one after the other. The violinist and pianist are both Viennese, and are first class.—I have had the good luck to meet two Americans, very clever sisters, and dislocate my tongue: unfortunately, they interrupt each other all the time, with identical intentions. It would make good material for a comedy. I get considerable amusement out of it.

Affectionately, St.

L.F.:

The sky today was again a gentian blue, with the air very mild; therefore, despite the frosts at night one can sleep with the window open. Meanwhile I think of all the things I've been missing.[1] Oddly enough there is a wicked Kaspar [2] here who growls at everybody, but comes to me in the friendliest fashion, sits down next to me as though he belonged to me. Give my best to everybody.

Your St.

¹ The disturbances during the Festival season in Salzburg.   ² Kaspar was the name of our spaniel.

L.F.:

It is as delightful as ever here. I go out walking a lot, inhale the invigorating air with relish, and would like to send you a package of it. I am reading a good deal and hear all sorts of languages, sometimes it is like the Tower of Babel. Few Germans—but every one of them has a loudspeaker in his throat, so that there seem to be more of them than of any other group.

Affectionate regards to all of you,

St.

8/14

L.F.:

Thanks a lot for your news. Here the weather continues to be fine. I am going ahead with preliminary work on the sketch on Fouché, talk little and feel well.—Wonderful place for quiet people. Every afternoon the noblest chamber-music from Beethoven to Mussorgsky and no concessions, consequently only about two people listen to it. In the evening they have to jazz and charleston—it is really a bitter pill for such first-class artists to have to slave away at such music. Of course, it is rather clever of them—they have a free vacation with pay and can practice their programs.

St.

L.F.:

I am still writing from Riffelalp; I am staying on. Really it is crazy to leave at all—the sunshine here at an elevation of from 2,000 to 3,000 meters is incomparable. But it is best for me to leave now.—My anonymity had been a great success; unfortunately, the past eight days have brought a number of Germans; four of them have already introduced themselves to me. I like a hotel as long as I don't know

189

anybody there and can watch everyone else; that will explain my brief stop-overs which you think are so weird. The fun ends with the anonymity.

Excitement here because two tourists fell off of the Matterhorn across the way: of course they were killed.

So I shall be on my way to Villeneuve on Friday, will stay there through Saturday, perhaps even through Sunday.

My best, St.

Riffelalp, 8/20

Today, just as I was leaving, I met Arthur Schnitzler in Zermatt with Mrs. P.—the only Austrian, and by no means the worst. This evening, Villeneuve.

Affectionately, St.

Villeneuve, Saturday

L.F.:

Thanks a lot for your two letters which were waiting for me here. I should prefer to stay here, because it is all so quiet, but I am afraid that my being so near might disturb R. I shall return to Salzburg either on Tuesday or Wednesday. The troubles in Salzburg don't worry me a bit, this time I am in a very peaceful frame of mind and without any anxieties because I am quite sure about my work.—I'll tell you about R. in S. Papa R. celebrated his ninetieth birthday on the tenth, is full of life and in good spirits.

My best, Stefan.

It is delightful here, but now I can appreciate how divine the air up yonder really was, an enchanted, improbable abode. Incomparably beautiful moonlight on the last night, Beethoven's last sonatas, "A little love and so on." Sometimes, really, life can be very wonderful.

My best, Stefzi

Lido, 9/16/26

Dear Stefan:

I am writing this in pencil because I am down at the beach. Thanks for the news. Leonhard wrote me that he was glad you were coming to Munich. Schmidtbonn will be there too. The children wrote you yesterday about our meeting some friends here. Felix (Braun) looked extremely well but seemed depressed. Then I spent some time with the dear couple, the Kahanes, your old friends. They seem to be very fond of each other. What happiness to have three sons by one's beloved! You wrote a sad letter to Felix. Dearest, if I could only give you my heart's blood to make you happy! How gladly would I plan our common life according to your desire! But, you hold back or are evasive. Yet trifles that don't signify anything at all, unfortunately, often upset you, come in conflict with your feelings and wishes. After all these momentary flare-ups are soon forgotten. They happen, generally, because you are so depressed, and, unfortunately, your shattered energies can't always cope with your spells of moodiness. That's all it is, so help me God! I hope I can help you in this too. Fresh strength gives fresh courage.

While enjoying the sun's healing rays here and bathing in the warm sea, it's comforting to know that hundreds of underprivileged children share all this with us. The Italian government has built several huge rest halls at the island's southern tip where convalescent children can play on the beach. The attempt on M.'s [1] life hasn't caused much excitement here. Even in Venice there was nothing, except the hoisting of those beautiful flags on the Church of San Marco and a parade of Black Shirts, just a handful of young fellows. But the people here seem less gay than formerly, though as charming as ever. And how handsome they are! Shall meet Stringa, who lives at Monte Baldo, on my return trip. Is Huebsch [2] going to publish the stories? Affectionate greetings,

F.

[1] Mussolini.   [2] His friend Ben Huebsch of the Viking Press in New York.

L.F.:

I didn't have a chance to phone you; don't get back home from rehearsals [1] before 2:30 or 3. Heine, Aslan are all fairly, in fact, very good, but the whole thing fails to catch the style, or really the basic concept. But I believe it will be better than I thought it would be.

Affectionately, Stefzi

1 Rehearsals for a first performance of *Volpone* on the sixth of November. (There are no letters about this performance or the one in Dresden because we attended them together. *Volpone* was produced in more than 500 theaters at home and abroad and later was filmed and shown throughout the world.)

LECTURE TOUR NOVEMBER-DECEMBER 1926

Hotel Hof von Holland, Mainz am Rhein

Dear Fritzi:

However did you manage to get back to our precious Salzburg by afternoon? I am very well taken care of here and the library is altogether at my disposal—too bad there isn't very much in it. Tomorrow I deliver my lecture in the famous hall, the second finest in Germany, where Mozart played for the Duchess. I hope everything is going along all right at home and that I won't be held up in Berlin by the play.—I really haven't the slightest desire to push into theatrical affairs; by the time I leave there I shall have swallowed people to the vomiting point. Do catch up on your sleep, my Colomba,[1] and hang a sign "please do not disturb" on your door and soul.

Affectionately, St.

1 Name of Volpone's wife.

(Written from Salzburg to Mainz)
My dear:

The trip was very pleasant this time. No lumps in my cushion except your reproachful announcement that you would forget everything because I had gone with you to the station. I am grateful for the trip to Dresden, not only because I could be with you and be at the celebration in the evening too, but also because I clearly realized how much we profit by not making our home in a large city where people, hounded by all sorts of ambitions, are full of pettiness. At least we have been able to hold fast to a bit of our faith in humanity. We would have lost it long ago had we been constantly confronted with these foibles of the people about us, or, as an alternative, we would have had to become as hard and callous as they are.

No news. Demands for Christmas contributions and the like keep pouring in. But I believe you should be a little less accessible, especially in the matter of these round-robin appeals, and so forth. Everybody is entitled to a little bit of privacy. Don't you agree with me? Naturally, the onslaught is at its height just now. The more need to apply the brakes, or you'll be swamped by all this ballyhoo.

Mr. L. Brieger wants to know what I, as an artist's "eminent" wife (probably should read "an eminent artist's wife") think of artists marrying one another. It'll be fun to answer that question.

Just received your sweet letter. Many, many thanks. Please take care of yourself. 1000 kisses.

Mumu

Hotel Hof von Holland, Mainz, Nov. 28th

Dear Lambkin:

Thanks a lot for the letter and things you forwarded. I have just finished lecturing in that ducal hall, two hundred years after Mozart, only I am afraid it was more crowded than for Wolfgang Amadeus. It was first-rate as a starter; tomorrow Wiesbaden. I am living here in an Edenlike quietude. I have a room with a bath (here the prices are reduced too, because I am entered in the register reserved for the hotel's guests of honor)—in short they spoil me here in Germany, but I won't let it go to my head.

By the way, please give my especial thanks to Mrs. Meingast, Therese and Franz for sending birthday congratulations. No other commissions for you except that you should keep well and not worry about me.

Affectionately, St.

Best to your youngsters.

Mainz 11/30

L.F.:

Dear lamb, thanks for letter-telegram. I lectured yesterday in Wiesbaden, afterward dined (terrific!) at Henckell-

Trocken's (whom I'd met some time ago at Rheinhardt's), go on tomorrow. I have had a complete rest here; everyone at the library was most charming. Now, of course, comes the Berlin whirl. I hope to have a message from you in Cologne.

Affectionately, Stefan

Cologne, 12/2

Dear Lambkin:

I didn't find anything from you waiting for me at the hotel here.—Well, I hope it is still to come. This part of the country is very interesting because it is so tremendously alive; you couldn't have the slightest inkling of what it's like. Essen, alone, has a bigger population than Dresden, and only twenty minutes away are Duisburg, Dortmund, Duesseldorf with between 300,000 and 400,000—huge complexes! When I get the chance I'll write you more about it.

My very best,

St.

Cologne, 12/3/1926

Dear Child:

I was thankful to get news of you. Please, dear child, be more lucid and concise. I know, my dear, how hard you try, but I will show you the letters and ask you if you, yourself, can make head or tail of them. I am doing wonderfully well here. Essen was a bore, because of the lecture, but on the other hand, I was even more successful there than in Hamburg. In spite of the Kreisler concert the hall was filled to overflowing; the beginning of the lecture was delayed because they had to put chairs around the lecturer's podium—the audience was splendidly attentive, many remarkable faces in it. After it was over I had to autograph seventy to one hundred books that had just been bought; there were some very pretty girls whom I'd rather have gratified in a different way. This worthy literary society hasn't had such a crowded hall for seven years, and so I was made much of, of course. All this affected me in an odd way, this alien world that I sense in Cologne: people do more solid and conscientious reading here, refer back to what they've been reading, comparing one book with another. I am going to the Museum tomorrow to look at the Cathedral treasures, but nevertheless have found time—please take note—to dip pen in ink and write you this lengthy letter. Tomorrow I shall be in Aix, Sunday Duesseldorf, where I'm to lecture. My very best to everyone at home.

Your Stefan

Dear Lamb:

Just received your letter. You complain that you can't concentrate—my dear, I gather that from your muddled letters, but I know that it isn't really tragic. I have had some good days here, and considerable success, as you can see from the newspapers (the national German and Catholic press). The students were awfully nice, they asked me to lecture for them next year, and there were several young girls (a new type, very jolly and at the same time earnest and zealous). Now for Aix. Farewell my child, don't complain, don't despair, there will soon be an end to your loneliness.

Affectionately, St.

This time several people came over especially to hear me, from Bonn, Koblenz, Godesberg, which moved me deeply.

Aachen (Aix), 11/5

L.F.:

I am in Aix, and, thanks to Mr. Witte, have carefully inspected the cathedral treasure—things you couldn't imagine. And the cathedral itself! But what impresses one most is that this was the center of the world long before Paris. To-morrow I am going on to Duesseldorf, where I hope to find some letters from you.

Affectionately, St.

Hansa Hotel, Duesseldorf, 11/6

Cara Confusa:

I had only one letter here, but not the one with the enclosures from Servaes, etc. Yesterday I had a good long visit with Berthold Viertel,[1] many hours in fact, and we talked together as happily and affectionately as we ever have. He was pleased because I attended the performance of the *Tomb of the Unknown Soldier,* which really was quite extraordinary. Then I also saw the Dumont [2] who invited me for today, but I won't go, they might think I want something from them in connection with the play.

Please, attend to all the Christmas presents, so that when I come back, it will really be quiet at home; there will be a lot to do. I will probably not be able to write you from Berlin. I have so insanely much to do there.

Germany impresses me terrifically. Here, in the west, resides all its strength.

Affectionately, Stefan

[1] Poet and producer of plays at important theaters.   [2] Famous producer who had her own theater.

Duesseldorf, 12/7

L.F.:

The Duesseldorf lecture was sold out again and very lively; after it was over there was a get-together, at which Herbert Eulenberg delivered an address at me.—Unfortunately, I can't learn how to look intelligent while this sort of nonsense is going on. However, there were a couple of incidents quite to my taste. It's a pity, although Henrici bid for it, skyhigh, for me, I lost the Beethoven, but I may have a chance at the variations on *Gott Erhalte* by Haydn. The prospect of Berlin is horrible—theater, lectures, rehearsals, conferences, women, friends—awful, because of the tumult and crowds.

Greetings, Stefzi

Salzburg, 12/7

Dear Stefan:

Am so happy that you are having such success and such a stimulating trip. I hope it won't be too tiring, especially in Berlin. Yesterday I sent you an almost complete list of your mail. Your nervousness about your letters is quite unnecessary. While you are away I shall have to decide what is important. You must rely on, and trust me. If there's anything urgent I'll attend to it. What I write will be neither mixed-up or unintelligible. So, my dear, let's forget about it. Felix Braun has been here since yesterday and we spent a very nice evening together. He told me a great deal about our dear Carossa.

Be embraced by your

F.

Harried like a wild boar, I can write you only on the wing. The première [1] is on the eighteenth. But I hardly believe I'll stay for it.—Party at Donath's,[2] very pleasant; I forgot to remind you to send him congratulations. Camill was delightful. Innumerable acquaintances, also many from abroad. Lernet-Holenia, Polgar, Bruno Frank, etc., etc., but I keep myself incommunicado. Sunday's lecture already sold out by Wednesday—really dreadful. I feel like a tenor. Several engagements for *Volpone;* Felix Bloch hopes for a big success. I myself am very tired due to too much alcohol, tobacco, too little sleep, and, on top of that, a head cold and a chill brought on by central heating and drafts. In Duisburg I had to stop in the middle of the lecture, my voice was gone, but the 700 people weren't. Saturday, my only free evening, big party at Fischer's, an invitation which I accepted, today. After the lecture I hope to sneak off for a couple of hours. Sunday, a dinner in my honor at the Bristol, with all the bigwigs. Horrible but unavoidable. *Oh, la gloire, quel saleté, quelle ordure!* But then, soon Salzbug and how I'll enjoy it— a metropolis is pure insanity, but especially Berlin, where things always happen all at the same time. All our friends are wrecks because of the telephone and daily invitations, all of them yearn for sleep. Because I stick to Salzburg, I am deemed super-wise. And you, my lamb, never complain, nor despair, e'en though your heart break in twain.[3] Forget me, practice your stenography and don't groan, you are doing better than your own

Stefzi

Best to Susi and all.

[1] Première of *Volpone* in Piscator's Volksbuhne.   [2] The art critic.
[3] From an old poem.

197

Salzburg, February 8, 1927 (to Vienna)

Dear Wife:

I am writing in great haste to give you some most important news. I was happy to receive the first copies of *Amok* in French today. The book looks wonderful, and Rolland's introduction is not only evidence of his really surpassing goodness, but also very learned and psychologically most important. I can't deny that I have been vastly pleased by it.

The weather still wonderful. Everything in excellent shape. Give my best to all my friends in Vienna, especially Felix Braun and Miss Korten! I would like you to see more of her because I feel she might perhaps talk to you more freely about many things and you could surely be helpful to this estimable human being. My very best to Mama [1] and Stephanie.

Affectionately, Stefan

[1] He didn't include a message to his father because the latter had already passed away, on March 2nd, 1926.

LETTERS FROM SWITZERLAND, AUGUST 1927

Buchs 8/6, Wednesday morning

We were an hour and a half late because of an avalanche at Lend, and so I didn't arrive till after twelve o'clock in Zuoz, but managed to get in a walk, past Hotel Raetia, the Reessli and other landmarks of former days.[1] But at that time we didn't notice how wonderfully ancient the old village castle looks perched on its terraces above the lake: at that time our eyes were sealed. Best regards to all,

Yours,

St.

[1] Reference to our stay at the frontier during the war years.

Assembly Rooms, Castell
Zuoz, Unter-Engadin, 8/8

Dear Fritzi:

And now I want to report that I am quite satisfied, after finally capturing a room (with balcony so that I can work out of doors and read, bathed in sunshine). The hotel is very decently upper class—only Swiss and Germans: unfortunately I was recognized by a chap from Karlsruhe, but I keep myself in hiding and, except for meals, never go into the public rooms.

As to the "cure," I have a confession to make: the most important part of the cure I prescribed for myself in Salzburg and since boarding the train haven't done any smoking at all and haven't drunk a drop of coffee. Everything else is just a framework for the symptoms of illness brought on by a too excessive consumption of stimulants. Now all this has been cut off with a single determined gesture. I drink in the mountain air and masticate like an American. The doctor found my blood pressure was that of a young fellow, no fatigue curves on the chart even after rapid exercises, (you will receive the original photos of my pulse for your collection) and prescribed nothing. The cure is as follows: I get waked up at seven. Gymnastic exercises begin in an open shack at half past seven (we do our exercises in the woods and meadows, which is sensible—I am causing astonished comment because I refuse to wear a sweater and go through the exercises in just my shorts, while the others shiver through theirs in woolens: nevertheless this all has toughened us up tremendously). At half-past eight I take a warm shower, and follow it with a cold one, after which a good-looking attendant rubs us down. Then breakfast, and then by nine you are free to do as you please. I haven't done any work as yet, but everything is ready,[1] and I feel very fit. I am taking today off, going to Pontresina to visit Ebermayer. On the whole I feel *very proud* of myself because I have managed this heroic non-smoking business without getting on your nerves or anybody else's. I am quite content to be sitting here enjoying the heavenly weather. Hope it all goes on as it has, and that I shall have good, cheerful news of all of you.

So, now you have *the* letter of the summer; from now on only lots of postcards, for life here runs along in a set pattern of monotony. I am absolutely determined to avoid meeting people and shall keep myself completely isolated.

Affectionately, to you all,

Stefan

[1] For the essay on Casanova.

(Picture postcard with a view of Hotel Calonder where we stayed in 1918.)

Souvenirs of Calondria days!

Affectionately, Stefzi

Most affectionate greetings. Pity that you aren't here!

Sincerely, Erich Ebermayer

Zouz, 8/8

L.F.:

I went for a glorious auto ride to Maloia today; also had a fine time with Ebermayer. Here, at the hotel, every-thing lovely except my precious anonymity: I have had the grandest invitations to go on excursions in a Rolls Royce, [in English] "very funny and amusing offers, you will be amused. . . . I would prefer to write my Casanova than to live it. You will be very amused. Truly yours,"

St.

Salzburg, 8/9 to Zouz

My dear:

Many thanks for letter and postcards. I took care of all the mail today. The whole house groans under the impact of the gas-men's hammers and chisels. Since the foreman seemed to be in a fog, I drew up a plan for the layout of the pipes.—Moissi,[1] who was sent by Metzel, comes up twice a day to study his parts in the garden behind the house. I don't bother him. My dear, play the Casanova as much as you like. It might be best to distribute your favors impar-tially. The desk stays in its accustomed place. Other things, as you often complain, are less stable. A thousand greetings from

Mumu

[1] The actor Alexander Moissi who was then playing *Everyman* during the Salzburg Festival weeks.

Letter from Zuoz, 8/9

Dear Fritzi:

I am writing you again just a few lines after yesterday's excursion to Maloia, which was really glorious; knowing it only in winter, one has no conception of the colors of the Engadine, above all, of the lakes from Sils Maria and Campfer. The auto took us so far that we could look down into Italy—really a wonderful day. Work sluggish-indifferent; I am still not in full swing, but now at last I am going to pull myself together and begin.—The countryside lures one away.—Haven't smoked for a whole week, and yet am still alive and hope to hold out till the end of the cure, also I haven't drunk any black coffee. My little remnant of will power is still functioning—let's hope that my head will clear up.

I am learning the difficult art of impoliteness here; I persist in refusing to get acquainted with anybody. Generally speaking, I don't understand people (here we have only a better class of them; but tennis seems to be the most important thing in the world).

In your letter you didn't specify what ones you answered yourself and what I ought to answer. I am leaving everything that isn't urgent for my return. Nevertheless, I like to know that someone is at home while I am away, looking after things generally, not only the letters.

The gymnastics regime agrees with me very well. At my age one's bones won't become completely supple again and I shall never become willowy or a young man again. But one does what one can.

My affectionate best,

St.

Salzburg, 8/16
My dear:
It was really darling of you and a great joy to me, one of the greatest that I've had for a long time. I could hear your beloved voice so distinctly that the miracle almost dazed me, and how sweet of you to phone at a time when you knew I was in the midst of such a mess. I am still happy about it today. The workmen are back but reduced in number to five. You can't imagine how terribly the house has been devastated. The whole place is messed up, the hall and your winter study excepted. On top of it all, I have to find lodgings for people who can't get rooms in this crowded season and therefore want to stay with us.

The following letters arrived: Inquiry about a lecture in Hamburg. Film offers. Maggs is sorry: the Goethe fetched twenty-nine pounds. Ponten wired to ask whether you were home. *Welt am Abend,* Berlin, is waiting for your declaration protesting about the Sacco-Vanzetti affair. I answered that you were away. Then an invitation from Max Reinhardt to Leopoldskron, after the *Midsummernight's Dream.* Warsaw wants you to lecture in October.

Susi is just copying the beautiful Rilke letter. (From Madame Verhaeren's copy that I sent to Huenich.) I hope it is accurate.

Well, my dear, most affectionate greetings. Hope the good weather continues. The rain is coming down in ropes here, which grieves me on account of the Reineclaude harvest [plums].

Thanks again for your dear, delightful inspiration. Be embraced by

Mumu

In September, my daughter Susi and I went to Gland near Nyon on Lake Geneva, where she was to attend a school under English Quaker management, where the students had the benefit of the most progressive teaching techniques. Susi was to study languages there for several months. For the time being we stayed on the opposite (French) side of the lake. The following letters are selected from a total of seventeen written by Stefan and many I wrote to him.

Interlaken, 9/9/27

My dear:

Up to now, everything went off according to schedule. We drank chocolate (the world's best) for breakfast at Spruengli's in Zuiro [Zuerich] and then ventured down to the lake. Then a marvelous trip to Interlaken past all the lakes. Darling, everywhere I think of you continually and consider this a sort of pilgrimage to the places we visited together long ago. Tomorrow the roundtrip Scheidegg-Grindelwald. Many kisses from

Mumu

Don't work too hard!

Salzburg, Sept. 12

Dear Wife:

Your telegram **just** arrived, and I solemnly beg you to forgive me for dictating this about a few important matters instead of writing you myself. My mail, after two days' absence and including today, runs to forty letters, and I don't want to keep you waiting.

The most painful business first: while I was away a veterinary had to be called in, not our regular vet; he gave Rolfe a thorough going over and decided that he couldn't be saved. The pus is weakening him so much that even those who love him dearly must agree with the opinion of the doctor. Nevertheless they waited till I returned, and so, today, Monday morning, (I was there) we put him to sleep; he didn't suffer the least bit of pain. You need not tell Susi about it. Otherwise everything at home is in good shape. When I was in Vienna I went to the cemetery with Mama, in order to be with her as long as possible. I saw Alix.

Kasper is very depressed and won't eat. He must have been aware of Rolfe's death or have noticed the chloroform; an animal's scent is uncanny. Take care of yourself.

Best to Susi and yourself,

St.

Evian, 9/15

(In French)
My dear:

Thanks for the dear letter. My poor little Rolfie! I loved him more than you knew, though I never like to be sentimental about animals. But your message grieved me terribly. You must have suffered too. I shan't tell Susi. Rolfie was so good and, what I loved most about him, he was like some sort of plant under God's heaven. Write me, if only a word. I embrace you.

F.

Salzburg, Sept. 19

Dear Fritzi:

I'm writing you in rather a hurry, to report the most important news items. At home everything in good shape.

203

Your room has been beautifully repapered. Today I had a letter from Susi in rather too good (for her) French. If it will interest her, you can tell her that she has become a grandma while she was away and that three young cats went the way of the other thirty-two of this year. I wish my business were as profitable!

The entire accumulation of letters contains so little of real importance that I wouldn't have anything to report to you with regard to them. But there is a very long and beautiful letter from Warburg [1] (about his impressions of America, an altogether outstanding exposé).—I hope you will find the house comfortable, but, of course, without your little lambs, which will, after all, provide you with something to worry about.

Most affectionately, Stefan

[1] Sigmund Warburg, formerly of Hamburg, now of London.

L.F.:

Today I am writing you to Noyon. Rain the last three days, rain. But it doesn't really bother me. Work proceeds rather slowly. *Tolstoy* finished in a second draft, now for the third and last; the same for *Casanova,* so that I will probably have gotten rid of both these incubi by the end of October . . . then only the third will be left.[1] I wish I were as easy-going and irresponsible as I used to be—but literature doesn't seem important any more; I am without ambition; remains only a longing to bring the machine to a full stop, to be anonymous, to be a real human being again. All this publicity takes the sap out of life, especially for people like us who can't feel that it is something that makes for increased happiness. Take good care of yourself, as for me, I am altgether tranquil and well. I mustn't complain, fortunately no visits, *Desbordes* [2] came, looked fine. I shall have the one-act play [3] printed at Kiesel's, just for me alone. I am not the least bit interested in it.

Affectionately, St.

[1] Stendhal. He refers to the trilogy, *Drei Dichter Ihres Lebens* (Casanova, Stendhal, Tolstoy).   [2] A new edition of the book about the poetess

Desbordes-Valmore, of which we were co-authors.   3 *Die Flucht zu Gott,*
epilogue to Tolstoy's *Das Licht Scheint in der Finsternis.*

Hotel de Nyon
September 21, 27

My dear:
        Just returned from Gland and am writing on my
glorious terrace facing Montblanc glowing in the sunset.
Many thanks for your letter. Now I want to tell you about
Susi, or rather the boarding school. I was really charmed with
it when I went there today. Everything radiant with sunshine,
flowers, youth, and a radiantly blond-haired and blue-eyed
young man by the name of Smith. He is the one with whom
I had corresponded. All the teachers are young, and the
Directress, Miss Thomas, is a good friend of the Rollands.
(The kitten, donated by Rolland, is called Jean Christophe.)
Susi's dormitory faces a bathing beach and a little harbor
where some boats lie at anchor. The children go swimming
two or three times a day. Susi rooms with two nice English
girls—that is, one of them comes from America where her
father, Mr. Cheney, an art critic, is also one of the group
that founded The Theater Guild. There are no servants, only
a one-armed gardener who is a part-time student and has his
meals with the others. So does the cook whose children are
pupils at the school. Children and teachers together take care
of the housework. Everything is decided by a joint Teachers'-
Students' Council. For instance, Susi accompanies the Director every morning to a farm where they get the milk. The
children take turns heating the bath water. No difference
at all between poor and rich. They all run around bare-legged
and are dressed in white linen smocks. The children may eat
all they want and pick all the fruit off the trees. There's no
meat at meals. Small classes with just a few pupils. History
is taught by a young Swiss, and they have a school orchestra.
The tuition takes care of everything, a few excursions excepted.
Montblanc looks more beautiful from here than from anywhere else. The back country reminds me of the landscape
of Hardy's *Tess of the D'Urbervilles.* Wealthy peasants. The
udders of the cows are spectacular. A single one could feed
an entire village back home.

205

Dear Stefan:

Thanks for the card. Don't worry about Susi. She feels completely at home here. So I feel quite reassured—especially after watching the physical examination given the older girls (Susi included) in a nearby sanitarium. It went off in fine style, and everything was done with Swiss thoroughness. It was interesting and lovely to see these fourteen- to sixteen-year old girls of six different countries and races as nature made them. I'll never forget the two sweet Singhalese girls. They seemed so plant-like—their little bodies (one was almost black) had something sacred about them.—On Sunday we'll go to Villeneuve. Shall visit Jaloux.[1] In the meantime, Affectionately

F.

1 Edmond Jaloux whose two novels I had translated.

Dear Fritzi:

Little to report from here; the Geigy-Hagenbachs were both charming. His modesty and unassuming manner, despite his great wealth, is touching. I still am not working with real keenness of mind. I feel as if there were some screws loose in the machinery; it ought to be shut down anyway now that I have reached fifty, and I could then make a try at experiencing the world instead of describing it. I am full of doubts about this ceaseless literary grind, it is an unnatural business if a person isn't the least bit ambitious. The less I hear of the St.Z. who lives in the mirror-world, the more I am myself: I would like to be altogether that and nothing else once more. Tomorrow Reisinger will be here for an hour or so.[1] I am so very happy, happier than you can imagine, that you are in such good spirits. I am often haunted by a sense of guilt because I have entangled you, much more than I like and much more than I can ever answer for, in this dreadful mechanism of my profession, the many people, the added work and the letters. I hear nothing from Paris,[2] luckily my desire to travel is negligible just now. I would like to get the book finished, so as to be free for a journey in search of adventure. Devotedly,

Your Stefan

1 Dr. Hans Reisinger, the biographer and translator of Walt Whitman.
2 The approaching performance of *Volpone*.

My dear:

Your card saying you were happy because I am feeling so well moved me so much that I found an outlet for my emotions in weeping over Chopin's death for I am just now reading Pourtales' beautiful book.—Hope Casanova is still your lively chum. If you feel "the screws getting loose" as you put it, this is due to the weight of your artist's conscience and nothing else. How easy everything would be if you were only more aware of your creative powers; you are a much too modest creature. Thanks for everything. Be embraced, my beloved, by

Your Lamb

From Nyon

My dear:

Must tell you of my visit to Jaloux in Lausanne. First I got my sleeping car reservation for the return trip before going to see him. Then strolled along the Avenue Leman, a very fashionable street lined with villas and grand hotels. It runs above the lake, in the direction of Vevey. Jaloux lives in a somewhat dilapidated house. No need to describe him to you.

I didn't find him as much of a snob as Erwin had said. Neither is he delicate, but rather pudgy and epicurean. I like him very much, and also the way he lives. He likes greenery at his windows too and to keep away from people. His wife looks boyish, with a serious face that masks all sorts of potentialities. Has black bobbed hair and bright eyes. Jaloux is immensely grateful to you. He felt slighted, because works by Dick, Tom and Harry had been translated, whereas he, who had done so much for the "rapprochement" remained completely unknown. He loves Germany because he loves the old romanticism and detests Americanized France. (I hope he won't be disillusioned.) That's the reason he is living in Switzerland. He was in Bayreuth last summer. The open score of *Die Walküre* lay on the piano. He would like to hear Mozart in Salzburg, but also wants to meet *you* there and knows it would be hard to combine the two. He was very nice to me. They have a small car and promised to visit me in Gland. He praised my French to the very skies. Gave me his latest novel *Soleils disparus* (Empress Elizabeth) with a dedication to you and me. Wants me to do the translation.—

On the way back to Gland I met a charming little lady. It turned out that she was going to Gland to see her daughter after a six months' separation. She knows Streinrueck,[1] worships you and has just read *The Eyes of the Undying Brother*. A very clever Hamburg lady. Lovingly yours,

F.

[1] The actor Albert Steinrueck.

My dear:

On Sunday we took the boat to Geneva. The view as one approaches by steamer is quite unique. The town has a distinction all its own, with beautiful estates lining the shorefront. We met Paule and her husband, both charming. Then took a long drive to Charles Baudouins'[1] house. Distressing to see how he lives, the place is more poverty-stricken than the one Jouves had in Mies. A house swarming with flies. Three darling boys making a lot of noise. His wife is a teacher. How I wished that this wonderful man (I love him very much) could have a comfortable, pleasant place to work in. At that, he seems to have quite a few patients.

Be embraced a thousand times by your most loving

Mumu

[1] Charles Baudouins, Professor at the Institut Rousseau, psychoanalyst, poet, and translator into French of Stefan's *Jeremiah*.

(From Susi)
My dear, good, Stefferl:

Am happy to spend Saturday and Sunday with Mama. Now, all this about my "prison": well, it's just the contrary. Nobody ever scolds us; but that makes one's conscience hurt the more. Stefferl, I hope you are well, and also your retinue of cats and so forth. Thanks and many kisses.

Susi

Dearest:

To begin with the most important item: the day with the Rollands was altogether magnificent. He looks well, doesn't cough any more. When he talks his voice is subdued but he doesn't seem to get tired as easily as he used to. At first I was tongue-tied, as I always am. But then we talked together quite freely and it was wonderful. Also Madeleine is fine, and Papa Rolland, more erect than ever, looks fine. Everything was beautiful, a real feeling of friendship. And to top it all, a divine day. Susi wanted to write immediately and tell you how wonderful it was. She listened in with her newly-acquired "French" ears. We stayed from half past ten until five, because they didn't want to let us go. Also I have a lot to tell you about Rilke, part of which was told me per Valmont (Rolland), and partly per Jaloux. Do you want to go on listening to me, your "Waterfall?"

Unless I wire to the contrary, I'll come on the Arlberg Express. Looking forward to you impatiently. I "buss" you many times.

Mumu

P.S. Enclosed is a clipping from *Comoedia* explaining why *Volpone* can't be put on just now. They are playing *Knock* and a one act play by our good Jules.[1] But at any rate, you can be sure that V. will feel at home in a theater where a little fun is still welcome.

[1] Jules Romains, translator of *Volpone*. Dullin played the lead.

1 9 2 8

Paris, March 25

L.F.:

This is to report my safe arrival. Good trip, in fact excellent, very nice room, no letters, freedom, soft spring weather, *cela suffit amplement*. Now for the *Boeuf à la mode,* then a walk, and meanwhile, kind regards to (in English) "at home."

Stefzi

L.F.:

Your card arrived just now. I was at the theater too yesterday with Frans, tomorrow I am to go to the Russian ballet, also will see Romains, up till now have had a good rest and feel fine. I have a horror of everything that smacks of society. I wouldn't like to live here, there is too much tumult. But it's wonderful for a few days.

Affectionately, St.

L.F.:

Thanks for your letter. Yes, I also felt there were repetitions in the Gorki essay; this would have been taken care of, as soon as I read the proofs (I never catch anything in the typed version except the mistakes in the typing). I am doing very well in a grand room here. I visited with Masereel, who is charming, but like me he withdraws more and more from people into his work. Today I am to see Romains, who continues to defend *Volpone* energetically. (Jouvet wanted to set a less favorable date). After that I shall go to Hannah Orloff's, a magnificent sculptress whose things have been the sensation of Paris.—I am making up for lost time in every direction, and being rejuvenated by following King David's recipe: Go out walking a lot. It was the wisest thing I could have done and precisely in the way I am doing it.

Affectionately, Stefan

L.F.:

Received your postcards from Vienna. Yesterday went to see Romains. Jouvet would like to produce *Volpone* as the next première, but R. won't have it, because even May isn't a good time. I am not getting myself involved—experience proves that a sparrow in the hand is worth more than a pigeon on the roof, but Romains won't stand for any nonsense. I hope you are well.

Affectionately, Stefan

Don't forget to send *Tolstoy* to the Pauls at the London address.

Saturday

L.F.:

Tomorrow I am going with Miss Vinant to Miss Schleicher's (Monod) at Versailles and will submit to being interviewed by Frédéric Lefêvre for the *Nouvelles Littéraires*. But there is plenty of time left over for important matters. Goodbye, dear Lamb.

Affectionately, St.

Complete chaos. Today Romains telephoned: the Theatre de l'Atelier would like to put on *Volpone*, instead of the Comédie des Champs Elysées, so perhaps I shall have to spend another day on this affair. Meanwhile, Easter without a chance of mail; a flood of Anglo tourists. Paris was wonderful. My best.

St.

1928, RUSSIAN TRIP

Stefan went to Russia to represent Austrian authors (an older colleague was unable to go) at the Tolstoy Centenary. He spent about ten days there.

(Postcard from Warsaw with a view of the Copernicus Monument.)

Dear F.:

Chaos begins right away: apparently that particular train to Moscow isn't running any longer. So I am staying overnight in Warsaw, with Dr. Stawski as my very amiable cicerone, and will not be in Moscow till Monday noon. Goodbye and take care of yourself.

Affectionately, St.

Norogovolje (Frontier already passed) 9/10
My very best to you. Traveling not at all exhausting. Already everything is interesting. I met a Spaniard who is going to Moscow, and all the passengers are very friendy. So there is nothing to worry about, despite all those stupid fairy tales.

Stefan

Dear Child:

I wasn't able to mail the postcard in N., continued the trip in a splendid, double-width sleeping car to M., feel as fit as a pig in clover, and happy.

L.F.:

I'll be in Moscow in another hour. Everything along the way already most interesting, the trains so comfortable that I'm sorry I didn't bring you along. My address for telegrams will be Woks, Moscow. I have had very pleasant company; a very nice Viennese tells me that you can travel for days by train, because it's so very comfortable. This is written from the train.

Best, Stefzi

Moscow, Grand Hotel, 9/11

Dear Fritzi:
Arrived yesterday. At two o'clock I was astounded to learn that I would have to lecture about Tolstoy and foreign countries this evening. I had nothing prepared but after thinking things over a bit, I decided to speak extemporaneously—although the big opera house (the finest I've ever seen, it seats 4,000 people) and the flashlights and electric spotlights for the movie cameras are really frightening; but nevertheless, it didn't go badly considering that I had to lecture shortly after a fifty-four-hour train ride. The celebration began at six o'clock, at eleven I delivered my lecture, and finally at one, I got to sleep. The audience was wonderful, extraordinary! It would have been impossible for us at home to get people to listen so attentively for such a long time. And the orchestra, I have never heard better. Today I am having a look around, at twelve, opening of the Tolstoy House, in the evening a concert, at twelve midnight we are to go to Tula, where we'll spend the night (arriving at three), and will go on by auto to Jasnaya. You will note that every minute is taken up with something, to top all of which, I have had glorious weather today.

Stefan.

Grand Hotel, Plaza of the Revolution

L.F.:
A few hasty lines. Today the Dostoievski Museum, the wonderful History Museum, then attended the dedication of the Tolstoy House, became acquainted with a thousand people, then to the Tolstoy Museum (my Tolstoy book is being sold at every street corner for twenty-five copeks and is cried out, like the time of day, by the book hawkers). In the afternoon to Boris Pilniak's where I met all sorts of Russians, after that

at antique dealers' and drove around all the streets in a droshky, in the evening *Eugene Onegin* at the opera, now, twelve o'clock, departure for Tula; arrive tomorrow, Wednesday, at 6 o'clock, then to Jasnaya Polyana; in the evening return by sleeper (what is a bed like?). Thursday four museums, ten visits scheduled, including Gorky, evening to the theater, later that evening, on the town, Friday just about as busy, ditto Saturday. Sunday evening I am invited by my publisher to take a "jaunt" to Leningrad, twelve hours in a sleeper, Sunday Rembrandts and Leningrad, twelve hour return trip. Monday, if the train is running, by sleeper to Warsaw, Tuesday sleeper to Vienna, will be in Salzburg Thursday afternoon, or, at the latest, Friday. Everything deliriously interesting. I am happy to have seen everything, the impression all this has made on me will last a whole lifetime. I am fine. I feel refreshed and better than ever; this is due to the intensity of the impression I have received.

Affectionately,

St.

Dear Wife:

I am getting along well, couldn't be better. I am seeing an endless lot of things. Everything is noteworthy, magnificent; I am getting acquainted with a host of extraordinary people and would like to stay months more. Everybody feels the same way. Professor Dana's six days became six months.

Your seven thousand times photographed, filmed and much radioed,

Stefan

(Short trip to Switzerland)

Montreux, 12/20/1928

L.F.:

I went to your Hotel Europe in Montreux, but, today, transferred to Hotel Monney, an old aristocratic hotel which fifty years ago was the finest. It has that lovely view of the lake, is quiet and congenial, and I have a broad balcony. I shall not write Rolland till today, because I don't want to be too close by and stay too long a time. Wonderful sun. I am feeling fine in an empty room.

Best to all of you.

Stefzi

Your Christmas present already in hand.

L.F.:

Thanks for the things you forwarded. I am still lazy, that is to say I went to Caux, and was really so enchanted by it that I wasted a whole day there. Tomorrow, Saturday, I shall be with Rolland for dinner. In a weird sort of way, I feel entirely at home in this forsaken village, although it is always a mistake to stay such a short time; but next year I'll do better, even this is a step forward toward achieving mobility. Take care of yourselves and don't wax too sentimental on Christmas! I thought of breaking in on your festive mood and telephoning, but God knows whether the telephone operators don't want to have a bit of rest too on that evening.

Best to all of you,

St.

Montreux, Hotel Monney 12/23

L.F.:

Thanks a lot for the catalogue you forwarded. I was at Rolland's yesterday; he looks to be in grand shape, even to the extent of being ashamed of the little pot belly he has developed.—*Le vieux papa* and Madeleine were touching. As in his letter, R. seemed to me to be less cordial than usual. I sense that someone or something has put him out of humor with me. Yet that is one of the few things as to which I have a clear conscience. He works terribly hard, is completely immersed in Indian and religious matters. What he told me about Bazal is really sad; apparently the poor fellow wants to do something for himself, now that it is too late.

I shall hardly be in Salzburg before the third or fourth. I thrive wonderfully on solitude, and it is a great delight to be able to sleep through all this Christmas [1] hurly-burly.

Doubtless your little herd is already crowding and bellowing around you, their gentle herdswoman, today, and you are happy—so don't miss your S. too much.

1 I only learnt later that Stefan's bitterness about Christmas and his frequent trips to escape the holidays were due to the fact that in his youth he never had the joy of celebrating Christmas.

L.F.:

Thanks a lot. Maggs is sending a Blake drawing and the Stravinsky manuscript. If it runs into trouble at the customs, tell them that you do not know the exact value; if they won't accept that, let them hold it until the fourth of January. Don't make any inquiries before they notify you. "Never to a duke do go, before that he does summon you." [Austrian dialect: "Gehe nie zu einem Ferscht, eh du nicht gerufe werscht."] I am leaving on the third, will be in Basel at twelve, dine at the Geigys and continue the journey at seven.

Best to your young heifers.

Affectionately, Stefzi

L.F.:

We had a splendid Christmas dinner here today; I'll bring you the program. As a windup each of us was presented with a bottle of liqueur by the owner, whom you know; he was manager of Hotel Byron in 1918. I am still not working here as I should, the machine must be somehow out of kilter; I am reading that incredible masterpiece, *The American Tragedy,* by Dreiser, and various other things, with a great deal of pleasure. But even though I am not working, nevertheless the isolation has done me a lot of good. After all, I have time to concentrate and recuperate from all that "busyness" which upset me so terribly. If you can find out about a masseur, I'd be very much obliged to you, because I should like to begin right after my return: I must really start living more sensibly, no more of this disgusting sedentary existence. Here, at any rate, I do go out walking, often three or four hours a day.

Affectionately, to you all,

St.

L.F.:

Hearty Christmas greetings despatched on the twenty-seventh. I was at Rolland's again today, he was much nicer and livelier. Unfortunately, bad news about Bazal. I have written him. Work feeble, but in any event, when I return I shall be less on edge than I was when I left. New suit turned out well, good-looking and durable; I am also buying the other things.

Affectionately, to you all,

Stefzi

Dec. 28

Dear Child:

Lots of thanks for your and Alix's letter—I shall have to try the thing out myself in Vienna [1]—It seems excellent to me. Rolland was also interested in it. Thanks for the catalogues—I must tell you I have been terribly foolish. I bid 12,000 marks for five pages of Dickens' *Pickwick* but was frozen out by a bid of 140,000 marks. Even I, manuscript addict that I am, have to admit that this is sheer insanity.

My work isn't getting on as it should, there is a kink somewhere in everything I've done the last year and a half. I need someone to point out the crucial mistake.[2] But I am not at all nervy, the complete rest has done me a world of good. How wise these Englishmen of fifty to seventy are: they turn over their homes as well as their businesses to their children and settle down here or on the Riviera and read their books and newspapers in leisurely fashion, and engage in a little non-competitive sport and play bridge in the evening! I would like to join them—get out of the whole "busyness" which doesn't mean a thing to me now, because I have left all ambition behind me. After the first of January all "joining" and playing the good Samaritan is going to stop—I have been helping all kinds of people, possible and impossible, for a quarter of a century—now I am giving notice!

Affectionately, Stefzi

[1] A dictaphone which my daughter tried out for him.   [2] The change that he felt was due to his periodically recurring restlessness, which, fed by various circumstances, recurred ever more frequently and was more and more difficult to overcome. There was an obverse side to fame—the growing

mental upsets, and less and less inducement to get back into harness, since the pinnacle had already been reached, and, at the same time, an intensification of his feeling of artistic responsibility, which affected the spontaneity of his work. The need for change grew apace.

1 9 2 9

L.F.:

Thanks a lot for your news, especially that you snatched Blake [1] out of the claws of those ignoramuses. Don't worry about Susi. Perhaps a vegetarian diet and some sort of tonic might be in order. I won't write again, because I arrive in S. Friday. I would like to meet Wildgans, but spare me that ball; as you know, I haven't much use for this sort of masquerade among friends, or for such unexciting affairs. So here is to our speedy reunion and (in English) "many thanks to Susi for her nearly perfect English letter; the next in shorthand!"

Affectionately, St.

[1] One of the Blake drawings.

LECTURE TOUR TO BELGIUM IN MARCH 1929

Brussels, March 15th

L.F.:

I arrived here safely and have just received your telegram. Oh, I am so little suited to the role of banqueteer, but what's the use, this too must be gone through with. As yet have seen nothing here and probably won't see much of anything—that's your inevitable destiny if you go places in an official capacity. Weather mild and pleasant, and the hotel likewise.

My best, your Stefan.

Gravenhagen, 3/18

L.F.:

Thanks a lot for your news. I have just been breakfasting, also have caught up on my sleep. Brussels was a big show.

I got a tremendous lot done in two days. Delivered a lecture (an astounding success, the best attended event of the kind this season), a *dejeuner* at the Penclub, a *dejeuner* with the cabinet ministers Huysmans and Vandervelde, visited Mrs. Verhaeren and the Museum, two more visits and interviews, then by auto with Messrs. von Buelow and Metz to Lier to call on Felix Timmermans, and didn't get to the Hague until midnight. Today I must drop cards at the Austrian and German legations, both of which have invited me, but I am rushing off to Utrecht and if I have some time off, would rather look at the Maritshuis again. After that the outlook becomes gloomier; I have to leave Wednesday morning—at six:thirty, and lecture at Goettingen the evening of the same day—it is farther than I thought; oh, I haven't learnt enough geography. Then Hanover, and then perhaps I shall go on at three a.m. to Berlin, to save a bit of time. In Berlin I shall see Z., my trusted Leader, and Mrs. V.—perhaps Victor too, but will that faze a chap who polished off twenty people in Brussels in two days and here in the Hague waits on his customers like a tailor? For the time being I am still in one piece; the weather is enchanting, but I haven't much chance to enjoy it.

Affectionately, St.

Gravenhagen, 3/19

L.F.:

I was (1) in Delft, (2) in Scheveningen, (3) in Utrecht, (4) at a *dejeuner* at the legation, (5) to tea at a book dealer's, (6) lecture, (7) supper afterward; besides that met some seventy people, and on top of it all, because this time you were angry with me and refused to worry about me, had a perfect auto-smashup, which left the other car a wreck, and nothing happened to us. This evening the supper will be over by one o'clock in the morning and I shall have to get up at six. I shall stay only a short time in Berlin, but before getting there shall sleep twelve hours in Goettingen, six to make up for the Hague, and six in anticipation of Berlin. Thanks for the mail and best from,

Your Stefan

I have never in all my life endured such a massive dinner as I had in the Hague yesterday; I am practically floating in bacon, which I can neutralize only by all the rushing about I have to do.

Affectionately, St.

Hanover 21/3

L.F.:

Today sees the last of my reading from my own works— I am tired of it all; nothing but the lectures makes sense. I wish I were back at work.

Affectionately, St.

Gardone, Savoy Palace Hotel
May 9

Dear Stefan:

It is cool and clear here after the hot trip. The houses and rocks and the snow on Monte Baldo are suffused in a peculiar burnished glow. This morning we were in Sopra Gardone. The church there is circled by a sort of rampart. Further inland lies D'Annunzio's Villa. In the park is the high mast, etc., of the Ship of Victory. The Villa must have been beautiful, but is spoiled by ugly new wings. The entrance is guarded by two gendarmes in fancy costumes. A huge dog chained to a bar above the garage barks ferociously. They say that D'Annunzio is out of his mind. Yet I believe there is still something in him of the impetus that made him a great and extraordinary poet. I wouldn't want to see him—or penetrate further into the twilight that broods over the magnificent gardens here. Too bad you have never seen Gardone; it's really wonderful. Maybe the lake isn't quite as magically blue as Como. We have been invited in such friendly fashion to go along on auto trips to Como and Bergamo that it would be churlish to refuse. Am a little anxious to know whether the new cook is doing the proper thing by you in a culinary way. Just mention anything you don't like to Johann.[1] Hope you can work undisturbed in the garden as much as you want. I offer you a loving heart, which often fails to please you but which can only try always to bring you all that is beautiful.

For instance, the light on the lake and the island with Prince Borghese's white castle—and the incredible clouds above—just as it all is at this very moment.

Stay well, my dear.

Mumu

[1] Our servant Johann, who was our faithful factotum for seven years.

Gardone, May 15

(In Italian)

Mio Stefan:

What a pity you can't embrace your Alberto! [1] Also had the pleasure of a telephone conversation with Borgese.[2] Stringa looks splendid, is the same dear fellow.

F.

[1] Alberto Stringa, Stefan's old friend, had come down from Monte Baldo where he lived among the shepherds.   [2] Giuseppe Borgese, author and journalist working for the *Corriere della Sera*. Later Professor in Chicago and Thomas Mann's son-in-law. Countess Greneville and I translated his play *Lazzaro*.

1 9 3 0

Trip to Germany for the production of *Lamm des Armen*, negotiating about theatrical business, etc.

Breslau, 3/12

L.F.:

I attended the rehearsal here of a strange comedy that reminded me a bit of *Das Lamm des Armen*. It wears pink netting around its neck and an awful amateur bleats away in the role of Bellilotte; [1] the men actors are pretty good. I was en route all night, rush off to Berlin again at six, and from there, tomorrow, to Hanover. Berlin meanwhile has been properly taken care of.

Affectionately, St.

[1] The chief female role.

(Correspondence from Berlin and Hanover.)

L.F.:   3/13

I am writing on the train, and that is why my hand-writing is so wobbly (not because we have been celebrating too well). So—now I am on the way to Hanover, then back again to Berlin, really only because Albert Einstein found out that I was there; to my complete amazement he turns out to be one of my enthusiastic readers. In order to make a meeting between us possible he begged off a date—so I'll meet him on Sunday at five and in the evening I'll go on right through to Salzburg. Hilpert, Ebermayer, Maass, Huenich, Beierle, are coming to Hanover. Fritz Engel and Diebold will come to Breslau for the performance; Dr. Horch will be in Prague. I met the Francés [1] on the street; I was rather high, and was coming out of our hotel with a lady, and the two of them, short-sighted though they are, recognized me right away. I tried to avoid them, but they took up the whole sidewalk. Romains was stuffy but Baroness Budberg [2] charming. On Tuesday Herterich [3] will come to Salzburg to discuss arrangements. A pity that Hilpert can't be there at the same time. I will arrive Monday, at eleven, if everything goes according to schedule.

Devotedly, Stefzi

[1] Raoul Francé and his wife, the naturalists.   [2] Gorky's secretary at the time we met him in Sorrento; later she was H. G. Wells' secretary.   [3] The director of the Burgtheater in Vienna, where *Das Lamm des Armen* was also being readied for production.

Berlin, Hotel am Zoo, 3/13

L.F.:

So it will be Monday anyway. I haven't anything more to do here because everything—Berlin arrangements, radio, records, amusements, visits—have been excellently taken care of. I have spent as much as your daughter's monthly salary for long-distance calls here, but today at last had seven hours of sleep.

Devotedly yours, Stefan

L.F.:

I had a wonderful meal in really "good society" in this wonderful hotel. It will be quite a good production.

Affectionately, Stefan

My warmest regards to you and Miss Susi,

Yours, Erich Ebermayer

Affectionate regards,

Your Joachim Maass

(Letters from and to Switzerland where I had gone to meet Susi who was taking a course in infant care in Geneva.)

Waldhaus Flims, July 7

My dear:

Just a word to let you know how much we like it here. I must admit that this is no ordinary big hotel but an Isle of the Blessed or a luxury liner, minus steerage, tied up to some primeval landscape. The greatest luxury of all is the spaciousness of the place, so that we can have peace and quiet despite jazz, roulette, and Packards roaring up the driveway. But when Susi tells of her babies and the fact that sometimes there isn't enough money to buy milk for them, it upsets me to think that I should be a passenger on this Noah's arc and a part of it all. But the lake is marvelous. The water isn't cold, just tingly, of an improbable blueishgreen. We can stay in it for quite a time without discomfort. Are you well, dearest? Please say yes. Susi, as always, is a good comrade and sends her best and her thanks.

Be embraced, my Stefferl, from your

Mumu

Dear Fritzi:

I had hoped that, because of the African temperature, people would be lazy about writing, but other people's "blue" Monday is, still, black and white with scribbled-over and printed paper for me. So I have to dictate this—it is one of sixteen letters—and report that everything is in good shape and that yesterday I escaped the "Boom-boom" of a Styrian festival and two flag dedications by going off on an excursion.

I have started the Freud job and hope to get on with it in energetic fashion. I am making no visits, except that I shall see Aslan [1] tomorrow; he is playing here as guest artist—Kippenberg won't arrive till Friday. We shall be thinking of you affectionately. My best to both of you,

Stefan

Alix went with me on yesterday's excursion. She is beginning to discover Nature in pleasant roundabout ways. My son Kaspar apparently perpetrated a piece of villainy. He must have managed, being crafty and cunning, to break through the enclosure while nobody was watching, for Henny looks absolutely as if she were soon to have a litter. Yes, it seems impossible these days to preserve female virtue.

[1] The actor, Raoul Aslan, at the Burgtheater, who played the part of Mosca in *Volpone*.

Flims, July 8

My dear:

I forgot to tell you I was a bit dismayed by the article in the *Neue Freie Presse* which said you intended to make a survey of the whole field of psychotherapy [1] (or something to that effect). Somehow, somewhere you must do something about this, either in your preface or introduction. The literature on the subject is impossibly voluminous. And an outsider, even if able to survey the whole field, can do no more than stimulate his readers' interest. Otherwise you'll stir up a regular hornet's nest of trouble! I can visualize the letters of learned gentlemen descending upon you and swelling your already unmanageable correspondence. You yourself are surely aware of the danger. For even if you don't directly provoke them, this unimaginative clan—the psychiatrists—will get after you. Hope you are well. Heaps of kisses.

Mumu

[1] Stefan Zweig's *Mental Healers*.

Might I ask, in all humility, why you began your little letter in such poisonous vein. It is doubtful whether you read letters that are quite explicit, or perhaps "etc., etc." *does* interest you after all. That sort of thing might be characterized as animus, not derived, however, from *animo,* meaning joy, or *anima,* signifying soul. In short, have you got caterpillars in your head? Yesterday I had a somewhat similar letter from Victor— the whole world seems to be feeling insulted. They all begin with phrases such as: "Doubtless you are not interested," and the end result will be that all the letter-writers will be right.

On the whole, quiet, which I have great need of because the Freud project is getting under way with difficulty. I must first of all work out the general outlines. The fact is, I'd like to lay it aside and write at something else, but I can't tear myself away from it now.

I think you'll soon know whether Flims is the right place. You have the whole of Switzerland to chose from. I don't know yet what I'm going to do in August. Perhaps I'll just travel at random, and stop off anywhere that strikes my fancy.

Affectionately, to Susi and yourself, Stefan

I didn't mean to be spiteful, but was only remembering certain unopened letters dating back to our "honeymoon"—that is what they call it—and that you are apt to glance at letters in a rather perfunctory way. But no reproach was intended.

Am amazed to hear that you've stopped working on the *Freud.* Perhaps you intend to take up the story of the *Young Lady at the Post Office*[1] again.

I read a lot of newspapers. Foreign politics are shot through with bare-faced double dealing. I found much of interest in Freud's lectures.

Embracing you, I am, my dear,

Your Mumu

[1] A novel that Stefan had begun but never finished.

Dear Fritzi:

I will scarcely have a chance to write you today because Professor Kippenberg is here. The radio people came today and asked me to show them through the house and tell them all about it and my life for their big program of August third; the Archbishop and others will talk for them, and it will all be done to a musical setting. I was pleased because it gave me an excuse to refuse the invitation. I expect to be a long way away from here by August third, although I'm not sure as yet. Apart from all this, things are quite peaceful here and I haven't anything to complain of. Kippenberg sends his best.

Affectionately yours, Stefzi

July 14th

Dear Fritzi:

I have already written you about moving on. Certainly, if you don't like the general tone of Flims—we belong in a museum for freaks, with our touchiness about social relations—don't stay a day longer than you have to. I would feel the same way. I find the vulgarization of all these resort hotels and amusement places simply insupportable. In warm weather Zermatt and Riffelalp are heavenly.

Affectionately yours, Stefan

7/16

Dear F.:

Heartfelt thanks for your letter. And let me know soon where you are going. Robert Rie plans to come on Friday, Felix Braun on Saturday. Today I received a prospectus from an indignant book-dealer: the Christian Scientists are using my essay [1] to launch Sybil Wilbur's book which I certainly ridiculed. And so they want to turn the interest [in my work] into money. Yes, business and religion go hand in hand beautifully.

[1] The essay on Mrs. Baker-Eddy, which later appeared in the volume *Die Heilung durch den Geist* with the essay on Mesmer and Freud.

Dearest Stefferl:

The *Mesmer* is doing very well. I want to buy another copy. Then I can study it more thoroughly and make some notes. Have you noticed how Freud begins each of his lectures by attacking his students' skepticism and their hostility to his theories? In each lecture he starts out by eliminating all possible objections. On the one hand, this makes the lectures very clear and comprehensible to the layman. On the other hand, they will in the future read as if they had been delivered fifty years before they were actually delivered, and as if Freud's audience had consisted of a lot of illiterates. Anyone who is familiar with the material and, therefore, doesn't have to be convinced, might consider that his presentation is oversimplified, too popular. Sometimes I have a feeling (without being unduly conceited) that persons of our caliber could easily romp through all sorts of University courses—excepting stuff that has to be memorized.—Susi is ploughing slowly through the *Lapses.*[1] Teachers could learn a lot from this chapter. It is amazing what a wide range Freud's teachings take in. But I am always repelled by his being so prosy. Also his emphasis on the "Oedipus complex" which many people find revolting. These things detract from the effectiveness of his otherwise eminently useful discoveries. I am sure any really objective psychic organism, one not obsessed by sex, will regard such obscure phenomena as the exception rather than the norm.

A desperate letter from Joseph Roth came yesterday. His despair is terrible. His debts are piling up on him in Vienna. His wife won't take any nourishment. Couldn't Huebsch [2] advance him a little cash? No doubt about it, you and I can't endure well fed, high living people, probably because all our friends are such tragic figures.

My beloved, farewell! Greetings to Lix. Susi and I embrace you.

Mumu

[1] Essay by Freud entitled in the German, *Fehlleistung.*   [2] B. Huebsch, his American publisher and Stefan's friend.

L.F.:

Nothing new. In connection with *Mesmer,* one of the archivists at the state archives wrote me that he had the documents covering the expulsion of Mesmer and would have them copied for me: so, anyway, the world will get some information through this paltry work of mine.

Best to Susi and yourself,

Stefzi

Flims, July

My dear:

Have just been reading *Louis Lambert*.[1] I wonder why you never urged me to read this remarkable book. It interested me particularly after your *Mesmer*. Have you read the novel recently? I know you quote from it, but can't tell whether what Lambert says about Mesmer and dreams is fresh in your mind. One passage would be a good Freud motto: "How little thought has heretofore been given the phenomena of sleep which reveal man's double life! Don't these phenomena point the way to a *new science?*" While reading *Lambert* and recurring to my yesterday's thoughts about your friends, my heart grew heavy within me as I realized that no one—except me— really knew you and that in the days to come the most silly, mischievous things may be written about you. Truly, you have let few people get close to you. You lock yourself up within yourself so completely. Your writings are only one third of you; and no one has managed to discover the essential you in them, which might explain the other two-thirds. Our poor Roth, who is astute and clairvoyant, has told me of some characteristic traits he discovered in you. But he is too much preoccupied with the demonic world in which he and his wife have become enmeshed.—I might be able to formulate what I would like to say. But for that I would need concentration, aloofness and would have to be completely uninhibited. Even so I would not know whether I could break through my subconscious restraints, and whether after I'd written it all, I wouldn't, as I have done so often before, tear the whole thing up again. Perhaps Leonhard feels things most. He wrote me a mournful letter. The kind of journalism to which he is condemned is utterly disintegrative of his inmost being. Still, there is another kind of journalism (like Krackauer's and others) that might be possible for him. But these younger people are more adapta-

ble—and the high regard one has for his gifts keeps one silent.
I love and embrace you.

Mumu

1 Novel by Balzac.

L.F.:

Welcome to Zermatt! If you go on an excursion to Riffelalp, I would strongly advise starting early in the morning. From Riffelalp you can proceed on foot to the top of the Gornergrad. Perhaps you will stay overnight up there. Oh, if only you have fine weather! As to coming back home, don't be in a hurry. I am not leaving until the morning of the thirty-first, and it will be all right if you get here on the thirtieth.

Affectionate greetings,

St.

L.F.:

It's high time for me to get away; visits every day. On top of that, this idiotic correspondence. I don't know yet where I'm going. I haven't had time to think about it, but I am already enjoying the prospect of getting away. Perhaps I'll meet Huebsch while I'm *en route*. I like to remember Riffelalp. Of course you have to have my luck with the weather. The financial situation in Austria is dreary. One hears only lamentation on all sides.

Affectionately, St.

Telegram:

Kippenberg writes today that Funkstunde is buying your novel, pays two thousand. Congratulations. Letter on the way,

Stefan

20/7

L.F.:

I hope Kippenberg's letter of today was a welcome surprise. Written in haste, affectionately,

St.

I find it hard to excuse your miserliness in not calling up; but my heart is inclined to be forgiving.

Hotel Seiler, Zermatt

My dear:

It wasn't stinginess that kept me from phoning you, but the fear that I might annoy you or couldn't reach you. But how I yearned to hear your voice! I came to the conclusion that I'd rather have half an hour every day with you than be puttering around at Flims. However, there are such moments of beauty here that one could easily lose one's mind over them. Went to the Schwarzee at the foot of the Matterhorn. The lake is a thousand meters higher than the Riffelalp. Returned by way of the Staffelalp. Incredibly beautiful flowers, also edelweiss. The falls drop in seventeen cascades from the terraced glaciers and their spray sparkles in the bright sunshine. The people here are very nice. Evidently glaciers attract a decent type. You should return to the Riffelalp. But, apparently, you have made your own plans and wrap yourself about in a shroud of silence, even from me. At any rate, I must thank you for all this beauty. I finished Roth's *Job*. The purity of style and economy of means give the impression of a rich abundance. You'll find it hard to review this novel with the same pen you would use to extol a Mr. so-and-so.

Thanks and embraces from

Mumu

Augsburg, July 31

L.F.:

My address here: Hamburg, Alsterglacis 10, care of Jaffe, and my very best,

Stefan

They tell me here that Julian Green is coming to Salzburg. Perhaps I'll meet him in Munich. What the name of the gentleman is who addressed me so familiarly, I can't recall; I am an idiot when it comes to remembering names.

L.F.:

The big diet [1] broke down miserably (see letterhead, herewith—Ehmke Restaurant at Gansemarkt No. 5 in Ham-

229

burg) after Schwartz's had already made a breach in my good resolutions in Munich. My quarters are charming, I couldn't wish for anything better.

Affectionate regards from Joachim Maass.

All my best, Stefan.

1 A reducing diet he had begun. Schwartz's was a restaurant in Munich, where he loved to eat its famous goose liver.

L.F.:

Arrived here in Hamburg on Saturday, also your letter today. Augsburg was enchanting; in the evening I was glad to get out of Munich, and traveled on, sleeping like a turtle after a stein of Bavarian beer, to Hamburg. My quarters are simply wonderful. Alsterglacis, once a very fashionable neighborhood —the house is the one where Hans v. Buelow lived for seven years. The bedroom is in the rear overlooking a garden—a little dining room and study toward the front of the house over-looking the Alster—bathroom. The owner, a pleasant lady, was one of the before-the-war rich. There is a good library: philosophy, history, literature, and infinite considerateness and quiet. The old lady stayed over today to show me the ropes, and leaves tomorrow.

And the city, it's so beautiful, one wants to bellow about it! Silvery light on the harbor, glorious ships, all one's heart's desire. I dined wonderfully with Maass at Ehmke's, there was even kangaroo-tail soup, but I ate my way around that tidbit. I shall send the money to the man from Leipzig who brought the E. Th. A. Hoffmann manuscript, incredibly rare. I imagine Julian Green would interest you. Is little Vildrac nice? There is a telephone in the house. You can always reach me between eight and ten.

Many affectionate greetings, St.

Hamburg 8/14

I repeat, I couldn't have had better luck.

True, it rains here every day, but it stops now and then, and I can always get in a walk, through all sorts of very clean and also some very sinister neighborhoods. I read the newspapers; it's dead quiet here. I have royal quarters, an excellent, charming lady secretary who has a wonderful all-round education.—It would seem that a friendly star smiles upon my travels, wherefore we might sometime venture on a trip to India. I haven't had a line from Roth and don't know where he is slaving away just now. And the list of visitors I have avoided elicits no anguished "what a pity's" from me. I note that you have become a radio addict, "on loan" [1]—here in the apartment there is one too, and, at the touch of a finger it immediately begins gurgling operettas and similar manure. God protect us from all such nuisances. I haven't had even one-eighth of a second of "nerves" here, and it seems as if the rest of the world were none of my concern at all which God knows is the truth, while in Salzburg I am conscious of it all the time, like an Alp pressing down on my chest. Farewell, and many best.

St.

[1] I had borrowed a radio during Stefan's absence; he had been against getting one for a long time.

L.F.:

Thanks for the mail; only a couple of lines now, because I telephoned you. Keep the manuscript, the Goethe item is to be exchanged for something of Kippenberg's, very interesting is the Louis XVI communication to the National Convention which was a prelude to the declaration of war on Europe. Prices are very low at the moment, four months ago I was offered the Bach in its unprinted form for 6,000 marks, and now it is offered at half the price: people can't manage to get along any more. Here you can have villas for a song; the very finest are empty or are being rented out. Everything is horribly expensive, twice as much as in Austria.

Please take care of the thank-you notes yourself. And my very best.

Affectionately, Stefan

Letters from Salzburg to
Hamburg, August 30

My dear:

Csokor came yesterday. He grows cleverer all the time and begins to have some success. In the evening the children and I were invited to Reinhardt's. A wonderful evening, with a serenade in the park. Among the guests were some Salzburgers, some actors and about twenty foreigners. The buffet fantastic. Tilly Losch's dancing was very beautiful. Mrs. Snowden [1]—believe it or not—wore a tiara and was every inch a queen. (*Ôte-toi que je m'y mette.*) Is it our fault that we don't feel at home in Leopoldskron? Maybe we are spoiled, or perhaps it's because Reinhardt is always holding High Court? Helene Thimig was very nice. But, of course, everybody told me how amazed he or she was that you weren't there. I am getting very tired of that sort of thing. Barbara Ring wired from Oslo that the premiere [2] is set for Saturday and we must bring warm coats along. Johan Bojer [3] is hereabout somewhere. Hope you will phone today, so that we can make plans. I'd like to get away from Salzburg with you for a few days. It's months since I've had a quiet hour with you. Away from the turmoil that you'll get into here! But there's one thing I am sure of: that you will do as you choose. Hope you are still feeling as contented as before.

Affectionately

F.

1 Former labor leader, wife of the Labor Party's Treasurer, who later was given a peerage.   2 Premiere of *Volpone*. Barbara Ring, Stefan's Norwegian translator, was often our guest and urged us to come to Oslo. 3 Johan Bojer, the great Norwegian writer.

My dear:

Herewith a lengthier report. I am enclosing Rolland's letter which please return. Two enormously long letters came from Madame Guilbeaux in which she says she will hold me responsible for anything that might happen to G. I am sorry, Stefan, but I'll have to drop the case. Apparently you made promises that can't be kept. I shall write that you were away and I tried to reach you. Guilbeaux wants you to advance money for the production of your own and Rolland's plays, the proceeds to go to Guilbeaux. Why just you and not Rolland, who has such strong faith in Guilbeaux? Of course, Rolland is always most anxious to help. But he also has this childlike belief in the efficacy of public protests, demonstrations—as if the world would progress more rapidly if it were generally known that Rolland's and Stefan Zweig's plays were being put on for the benefit of the revolutionary Guilbeaux. The sad thing is that neither Rolland nor Stefan Zweig can get their plays produced whenever they want. Then the Guilbeaux claim you had promised to come to Berlin. For God's sake, do be a little more chary of your promises. Your careless amiability merely provokes people to resentment and anger and you end up with a guilty conscience. You simply *must not* get involved in this sort of thing. It's much wiser to be frank and honest at the very outset and so avoid being swamped by appeals and having to weasel out of futile commitments; all of which wears you out, makes you irritable and horribly glum. You may insist that you are in excellent spirits at the moment. But that doesn't count because it's exceptional for you to be so. It would be fine to take Rolland as your model; he is wonderful. But he seems to want to burden you with more moral responsibilities than you can cope with unless you take them in smaller doses.—Besides, my dear, I simply can't continue dealing with such irregular situations; I become too deeply involved in them if I am held responsible. So please don't overdo it; for my sake, please. Greetings and kisses. Please forgive my frankness. You don't have to answer. I know all the pros and cons.

Fr.

Munich, Nov. 18th/31

Dear Fr.:
  Many thanks for the phone call. So here goes: Richard Strauss writes in a very amiable way that he must come to Munich again. I shall be with him on Friday; am invited to *Electra* in the evening, meet him perhaps again on Saturday— that means that I shall stay here the whole week. I am feeling very fit, because I *dose* myself exclusively with good things; yesterday at the Weisses Roessl [famous restaurant] with that young girl; this evening Carossa; Friday, Richard Strauss and *Electra*—could one do better than that? I'll squeeze Adelt and Bahr into my schedule somehow. You'll admit my stay here is cleverly arranged. As far as work goes, there isn't much doing, but to make up for that, I haven't done any smoking for two

whole days and am not drinking any coffee. You will admit that I am being more sensible than you imagined.

Affectionately, Stefan

Hamburg, August 19th, 1930

Dear Wife:

Today is the day of the big battle of the letters, and so you are getting a very detailed one too. The list of all the visitors I have avoided has put me in excellent humor and strengthened me in my resolve not to go out in this downpour before I have to. Quite possibly I shall return by the end of August, but only to go immediately to my old refuge, Zell am See, for I doubt whether I shall decide for Oslo. Firstly, I don't like to interrupt my work, secondly, I don't want to spoil Scandinavia for myself by a hurried visit, thirdly, I haven't a "smoking" with me, and it would be an insult (to my hosts) [if he didn't wear one], fourthly, they would give me a big reception and you know that I can't stand that sort of thing. Today I shall have to send the telegram which will be easy, and a letter which will be difficult to Barbara Ring, and will have to consider what excuse will be most convincing. My ability to make public appearances and to lecture diminishes from year to year. One wants to go places and live in them anonymously; I sense that here very pleasurably. I'm going to pay my first visit here today and am dining with Sigmund Warburg. He called me up just now and asked particularly whether you were here too. Then day before yesterday and yesterday Vladimir Lidin visited me; he is an intimate friend, by the way, of Joseph Roth's and especially of his wife. The situation of the Russians is indescribably horrifying. It was tragic indeed to meet this splendid human being who brought his wife, who was becoming blind, to Germany, and found out when he got her here that she couldn't be saved, and in spite of this (it is incredible) he reckons these days spent abroad are a slice of paradise. All this ought to be written up so that people could have some appreciation of how well we all are living and some realization of the difference between real hardships and the kind of life we lead even in these critical times.

I am delighted that you are still enjoying the radio while I'm away; you know my opinion of it, and it isn't necessary to waste any words over that. I am anxious to have the Freud essay and the preface to the book finally behind me by September, and so be entirely free for the winter for the trip, work and no-work.

All my best and many regards.

Stefan

8/20

L.F.:

I am answering your letter of lament about Guilbeaux in this wonderful weather. I have interrupted my work, because this everlasting going around the psychic treadmill gives me the creeps. The preliminary digging is all but completed; now it's a matter of working it over, and then of writing. I shall be glad when all of it is behind me!

And so I have put Barbara off, mendaciously hiding behind a lecture. After all, it's a two-day trip to get there, and two days return, besides the feeling of having by-passed Stockholm and all the rest of it. Perhaps we'll go up there next year for the whole of August. I am upset about Barbara.

Friedenthal is coming today; he delivers a lecture here, and so I'll learn something; it might do me good. In general, everything is very pleasant for me; I see a thousand interesting things. Nothing more delightful than to live in a city and yet not be of it; after all, how much more delightful it is to be on the outside instead of eternally in the middle of things.

I am thinking of going to Berlin on Monday and of arriving in Salzburg Tuesday forenoon. We could leave right away on Wednesday for Zell am See and stay there a few days until the uproar has died down. Please, if you agree, get everything ready. For a moment I thought of flying to Copenhagen and then going to the Danish coast, but I can't do that because of the "Affaire Oslo." I mustn't get too near Norway.

Affectionately—will be with you soon,

St.

Dear Stefan:

Want to write you while *Freud,* which I began to read immediately after you left, is still fresh in my mind. Today I read the beginning a second time. I find the work excellent and want to thank you for it, as all your readers will want to do. At first I was a little suspicious. The first chapter is the weakest, although it improves on a second reading. Perhaps you could add a little more color or a more detached criticism, perhaps in somewhat lighter vein, of the age; for instance, you might describe the old, outmoded methods for teaching natural science, and the like. But possibly the chapter would become more provocative if it were worked over, polished, and shortened. As always, you succeed admirably in giving a vivid "picture" of your central figure, a picture quite as exciting as your *Tolstoy* and quite as significant. The chapter on dreams is outstanding. The way you develop the exposition, as well as the analysis, of his theory of dreams is beautifully lucid, yet most absorbing, although you stick close to the factual. But I still have my reservations about passages in which you, personally, venture to evaluate, to pass judgment; these judgments are superlative in themselves, but just because they are so, appear to be flaws in an otherwise noble factual presentation. They will rather tend to weaken the general effect, and may alienate your more serious, thoughtful public which reads with a deeper understanding. On the other hand, the Freudians will consider you too detached. Yet your decisive but dispassionate approach will do them a great service. I discovered two contradictions and one lame analogy. Although the two other essays are original and interesting, this one far surpasses them both because the subject is much greater and much more difficult. I feel for the first time that you have studied philosophy to some purpose (which I had often doubted). But you never point out that the unconscious has *not* been unknown to pedagogical psychology. At any rate, you have been amazingly successful, perhaps because you refused to give detailed expression to any of your own personal points of view. In this essay you show a wise balance, the ability to grasp your subject matter as a whole (except for my previously mentioned objections which, however, concern only the first draft) and, what is more, you come out of it all, a kindly, not at all autocratic, objective (which I consider the highest praise) human being.—Good wishes for Munich. Remember me to Kippenberg.

Yours, F.

Frankfurt, 12/26

L.F.:

       Was in Hamburg today, tomorrow Kassel, Sunday back again in S.

Affectionately, St.

Kassel, 12/27

Cordial salutations from twenty-one Rembrandts and five even more fabulous Franz Hals's; very contented and in good spirits.

Your S.

1 9 3 1

(From Salzburg to Tummersbach near Zell am See)

Summer/31

My dear:

       I enclose only that part of the mail which won't worry you too much. Various catalogues, reviews, criticisms and so on. One article claims you have become a communist and were writing for the *Red Flag*. This refers to the answer you sent in to one of their newspaper questionnaires. Perhaps this matter should be followed up, since it is an obvious lie to say that that kind of thing makes you a contributing editor.

       I enjoyed the days in Marienbad very much. Mama stood the excursion to Karlsbad well and, in spite of the great heat, reveled in the unbelievably luxurious shops there. She was so sweet. It made me happy to give her a little pleasure. I still maintain that a woman, if she loves a man, also loves his mother. A thousand greetings from

F.

L.F.:

Today I tried to reach you by phone, but couldn't. This afternoon a heavy shower, now fine weather again.—I am leading a completely timeless existence since I broke my watch—it is a bit weird but I believe it's good to feel that way. I haven't really begun work yet, but lots nevertheless has happened, because I found out, after thinking things over quietly, what was wrong in the first part, and now I hope I know how to do it the right way. That is something after all. Also I am feeling wonderful here, go swimming, take walks, and at last belong to myself a little.—If, as you tell me, the review by Krakauer is worth reading, I would like to read it; please send it to me. Even unfriendly things don't bother me here or my work.

Affectionately, St.

L.F.:

Here everything quite pleasant, (in French) only a few more National Socialists among the hotel guests than I'd like to see, otherwise the young people are quite *sympathiques* and polite, but wear swastikas, which shows how this movement has grown among the upper bourgeoisie.

See you soon, S.

L.F.:

Everything here all right, only, just at the moment, frightful people, lower-class Germans. This swastika business has got hold of the middle class, which turns everything it touches into caricature—socialism, religiousness, education—it (the swastika cult) inspires these people, who would be tolerable only if they were modestly self-effacing, with a stupid belief in themselves as a master race, or rather, a would-be master race. Interesting, nevertheless, to observe at close quarters. I'm sorry about Silbergleit [1]—he received word here that his tiny but steady job on the *Funkzeitung* is to be rationalized, in other words, dismissal! The poorest ones are always the hardest hit. My work goes along only so-so. There is a big, broad ditch down the middle of it which I can't jump; I have been standing, planted at its edge, like a balky horse for a month. (In English) If you wish to come you are welcome.

Affectionately, St.

[1] The poet Arthur Silbergleit; St. often was deeply concerned about his health.

Dear Fritzi:

After the phone call, just a few lines. In case I don't phone, then I'll be arriving tomorrow evening. Zell am See is empty, and that is why I was astonished last night to meet someone for the first time quite by accident who has been staying here too—three weeks—and who was quite as surprised as I was, Mrs. Bahr-Mildenburg, who sends you her very best. This Saturday [1] I hope to get my hands on Shalom Asch. If Paul Stefan should happen along or anyone else close to us, from Berlin or Vienna, do invite him, but no Salzburgers, because of hurting someone's feelings or insulting someone. I suspect you will also welcome the end of the Festival performances. So many visits wear one out.

Affectionately, Stefan

[1] In order not to alienate our friends and acquaintances completely because Stefan was away during the Festival performances, I invited some people now and then, and Stefan sometimes came out of his "Retiro" to join us. In later years he came because he wanted to welcome Arturo Toscanini and Bruno Walter and their wives at Kapuzinerberg.

(Letters from Stefan to Crkvenitza, in Yugoslavia (near Fiume), where I spent two weeks with my daughters.)

Sept. 4/31

L.F.:

Only a few lines. I haven't any news as yet today. The Moissi [1] affair is stirring the newspapers up terrifically; today again interminable articles, great excitement. I realize how wise I was to be hyper-cautious and keep out of everything. In Vienna tremendous excitement about making public the names of the creditors of the Amstel bank. People are calling for drastic action to put an end to all this tax evasion.

Yesterday I had a fine, two-hour talk with Professor Schroedinger; [2] it was really very gratifying. Here was a man of great intellectual accomplishments, though in an entirely different field. Rieger is coming today, and I am looking forward to meeting him with pleasurable anticipation.

Affectionately, St.

1 A crusade, with political overtones, which developed out of a nasty crisis. The famous actor was accused of having unintentionally committed indiscretions.   2 The physicist, later a Nobel prize winner.

Salzburg, Sept. 7th/31

Dear Fritzi:

Your two postcards (Trieste and Crkvenitza) both arrived on Monday. Connections aren't exactly outstanding, but, to make up for that, you have sunshine and we, here, cold weather, so one has to be satisfied even if the mail is delayed. I wanted to remind you to congratulate Ginzkey either by telegram or letter; I shall deliver a short radio talk on the ninth. Rieger arrived yesterday and has managed to dig up some really interesting unprinted passages out of Marie Antoinette's correspondence for me in the State Archives. This material actually interests me more just now than my current work, which has stalled.

Take care of yourself. My very best,

Your Stefan

Salzburg, Sept. 13th/31

Dear Fritzi:

Just received your special delivery letter.—Just this minute heard about the Heimwehr *putsch* in Steiermark: Good preparation for Geneva! A shameful business!—You are always the same. If I hadn't forced the 500 lire on you (you wanted only 100) you would now be left high and dry. After all, there is a possibility that you might become ill. If you need more, wire.

In great haste, St.

Dear F.:

I am glad that you are having fine weather. I can't say the same for us, but just now it doesn't bother me; anyway I feel very well in the company of the Dauphiness 1 whom I hope shortly to make Queen. Next week I'll finish up Louis XV., although, of course, only in a first draft, then she will take over the government.

Affectionately, Stefan

1 He had, without really intending to, begun to work on *Marie Antoinette*.

L.F.:
I wired you to Graz at the time when the Heimwehr affair was in full swing—of course it was more serious than appeared from the newspaper reports, for they ordered out the Wehrmacht six hours too late, in the hope that the thing would succeed. I was uneasy because, due to your unhappy tendency to want to be an inexpensive family, you didn't take any more with you—you must always keep a reserve against the unforeseen (airplane, sickness, a longer stay). So we expect you on Friday, but if you want to stay on, pray do so.

Affectionately, your Stefan

Salzburg, 12/31/1931—to Paris

My dear:
Let me say once more, may the coming year be as good to you as will be possible under present conditions which, of course, affect you terribly too. I would so dearly love to give you peace and tranquility. But I am no longer so sure of myself and I find it difficult to keep a sense of balance, just sitting here, doing nothing. The house isn't enough my home anymore; what I have to say matters too little; I don't own it; it is too big for me, a too ample cloak for a sometimes chilled and shivering soul. You know—and I promise it again—that I shall do all in my power to make life easier for you and do my duty.

Lernet-Holenia and Zuckmayer [1] were here today. The latter was in Berlin and is going on to Vienna. The Wertheimers are in Igls for the skiing. Gertrud writes that she and Egon [2] had just come from London where the general mood was very chauvinistic and disagreeable. The Italian edition of *L'Anima que Guarisce* is beautiful. Please write to la Mazzuchetti [3] who also sent you a Pascoli autograph.

Hope I'll be able to spend a few days in Paris with you

after returning from Geneva.[4] Please make a note that, after the fifth, my address will be the following: Geneva, 12, Rue du Vieux College.

A thousand greetings from

Fr.

[1] Well-known writers.   [2] Dr. Egon Ransholen Wertheimer of the League of Nations, and his wife.   [3] Lavinia Mazzuchetti, Stefan's translator and faithful friend.   [4] My daughter Susi, who had been devoting herself to the work of infant care for two years, wanted to establish herself professionally in Geneva. I planned to accompany her and also visit my "Pacifist Women Friends" at International House.

1 9 3 2

Salzburg, January 1
To Paris, Hotel Louvois

Dearest Stefan:

Thanks for the wire. Have just written to Dr. Burnet.[1] *Pasteur* stirred me to such a pitch of enthusiasm that, if I had a moment's leisure to sit down and do it, I would like to tell everybody about this Healer-Savior, let them see him in his true light.

Susi's trunk has been shipped to Geneva. Please don't worry about anything. Attend to your work without giving any thought to our arrangements. If I could only write a book like this *Pasteur*! How much that would do for my inner life! If I were only allowed to concentrate and give forth some of the riches, the abundance that is in me. Perhaps I can make preliminary studies at the library of Geneva. Am also happy about Rolland's invitation.—The weather is terrible. Everything covered with sleet. Stay well and don't drink any of the water. I am told that sanitary conditions in Paris are none too good. A thousand greetings and kisses.

Fr.

[1] Dr. Burnet, Pasteur's pupil, was head of the League of Nations Hygienic Commission and later Director of the Pasteur Institute in Tunis. Romain Rolland had interested me in Pasteur's biography, and I was possessed by an urge to contrast the life of this marvelous benefactor of mankind with

the glorification of the lives of warlike heroes. Dr. Burnet, a friend of Erwin Rieger, gave me information on many points and also gave me introductions to Pasteur's grandson, Dr. Pasteur-Vallery-Radot, and to the Paris Pasteur Institute.

(To Paris)

Geneva, January 8/32

Dear Stefan:

Am writing in the train on my return trip from the Rollands. It is wonderful to be near him, to feel his reassuring eyes upon one. He looks pretty well, coughs a little but his voice is a bit stronger. It's good to be able to report that he has engaged a secretary, a good-looking Franco-Russian girl who apparently lives in the house with him. Unfortunately Madeleine's heart and nerves are in bad shape because of overexertion and she feels that the damage can't be repaired. Rolland spoke of the panic in Germany. For instance, Friedmann is afraid of being expelled from Leipzig and is terribly upset about it. And when Rolland sent his Malvida correspondence to Weimar, it was rejected. In a few days the situation will have become somewhat clarified. R. spoke a great deal of Gandhi. He was amazed that the detective who was assigned to accompany Gandhi wherever he went was once at Rolland's as his guest. But these detectives, it seems, idolized Gandhi and took the best care of him. R. was lovely to me, and Madeleine friendlier than ever. Yesterday I chanced to meet Miss Hartock, a friend of the Rollands and a teacher at the International School, whither we went to visit the little Wertheimer girl.— As regards your plans, my dear, I implore you not to go home. I enclose an article of the *Neue Freie Presse*. There'll be disturbances. I know you disregard your friends' advice to find a quiet place where you can work, and since you won't listen, at any rate do go on as you are going for the present. Will write again soon. Farewell!

I embrace you.

Fr.

Dear Stefan:

Just returned from a marvelous walk which afforded me a fine view of Mont Blanc. Thanks for your letter. Spent a nice evening with Egon Wertheimer. Now we are off to the

Baudouins'. The visit to Claparède was also pleasant. The old Professor [1] is a genuine scientist with the head of a Christ. The daughter looks very oriental. Madame [2] babbles on like a waterfall. She is well informed, is full of lamentations because Friedrich Foerster makes it so difficult for people of good will to work for Germany. Lord Cecil is supposed to be very much distressed about it. F. foments trouble in Paris and opposes disarmament because of Germany. Well, dear Stefan, I hope you are enjoying yourself. I'll phone very soon. Susi's work permit is still pending at the City Hall. Many greetings from Susi.

Be embraced by

F.

[1] Professor at the Rousseau Institute.   [2] His wife, daughter of Spire, a friend of Tolstoy.

Les Rasses near Ste-Croix, Jura
1/16/32

Dear Stefan:

As I write, the most incredible range of mountains I've ever beheld looks down on me, and a hot mountain sun pours down upon me. The view takes in innumerable peaks; the aristocrats among them, Montblanc, the Jungfrau, the Matterhorn, are quite distinct from the rest but do not overshadow them at all. And below the peaks and around them, an ocean of mist. And then the forests edging this mountain plateau round about—. The place is absolutely unique. It's not merely the dizzy altitude of these peaks and glaciers that is so overwhelming, but also the vast extent of the ocean of billowing snow, tossing in myriad shapes up into the sky, which itself seems to be much further away because it is far up above these sky-scrapers.

For the time being the silence has been wonderful. Shortly, in the next few days, some Malayan, English and American children will come up from the school in Gland. Aside from the teachers there will be only one adult: a young Hindu of whom Madeleine Rolland and Claparède spoke to me. The Hotel is like an Alpine hut; the food vegetarian. The door to my balcony is open while I write. On the table lie several books on Pasteur. They will help me to get at the job.

244

Rolland's and Baudouins' suggestions (the former knew Pasteur personally) will help too. I have discovered three or four novel aspects of the subject.

Well, my dear, many thanks for the cards and letter. Your list of names really flabbergasts me. But now you are on a new track. First you wrote that you wished to be free at meal-time. Now you hold up everything we have agreed on. You know that I got here only yesterday. Please, can't you stay two days longer and do let me have six more here? I feel much better already—without headache and the pain in my arm that bothered me so. Besides, there will be such interesting meetings in Geneva. At the beginning of February the Women's League will muster four million votes for disarmament. Salzburg is represented by 150 voters. But I have left Geneva behind me. I wanted to be here in the mountains to digest all the impressions I received at Rolland's. I think so much of him and the different mood that prevails in his house now. How youthful he has remained! And how true and yet how false is his concept of the world. He is a sun whose rays have somewhat the effect of a crystallization which spreads in both directions, to the right as well as to the left. He dwells in a higher reality, too far removed from common experience, and almost vanishes in the clouds.

What a pity that you refuse to come here for a few days! I mean to Rolland's and Geneva. In many ways, the city is again "the heart of Europe." [1] Perhaps not an entirely sound heart. Yet it tries to cure itself, with more or less sincerity, before giving itself up as lost. If you were only willing to buy a small house on the shore of this beautiful lake where the flowers bloom in January! Evil days are coming. In my sleepless nights, I have visualized Hitler bombs crashing down on our house. Who would ever have thought that we'd pray for Hindenburg's re-election? And there's no time to be lost. We must make decisions now. Don't hurry back. The accounts I have of incoming mail convince me that everything can be postponed.

Affectionately

Mumu

[1] Refers to Stefan's "Heart of Europe" brochure on the International Red Cross, written in 1917.

L.F.:

Thanks for your letter. Please let me know your plans—I have to know whether you'll be here, because of the many invitations which I have for next week. I am staying till the twenty-eighth. Would have loved to spend another two months here, but I cannot work without a secretary; it is the old misery. How much further along I should be if I had someone with me to whom I could dictate my work and letters; I would have turned out twice as much with half the effort and none of that got-to-go-home fidgeting.

I shall have lunch with Schalom Asch today; this afternoon I'll be with Benaroya (my Bulgarian biographer); in the evening with the Masereels and Luchaires; some day in the near future a visit to (charming) Helene Eliat, whose husband is a big wig in banking circles here, and whose two dogs I have fallen in love with. I shall have to see Levinson [1] once and the Schiffs; Thursday with Duhamel; Friday I am delivering a radio talk, and I must still call on Julian Green and autograph the Freud books. Moreover, I want to go to a manuscript auction on the sixteenth, and despite all this, I seem to be doing nothing but refusing invitations and apologizing. But it is wonderful here and I feel like a carp in fresh water. Arrange matters any way you want to.

Affectionately, Stefan

[1] He wrote essays on art and the dance.

My dear:

I don't feel at all guilty because of your complaints that you haven't turned out enough work. I don't see how you could have published more books than you have, or more successful ones. And year by year, you have acquired greater stature in your books. Perhaps the human being in you has shrunk a bit because of the daily grind. But it will expand again if you put away from you all these pettinesses. The craftsman in you has nothing to complain of; you have not failed him. Since you've been with me, my dear, your work has shown a steady *upward growth,* and, though I wasn't your stenographer, I have given you all the peace and quiet and protection against the outside world that an artist needs. This doesn't come about just by itself. Don't underrate it or try to make a stenographer of me, especially now, when my hair is turning gray.

Be embraced, by your

Exmumu

Paris, Hotel Louvois, Jan./32

L.F.:

It was very pleasant at the Luchaires'. They had invited Paul Valéry on my account, also Perret (Secretary of State and a great mathematician), René Jouglet, Channa Orloff, Cremieux and Julien Cain, director of the National Library, who was most cordial and with whom I am to *dejeuner* on Friday.[1] I had already been to call on him at his home in the old Mazarin Palace. Everybody is very kind to me. Today I am dining with Lefèvre; I have invited the Schiffs[2] for tomorrow; am still to see Gide, unless he has already left. I ought to pay Jean Richard [Bloch] a visit; meantime Roger Martin du Gard is going to pay me a visit. If you meet up with Rolland or his sister, say that I shall be writing him shortly and will have a lot to tell him. If you want to phone me that you are coming, the best time is about nine o'clock in the morning. All my best and lots of greetings,

St.

Another idea! Couldn't you start early and interrupt your trip for a few hours at Dijon? Very worth while! A wonderful city, lovely museum, etc. But if it wears you out, then don't. You mustn't arrive here all tired out.

[1] This was the beginning of a very close friendship with Julien Cain, the noted Director of the National Library, and Lucienne Cain; the friendship between them and me has continued to the present time.   [2] A married couple, both physicians, he a psychiatrist, she a famous eye specialist; they were in close touch with St.'s literary friends.

Salzburg, April 20th/32—to Vienna

L.F.:

Everything in good shape. Maass[1] very pleasant and youthful; he is putting up at Junger's. Received a charming letter from Dr. Lava,[2] who writes me about "mental healing," also from Richard Strauss who would like to come for a conference in May.—Alas, I have a terribly hard time getting things done. No mail of any consequence for you. Give my best to Mama and don't wear yourself out tearing around in Vienna. Robakidse is coming on Friday; [3] take a look through the train, perhaps you will be traveling together.

Affectionately, St.

1 Joachim Maass, the author, later a professor at Mount Holyoke.   2 Belgian physician and step-father of Masereel.   3 Author, native of Georgia, Russia.

Lecture tour to Florence, May, 1932.

Excelsior Hotel Italie, May 2

L.F.:

Just arrived. Hotel fantastically elegant, actually unpleasant J. P. Morgan type of place.—I got a room on the fifth floor with an enormous terrace and wish I had nothing to do the livelong day but lie back lazily and admire the view of the river. Enrico Rocca [1] is coming this evening and I am delighted at the prospect. Otherwise everything here enchanting, the same old silly shops still selling marble this and that and at the same time, all those lovely things. I made the trip in fine style, compartment all to myself, baggage not even inspected—I appear to have a thoroughly trustworthy countenance.

Part two: I am sitting alone in the Buca, and am dining. Barfutti is very nice and very clever, he manages to see to it that I am left in peace. There is to be a small gathering this evening, *without* my having to talk, at least that is what they promise me. I shall be free all tomorrow, that is, I can go to the Exposition with Rocca; in general I have been left undisturbed, have already spent an hour in the Uffizi. The lecture is worrying me. I am in awe of the Palazzo Vecchio where I am to lecture.—We wouldn't have believed it possible ten years ago, nor the lords of the Signoria 800 years ago, either.

I am immensely pleased with Rocca. The weather is

248

mild, the air tastes of mignonette and great quantities of flowers are for sale in the streets.

Affectionately, Stefan

N.B. The fresh wild strawberries taste awfully good!

1 The journalist Enrico Rocca who, it appears, committed suicide.

May 3rd

· *L.F.:*

Splendid weather, the women and men so beautiful in the springtime, it makes you want to whinny for joy. I am turning invitations down whenever possible. But on Thursday I am going by auto to Sienna with young Olschki and Mrs. Selden. I was delighted to accept their invitation (an hour and a half through the Tuscan countryside). Will be back at about four o'clock and go to Milan at five, and leave there at midnight of the next day, and should in that event be in Salzburg on Saturday (but one should make one's home in Florence). Everything has worked out fine here, nothing at all like what we were afraid of, utmost tact on all sides. The women beautiful to the point of distraction! Oh, I am frightened at the prospect of our mountain yokels.

Affectionately, St.

(Postcard with view of the Palazzo Vecchio.)

Firenze, May 4th

Cara consorte:

I shall be stammering Italian in this Palazzo tomorrow. We were in Fiesole today. Thursday to Sienna; springtime is indescribably wonderful here.

Affectionately, Stefan

Livia Rocca

Dear Mrs. Friderika:

Why aren't you here? We are happy to be with Stefan Zweig. Kindest regards from your devoted,

Enrico Rocca

249

(Postcard from the Antica Trattoria già Paoli.)

May 5th

It's all over! The most splendid hall imaginable, moreover, packed full of people. Pity you weren't here.

Affectionately, Stefan

Confirm, enchanted,

Enrico Rocca

Idem, the lecture, enchanting.

Affectionate regards, Lavinia Mazzuchetti

Hotel Excelsior, Italie, May 5th

Dear Fritzi:

So I have gotten through with it and I must say it was astounding.[1] The divine hall of the Signoria, a dream *di bon dio* and, moreover, packed to bursting, over a thousand people and no Germans, only Italians, and what incredible women!— *grand événement artistique,* and afterward I had to autograph some two hundred books, ward off invitations from the Podestà and all imaginable kinds of Marquises and Principessas, and I believe I really spoke well, probably better than others [they have had here]. The whole business had a marvelous *cachet.* I can't imagine how this could be surpassed anywhere in the world. Pity you weren't there—it and Moscow—at the opera house there, were the most impressive moments of my aging career.

I shall probably have to let Sienna go because of the bad weather and because, after all, this Italian, from morning till evening, and the continuous visits, would be too much of a strain. At the moment I am as lively as Kaspar [2] when he is allowed to take a walk into town; I have a number of amusing things to tell you *a casa.*

Affectionately, St.

[1] This lecture, "European Thought in Its Historical Development" (included in *Time and World,* Collected Essays, Bermann-Fischer-Verlag), was one of his best and is still pertinent.   [2] Our beloved spaniel.

(Letters from Switzerland and Grenoble, where I attended the Congress of the Women's League for Peace and Freedom as Austrian Delegate. At the same time I visited my daughter who was working in Champel near Geneva as baby nurse.)

Dear Stefan:

Although fewer cars seem to be coming and going and things in general are slow, this country impresses me still as an Island of the Blessed. A lot of building is going on, probably for investment and to give employment. People look prosperous, but not care-free. I met a young Dutchman who said that prices might rise again in Holland and disrupt business in a catastrophic manner.

Unfortunately Jane Addams' [1] weak heart prevented her from coming over. It grieves me so much that I'll probably never see her again, for she is old and unlikely to recover her health. Many greetings from Susi. When I spoke of you, she began to long for you so much that tears came into her eyes and she felt like writing you right away.

Affectionately,

Mumu

[1] President of the International League for Peace and Freedom. Winner of the Nobel prize for Peace. She had visited me while attending the Salzburg Conference. Founder of Hull House Settlement in Chicago.

Dearest Stefi:

Am writing you after the second day's battle, and I am not through fighting yet. Madeleine Rolland is here, feeling much better. Also R.R. is well, Andrée Jouve, Mlle. Gobat and many others are here. But it's tremendously difficult to get down to work, because Conferences are managed with such fossilized procedure. Three splendid men are here: Michon, Lehmann-Russbuilt, and a Dutchman who lives near Geneva, is tremendously active in the work and has all the money he needs so that he can devote himself to it. Charming young people from Paris, all of them your admirers. Such good-looking boys and girls. I invited them all to Salzburg. Will have so much to tell you. It is so incredibly interesting to feel that one is finding out about the mental processes of a whole continent. Einstein, Gorki, Rolland, Thomas Mann and Barbusse have promised to attend the June Conference in Geneva. Everybody is asking whether you will be there. I want to find out who's sponsoring the Conference. Possibly Barbusse who asserts that it will be a nonpolitical affair to promote the cause of disarmament. At any rate, it may impress the League of Nations, if it goes off without too much sound and fury. The town of Grenoble is very attractive and not spoiled by politics. The air mild without sultriness.

Avidly waiting for your letters. Wanted to phone from Geneva and regret that I didn't.—The Municipalité is giving a reception today.

Be embraced by your

M.

Grenoble, 5/17

Dear Stefan:

At last, two of your letters, my beloved. Am glad you had such a pleasant reunion with Friedenthal. Remember me to him. So sorry to have missed his visit. Am going back to Geneva on Thursday.

My dear, yesterday and today were immensely interesting. Met two splendid Chinese women. What a whole wide world these people bring here, although they themselves, may often be rather narrow and limited. And how marvelous to feel this common bond of humanity, what happiness in the midst of world tragedy, which is and is yet to come. The French women are magnificent. They are intelligent, and passionate, too, and think with their hearts. They make you feel more real, genuine. What a cleansing soul-bath! What I myself may have gained is still up in the air. But it doesn't matter much whether I get anything out of all this or not. And the Swedish women! At yesterday's reception, at the City Hall, they were so friendly, especially to me, largely on your account. A certain M. Cornou, who teaches German at the local University, worships you. There's so much to tell. I love you and greet you, and embrace you.

Mumu

Dearest:

No letters. Hope to find some in Geneva. Yesterday afternoon I played hookey, in which I was aided and abetted by some very nice people. We paid a visit to the Cartusian Monastery, the order's chief establishment, up on a 1300-meter mountaintop; wonderful view and a glorious drive. Reminded me of Lofer.[1] One of the party was Emil Ludwig's sister whose son, Dr. Hamburger, is instructor at the University of Geneva. I intend going with him and Susi to see the narcissus fields in Les Avants. Yesterday, while I was away, I was nominated for the Executive Council. They picked me out of one hundred sixty delegates. I left before the voting, because I didn't want to obligate myself in any way. In the evening we had a meeting in the theater. Enthusiastic applause for all of us. At the moment I am passing through the greenest landscape I've ever seen. Spring, lush and succulent, plus southern sunshine. Poplars and cypresses crowding each other, and those oppressively fragrant Judas trees. There isn't a bare spot of ground until you get up to the 2000-meter level, fruit trees in bloom and vineyards. From Monday on I'll be very busy writing reports for the Vienna press. Then a few days of leisure, topped off by our reunion. Just passed the Lac d'Annecy. Savoy is a glorious country. Give my love to Lix. I'll write her soon. Be embraced, my dear. I felt so close to you all the time.

Fr.

[1] Austrian summer resort near Salzburg.

My dear Stefan:

Here we are, way high up, facing Rochers-de-Naye, above Les Avants. Far below are the lakes at the points of a sort of triangle and nearby here is the tree which you see from the Hotel Byron in Villeneuve, where we spent such never-to-be-forgotten days when visiting Rolland for the first time fifteen years ago. Next to us are the heaps of narcissi we have picked, which we shall send to you and Mama. The meadows are so thickly sprinkled with them that there would be enough for a horde of flower fanciers. On the mountain-tops here they are still only buds, which survive shipping better than those in full bloom. Found your letter in Geneva, and was glad to hear the nice things Josefine[1] said of her guest Friedenthal. This evening we'll meet the Masereels at Paule's.[2] You can imagine how I am looking forward to Frans. They have motored down from Paris and are going on to Germany. So we'll see them in Salzburg too. Probably I'll arrive about the same time they do. I found Susi looking worn out and am glad to have her up here in the fresh air. Many kisses from

M.

[1] My friend Josefine Junger who often entertained our friends in her beautiful home in Salzburg.　[2] Masereel's step-daughter.

My dear:

It was good to hear your voice. But a terrible homesickness, yearning, gripped me too! Spring is here with a vengeance, the most vivid, intensive spring I've ever seen in any landscape. What a dream, this blessed isle, this Switzerland! The difference between this country and the others is again as marked as during the war. The reports I read in the papers are most distressing. Like Herriot, I foresaw it all, despite his friend Foerster, who is quite sure he knows all about Germany. And now Stresemann! Probably there'll be a moratorium, unless Lausanne produces some results.

Affectionately

F.

Geneva, 5/23

My dear:

Thanks for today's letter. Am glad you are enjoying the good weather and a measure of tranquility. Tranquility is all-in-all these days, and I'm afraid we won't have it much longer. Yesterday evening, Masereel and Salive were anything but *reconfortant*. Nobody could predict a darker future than Masereel.

My dear, don't worry about my being elected. I refused the honor, although pleased by it. As Mrs. Hamburger says, we wives and mothers are only part-time workers for the League. Though the fact is we are all involved in this for life, and there's no retiring on half-pay.

Les Avants was a dream, a creation as wondrous as on the first day.[1] Greet everyone at home, including Erwin if he is there. Be thanked and embraced by your

Mumu

[1] Quotation from Goethe's Faust.

Geneva, Monday Night

My dear:

Believe it or not: I've just met Einstein. The Peace Council arranged an interview and meeting with the Press. Lord Ponsonby and Einstein presided. He is so simple, so straightforward, so steadfast. Of course, he sends his best to you. Said he enjoyed reading the views you expressed in your various publications. There's so much to tell. Many thousand greetings.

F.

My dear:

Just received your letter, as well as the one for Susi. As Lix (to whom I wrote yesterday) may have told you, the Director of the Clinique was most enthusiastic in his praise of Susi. My dear, I'll arrive in Salzburg Sunday at the latest. My heart is going pitter-pat all the time, but I hope it's now, more than ever, in the right place. A thousand kisses.

Mumu

(October 1932, during a short trip to Lake Garda.)

L.F.:

You probably didn't receive my telegram—the reason is that I don't want to settle down so quickly. The weather here in Bozen is divine, simply indescribable, brisk and at the same time warm, just what I like. On the other hand there's trouble about getting quarters. Gries has been completely ruined by innumerable recently-erected government buildings, the good hotels of yore (that is to say of twenty years ago) are still standing but in a state of decay, or have become regular sanatoriums. Bozen also doesn't appeal to me because at every step the names of the streets compel one to think of politics—one doesn't have any such feeling in Naples. Moreover the city has lost much of its paintable picturesqueness. So I shall go on, either to Meran or Gardone. Which won't be easy because no autos are to be had, just the same old slow-poking via Rovereto, Mori, Riva, as formerly, though almost everyone here has his own auto!—the trains are for the *terza classe*. I shall wire you at once as soon as I am settled. Wrote this at midday on a bench at the Talfa River. The mountains remain divinely unpolitical, likewise the sky. But one ought to go to Switzerland for relaxation, to a neutral country, where you don't sense, in a thousand trifles, the tensions that afflict our times, tensions from which one wants to have some relief after all.

I had decent quarters in Hotel Greif, but the place is more primitive than it was twenty years ago. It appears that we, in Austria, were much more demanding than we think we were.

Affectionately, St.

Gardone, Pensione Garda, 11/6

Dear Fritzi:

I wired you my address today and now I am sending you my first report. Actually I got here too late, for the good auto connections have already been discontinued. A few of us who had been disappointed scraped up an auto and got safely to Gardone. I thought the Savoy Hotel was frightful; I don't understand how you could live in that kind of a barracks. I took flight right away, finally found a little pension on the lake, which despite the fact that it is rather primitive, suited me better, a quiet little garden and a little balcony out toward the lake. I would be telling a lie if I were to say that I like Gardone; the walks that made Montreux so enjoyable are missing here, and I'm not enraptured by the *Zanzare* [mosquitoes]; I don't have much use for the music they make in the evenings. Gray weather today, but warm. I am feeling pretty fit and have begun work on the opera; [1] perhaps I will shortly be sending Mrs. Meingast the text. It may be that I shall return by way of Munich—you will receive news of all my plans by wire.

Goodbye, Stefzi

1 After Hofmannsthal's death Richard Strauss asked Stefan to write his librettos, including the lyrics. He (Stefan) was at work at this time on *The Silent Woman* based on one of Ben Jonson's plots.

¹ 9 3 3

(From Salzburg to Vienna and Semmering.)

L.F.:

I was very much stirred up just now when I read the news that Hotel Byron in Villeneuve had burnt down.—How memorable and beautiful were the days I spent there! I shall write Rolland at once. I received a charming letter from Richard Strauss; he writes out the notes of the song (I believe it is by Brahms):

> *To have found thee, dear child,*
> *Fills all my allotted days with joy*

He is making a rough draft and says the composing is getting along splendidly. Take care of yourself.

Affectionately, St.

L.F.:

At last, good news today. Huebsch wires that the American Book Club ¹ has taken *Marie Antoinette*—that means, probably, some 20,000 to 30,000 copies, although they pay less. Otherwise only vexation. Tonfilm won't pay and will have to be sued, which will cause another public uproar; I am about fed up by the "affaire Volpone," in connection with which I was bitterly attacked by Messrs. Ihering and associates; indeed, not a day goes by without some sort of annoyances or wrangles. A kind of malevolence grips the whole world; it is intolerable. Kippenberg, with whom I just had a talk by phone, tells me that, because of the political situation, the bookstores and theaters are in complete stagnation; an abominable era, but perhaps better than what is yet to come.² My best to everyone in Vienna and let me know in time when you are arriving. Don't hurry on my account.

Affectionately, S.

257

1 The Book-of-the-Month Club. Their edition was much larger than he anticipated.   2 His pessimistic prophecies now began; unfortunately, they turned out to be true.

Munich, 1/31/33

L.F.:

I am staying over today, Tuesday, in Munich (to hear Verdi's *Othello* at the Opera) and will travel on to Garmisch [1] tomorrow, where I shall surely stay two to three days. I am going to visit Bahr today.

Affectionately, Stefan

Give my very best to Mama.

1 To visit Richard Strauss.

Salzburg, January/33

L.F.:

I have just been listening on Johann's [1] radio to Ernst Bloch's concerto in the Augusteo at Rome; instrumentation quite incredible, and in other respects far above the modern music I am familiar with. There is another program from the Augusteo on the twenty-seventh; perhaps you can listen to it at five o'clock in the afternoon. Of course, chamber music will not have an orchestra's marvelous wealth of color.— A happy telegram from Triest came last Friday, which means that the letter reached its destination. [2] Otherwise nothing out of the ordinary; Sunday, and praise God, no mail.

Affectionately, St.

1 Our butler's radio, as St. still did not want us to have one of our own.
2 This refers to Stefan's intercession on behalf of a man who was being prosecuted by Mussolini because he had been a friend of Matteotti.

L.F.:

There are a lot of things afoot. Today a gushing letter came from Mrs. G. from Trieste. Her husband (and this is especially amiable on Mussolini's part) has been lodged in Trieste prison until a final decision as to the place where he is to be exiled is reached; she is allowed to visit him every day, and he has seen his child again after two and a half years. Then a really delightful letter from R. Strauss, who is hard at work composing. Then something very pleasant from X.

258

He has sent me the original of the letter with the attack on me that was circulated among all the "nationalist" papers in Germany and Austria for them to print. (With it went a request by the National Committeeman Prodinger that it be printed without fail.) Now at last we know who is the prime mover in this affair: The German Commercial Workers Union, which has bought up the publishing house of Albert Langen-Georg Mueller and through it will give Insel Verlag some cut-throat competition. I sent it right off to Kippenberg, so that he can force a showdown with his "German" colleagues.

Vienna is becoming a regular rat race. Moreover, Jean R. Bloch is here and I shall doubtless meet him at Zolney's [his publisher]. And I'd so much prefer to go out for a walk now and then or to the opera.

Affectionately, in haste, St.

Today, they are having a radio book forum about *Marie Antoinette* all over Italy; perhaps I'll listen in, via Johann.

I shall go right on from Vienna through to Munich-Garmisch-Partenkirchen.—Strauss wrote Kippenberg that it was the best light opera libretto since Figaro. Anyway, I am delighted that he is getting at it with so much gusto and love.

Affectionately, St.

(Lecture tour in Switzerland, March 1933.)

Bern, 3/7

Dear F.:

Up to now everything has been going along better than I expected. I wasn't waked up by the customs people during the night and slept right through to Zuerich; the weather was very fine and I went for a walk all alone, visited the *Lesezirkel Bodmer* (my lecture is already almost sold out), I also went for a two hour walk in Bern and got your telegram. At the moment I am alone at a café and am looking at the "Maitschi" [Swiss dialect for "Mädchen," young girls]. This evening, the lecture.

Affectionately, St.

(*En route* from Bern to Olten.)

March 9/33

L.F.:

Bern and Zuerich finished, very happy about both. Zuerich presses for a repeat performance, because the hall there, as in Bern, was sold out, and the people who were turned away are making a fuss.—I had to autograph 800 copies of the book in the two bookstores. It is still being bought here in good quantity. I saw a few of the refugees from Berlin. Doeblin is very nice, he was at the lecture and met me afterward. (He treated Roth's wife; she is a hopeless case.) Then I met Max Hermann-Neisse and Toller from whose home in Berlin they have cleared out everything; also Wilhelm von Scholz, Councillor Wettstein and, in Bern, the indestructible Benno [1] with his Italian Ida (a real beauty). The panic that has gripped the intellectuals is fairly widespread, articles attacking Jewish writers with ever-increasing violence appear day after day and it would seem likely that more is happening than is reported in the newspapers.

I have been quite all right up to now, although I didn't manage to get any sleep at all. I am scribbling this letter on the train, with a pencil, because my fountain pens are worn out with overmuch autographing. There isn't any lack of new appointments to see people. On the fifteenth I shall look at the Beethoven manuscript collection and listen to a private concert at Ernst Bloch's.—Everywhere the most unlikely and forgotten people turn up. On the whole, however, this lecture tour was the right thing after all, because here the air is still clean and people are disgusted by these Hitler antics. There will soon be quite a big German colony here.

I am looking forward to a day of rest. The lecture at Strasburg would have been too exhausting in any case, aside from political considerations. I shall be with Rolland at noon today, and, as in the old, difficult days, I am looking forward to his wise counsel. The evening in Geneva will be hard work, a lot of acquaintances and, in addition, I am supposed to autograph books for Payot, a new plague for lecturers, but one shouldn't avoid people who are well disposed toward one, for now there are millions of others who will hate and despise you by command. Farewell, my child, I shall shortly be passing through Bern; the indestructible Benno will be at the station to welcome me. I regret to say that I found it difficult to resist the imported articles offered me but, as a matter of fact, had no time to buy even a package of chewing gum.

Affectionately, St.

1 Benno Geiger, poet, art historian and art dealer, a pal of Stefan's younger days.

Postscript on an envelope:

The weather here in Montreux is enchanting, I would like to howl to high heaven because I have to leave.

Geneva, 3/10

L.F.:

Terrific rat race, but I am going through with it indomitably and now am already looking forward to the end of it. Here things were very pleasant, but I note that the *Neue Zuericher Zeitung* gets after me in pretty unfriendly fashion,—this is partly due to a personal feud with the *Lesezirkel,* and all this confirms me in my determination to make an end of these lectures, a decision I arrived at long ago anyway. It is fun for the first few days, the rest tires one out and besides it takes one away from one's work. One ought to travel, but with the least possible restrictions.—How wonderful it would have been if I could have stayed on here.

Affectionately, Stefan

Wintherthur, 3/14

L.F.:

Thanks for everything. I am quite distracted, leave something behind at every hotel in this rat race. The fact is that Goebbels now controls the entire German press, and therefore, from now on not a line of mine or about me will be brought out there. I would still like to hop over to Sweden.[1]—Travel nowadays means being under a constant strain if you are tied down to a daily schedule. I am writing this on the train, with a poor pen, because I left my good one in the hotel. And this rush of appointments. Well, it was my swan song.

Affectionately, St.

1 A lecture for Sweden had been planned but then was abandoned.

Bâle-Mulhouse

L.F.:

 I walked across the frontier into France today; the guard examined my passport and then announced: *"Mais votre nom m'est bien connu"* (but your name is very well known to me); fortunately not unfavorably, as at the German frontier. Joseph Roth arrives this evening; I shall be with him on Sunday and perhaps spend a little time with Geigy. Tuesday home.

My best, St.

Bad Gastein (en route to Salzburg), May 23

L.F.:

 Arrived here with the most beautiful weather. I had one of these disagreeable difficult encounters on the train—all of a sudden the gentlemen of the German (new-German) delegation to the Pen Club greeted me; they are going to the Congress at Ragusa; there they will have to face a lot of things; naturally I was polite, especially as Hanns Martin Elster, my former biographer, was with them, but we sniffed at each other cautiously and talked about the green meadows of Gastein.

 I ordered three beautiful shirts right away here, just to please you, of course. Take care of yourself.

With all my best, St.

(To Bad Gastein)

Salzburg, May 23/33

Dear Stefan:

 The enclosed wire just arrived. I answered: My husband left yesterday and will not attend the Congress. Signed, Mrs. Zweig. The people will probably take me for an idiot who doesn't know what it's all about. But, at any rate, you will now have time to think the matter over. You can write directly to, or wire Felix Salten. There'll be no declaration of protest the first day and, in my opinion, those whose books weren't burned should also protest.[1] Public opinion has protested on your behalf; among others, Mr. Bryan; and your *Erasmus* will have something to say, too. If you decide to come out of retirement and speak out, this is not the way to do it—as a sort of tail to some Club's kite or sponsored by or at the instance of some political organization. I am sure you share my opinion. Besides, how can one join in a protest without knowing the way it's to be worded? The whole thing comes much too late. The Pen Club, if it had wanted to get results, should have convened the Congress at an earlier date. All the presiding officers should have undertaken a joint trip to Berlin. Such a protest, even if it produced no positive results, would have been to some purpose. Of course, they'll take some kind of action in Ragusa, as you indicated in your letter. They've got to do some face-saving. I am astonished that the pleasure people take in going to Congresses should be so great that even a man like Elster should be willing to expose himself to all this chicanery. Please write and tell me if you think my (I regret to say) not altogether ingenuous answer was justified. Nowadays we must be diplomatic, more's the pity. But, really, people should be told the truth; namely, that their bickering and lack of solidarity make a farce of all Clubs and associations.

Affectionately

F.

[1] Concerns the protest against the Nazi book-burning.

To Bad Gastein, 5/24

Dear Stefan:

The reason I didn't send a flat refusal, as I wanted to do, is the following: I had heard you say you would know what to do if they didn't behave as they should at Ragusa. At the time I had no idea as to what you had arranged with Salten. Immediately after our telephone conversation, I wired a second, more definite refusal.

Katharina Kippenberg wrote she was at work selecting the Trakl poems,[1] and was thinking a great deal of Salzburg and us. She said that the poems were beautiful but had no prospect of publication at the moment, because everybody was

263

listening to the radio, or was so excited or in much trouble, and, therefore, no one was reading any books. The letter tried to express sympathy but was by no means at all cheerful. Also the Ruetten and Loening Publishing House are demonstrating that people are beginning to open their mouths again.

Read the two manuscripts. Shall report on them later. The French letters (5-6) have been written. Last night I attended a concert at which ancient instruments were played and this calmed my nerves considerably.

Affectionately M.

1 Georg Trakl, Austrian poet.

Salzburg, May 27/33

Dear Stefan:

Forgot to say while phoning you that (as you may have read already in the papers) our dear friend Leisching [1] has died. He was my favorite among our men friends in Salzburg, and the only one who indicated by a few remarks made when we last met what he thought of current events. One of the finest men I've ever known. So we are losing another friend here. Josefine [2] is a storm-swept rock of comfort. She calls up every day. Also Mrs. Worafka, the General's wife, phoned immediately; said very nice things and was indignant at this and that.

Mrs. Trebitsch asked whether you wanted to sell the house. She knew someone who might buy it. I said no, that I was more likely to want to; and only in case it rained for three weeks on end [as it frequently did in Salzburg]. I told Mr. Trebitsch you were receiving as many nice letters as on your fiftieth birthday. He is greatly worried lest Fischer refuse to publish his novel. Now the publishing houses won't have to hunt so hard for excuses. Frieda Richard told me a lot of things. She's a splendid person. It's her greatest wish to be taken on by the Burgtheater. Since the theaters are stressing the "Austrian Front," this might be the right moment.—Read Morand's amusing book about London which inspires dread of that city rather than curiosity. Morand is obsessed by an aristocracy-mania and very worldly, but has a pair of eyes in his head!

Don't freeze to death,[3] my dear. A thousand kisses from me and greetings from the children. Yours,

Mumu

[1] Privy Councillor G. Leisching, Custodian and Renovator of the Salzburg Museum.   [2] My friend Josefine Junger. Evidently the papers had brought extensive reports on the burning of Stefan's books.   [3] Gastein was still cold at this time of year.

From Salzburg to Vienna, June/33

Dear F.:

What a pity! Just this minute H. G. Wells called with Baroness Budberg [1] and we had a grand talk. I am to dine with them this evening. You would have enjoyed it a lot.

S.

[1] Formerly Gorki's secretary; we got to know her when we visited him in Capo di Sorrento, and later saw a lot of her in London. Gorki, it was said, saved her life during the days when the aristocracy was being hounded in Russia.

6/2/33

L.F.:

Nothing new. Rieger is coming next Sunday.—Wells was delightful, we were together five hours; he is as wide-awake as the day and the Budberg woman is very *sympathique.* —Good news from Huebsch; they haven't sold *Letter of an Unknown Woman* as yet, but have gotten cash for the option. —Bruno Walter is here already, but I haven't seen him yet.

Affectionately, S.

Dear Fritzi:

We visited Frieda Richard [1] yesterday and had a wonderful day. That report is all idle talk; the books were burnt, I read about it in the *Berliner Tageblatt,* and actually saw a picture of the shameful pile.[2] But we shouldn't think too much about these things.

Affectionately, your St.

[1] The great actress.   [2] Apparently an official denial of the book-burning.

(During the following months we exchanged comparatively few letters, because we were so seldom separated. We spent several months together in

265

London and we made some longer trips together in '33 and also in '34. Unfortunately, not a single letter from '34 has survived. The year of 1935 also began with an extended stay at Nice, his sixth or seventh southern trip. From Nice Stefan proceeded with Maestro Toscanini, Schalom Asch and their wives and some more friends, to the United States where he went on a short lecture tour. He had finished Mary Stuart's biography in Nice.)

¹ 9 3 5

(Letter found in the hotel)

Nice, January/35

L.F.:

    I'm going out to get something to eat because I have to be back by three-thirty for a conference ¹ with Reece and Dr. Bing. To make sure no one will claim that something was overlooked, you could join us. Please be here by three o'clock at the latest.

St.

¹ Negotiations with publisher and agents about international arrangements, but in the end nothing came of it.

(On his return trip from America, Stefan stopped over in London for about ten days and then came back to Austria, after which, in the spring, he went on to Zuerich to work.)

Zuerich, May 10, 1935
(To Salzburg, Kapuzinerberg)

L.F.:

    I am at Hotel Bellerive, Utoquai, the new apartment house, and have rented an apartment which, however, has only a slanting view of the lake; the others are too expensive. And even this one is expensive enough, more than in London, but the owner (a woman) when she heard that I was the tenant, gave me a reduction of three francs per day. Conditions here are quite unhappy because of uncertainty about the currency; everyone insists that the speculation originates to the "east" in "international" quarters—when they are by themselves they call it by its right name. Seelig ¹ sent me a secretary; I'll try her out on Monday. This is always a very important matter. I haven't seen anyone else and have little desire to, I am still in a state of exhaustion due to Vienna and all the people, and all day today I felt as if I were in Paradise, in the peaceful isolation of this apartment. I am still undecided as to whether I shall stay here a long time. I shall have to find out how the secretary works out and about the library. The telephone is: 27010 and right next to my bed, so, if necessary, I can be reached early in the morning.

My best, S.

1 The author Carl Seelig.

Zuerich, May 18th/35

Would you please take the little Goethe poem, "Will Einer Sich Gewöhnen," out of the chest in the library and send it to me? I should like to give it to Thomas Mann on his sixtieth birthday. But please, not only cross it off the inventory but also take the card out of the card catalogue and destroy it. I can't, I regret to say, get anything I might write about him published anywhere, and I do want to give him a little pleasure on this occasion.

Fuerstner notifies me that the proofs of *Schweigsame Frau* will be ready by Monday. Unfortunately the situation is getting serious, which doesn't stop them from making all sorts of trouble for *Mary Stuart* in Germany. I still get a great deal of mail.

St.

Hotel Bellerive
Zuerich, June 26th/35

L.F.:

By now I have gotten a general idea of what happened in Dresden. People agree on only one point, that the city was in the grip of an African heat wave. What nonsense to delay the opening until the dog days. As for the opera itself, one thing is certain, it is *very* much too long, secondly, it is an atrociously difficult work and so the very opposite of my original conception of it—not a light opera, but over-loaded with all the *raffinements* and really oppressive because it is too replete. Single passages are said to be outstanding and the first act well rounded. Then it gets to be tiring, like *Arabella* and *The Egyptian Helena*. His technique remains intact. But the dynamic isn't there.

From several of the reviews I sense the animosity against Strauss that prevails in Germany at present. Even official people seem to shy away from him a bit. Goebbels didn't come to the opening and the other high muckamucks luckily weren't there either. I suspect that the opera will have a sort of historical, twilight-existence, like the *Woman Without a Shadow, The Egyptian Helena, The Intermezzo*—disinterred now and then, but not a regular repertory opera and probably (quite the opposite of what I wanted) impossible for smaller opera houses. It appears that only La Cebotari and the orchestra were tops in the Dresden performance, the others couldn't cope with the terrific difficulties. This appears to be the most difficult of Strauss's difficult operas. I am anxious to hear it on the radio. Perhaps he will, by then, have made the necessary cuts.

It is terribly warm here, as it probably is everywhere, but my quarters are quite bearable. The material for the book will soon be complete and I am getting along reasonably well with the actual work.

Now about my plans for the summer. I shall probably substitute Marienbad or Karlsbad for Gastein. I will certainly be allowed to take out quite a bit of money, seeing that I would have to defray the cost of a visit, which included myself, my wife and probably my secretary, to a Bohemian resort.

That's one point to consider. Here's another. I would have to come down frequently from Gastein to Salzburg to meet this or that friend (Ojetti [1] and a hundred others), which would mean at least two days wasted every time, while my secretary would be left high and dry up there with nothing to do; and besides, in Gastein I am bound to be harassed daily by visitors, which involves a constant scurrying hither and thither, whereas all I want is to go ahead quietly and undisturbed with my work, the way I do here. I've seen enough people this year, in fact too many, and I have absolutely no inclination to plunge into that maelstrom. Now that mother is well again, another obstacle has been eliminated.

I should like to leave Salzburg after the *Falstaff* première and stay about a month in Marienbad. I imagine that will be agreeable to Mrs. Meingast.

I am curious to know what is to become of the Strauss opera; I hope he has cut it.

Affectionately, S.

1 Famous Italian art critic and Senator.

L.F.:

I may meet Huebsch in Paris. I am quite comfortable here, but that we have a south wind every day; reminds me too much of Salzburg.

S.

Hotel Bellerive, July 15th

L.F.:

Mr. Huebsch left yesterday, Sunday. As he was going via Selzthal direct to Vienna, I couldn't let you know in time. But there is a chance that he will come to Salzburg on the twenty-ninth. At any rate I would like to have a ticket to *Falstaff* reserved until the day before the performance, in case he should come; they gave me such a friendly welcome in New York that this would be only a very modest acknowledgment on my part of their kindness.

Yesterday evening *Der Morgen* called me up from Vienna and wanted to interview me about the Strauss matter. Of course I told them *nothing,* but it made me realize how dangerous it would be to be in Salzburg and have to face the inevitable domestic and foreign newspapermen. The wisest thing is for me to keep under cover. I haven't heard anything more from Strauss himself.[1]

My plans then are: arrive in Salzburg on the morning of the twenty-ninth, go to *Falstaff* in the evening, meet Toscanini the next day if possible, and leave on the thirtieth and get to work as soon as I can. I don't want to stay any longer than this under any circumstances, because this continual onslaught of people wears me out more and more and, after all, they and I have no interests in common. I don't need any more books from the library; possibly I shall have to pass through Geneva again, in the fall. A book by Kamp-schulte about Calvin is being sent on from Vienna—please keep it for me, because I shall want to take it along with me.

A lot of people are passing through here: day before yesterday Robert Neumann; yesterday I visited Thomas Mann, today I'll say goodbye to Faesi; I met Benno Geiger, who, to my amazement, was beautifully turned out and very elegant.

Affectionately, Stefan

[1] Stefan had tried in vain to induce Richard Strauss not to allow the Dresden performance. The correspondence which covers their collaboration is to be found in the archives of the Vienna Philharmonic Society.

(After a stay together in Marienbad, where Stefan worked with Mrs. Meingast, who had been his secretary for years, on the Castellio book, and I began the biography of Pasteur, Stefan went to Vienna to visit his mother and confer with his publisher, Reichner.)

Vienna, Hotel Regina,
Sept. 2nd (to Salzburg)

Dear Wife:

You have, I am sorry to say, not told me where Baron Franckenstein is staying. I certainly should drop a card at his place.[1] Everything is in good shape with Reichner and some good orders have done a lot for him. Then on top of that, by a stroke of good luck, young Neumann, of Ruetten & Loening, suddenly pops up in Vienna. It is not certain whether he [Reichner] can give him a job, but in any case he will be able to use him in some capacity in his business setup. The poor boy who is half-Jew, was summoned to the police station because he had an Aryan girl friend and was given to understand that in order to avoid further complications, he had better get out of Germany as fast as possible (he is an Austrian), which he did the same day.

Ruetten & Loening, like Fischer's, will be liquidated by January or be handed over to someone else. I see that I did the right thing and didn't leave them either too soon or too late.

Yesterday I went with Mama to the cemetery. I saw Rieger, will be with Gregor today, and tomorrow with Mrs. Privy Councillor Zuckerkandl. And I am surely going to visit Czokor.

I was, of course, sorry to miss *Fidelio,* but a single beautiful evening that has to be paid for by four weeks of time lost and a nervous upset, is, after all, too expensive. Let people do their own work, and me do mine, and with all due respect and without making any comparison between the value of their work and mine, I merely insist that my work is more important to me.—The Castellio Biography arrived today.

Best, Stefan

1 The Austrian minister in London who had just visited me in Salzburg.

About Sept. 4th.:

L.F.:

Today no mail from Salzburg. Yesterday a dinner for Czokor; a lot of people were there, but I am really ridiculously clumsy on such occasions; I gave him a present in private; I can't get anything published anywhere (Werfel wrote a beautiful piece in the *Fledermaus*). Lunch today with Frankenstein, very pleasant. Mama is impossibly brisk, altogether too active, it worries me because we can't prevent her going out at least twice a day.

My best, St.

Vienna, Hotel Regina, Sept. 6th/1935

Dear Wife:

You will have to plan things as best you can yourself. I don't know whether I may not suddenly go rushing off to that affair,[1] as a matter of fact, I should have been on my way yesterday already, but sent, instead, some suggestions for a plan. I hear that Schalom Asch is there. I would like to talk to him about a lot of things. As a rule there isn't much point in making these short trips to Vienna, although you will have to stay here in December, because, in spite of the critical situation, we don't want to leave Mama without anybody.

Otherwise nothing of special importance.

Affectionately, your Stefan

1 There were plans to get some well-known people in the world of the arts and letters together for a "demonstration."

I will have to go to Paris for a few days, will stop over in Salzburg only from forenoon till evening, and won't go out or see anybody. Please don't let anyone know about my coming to Vienna; tell people that I am coming the week after Christmas. I absolutely need a few days all to myself (Reichner, dentist, and suchlike) and don't want to see anybody until I have attended to my own most pressing affairs.

Dec. 9th, from London to Vienna

L.F.:

Just received your letter. I haven't negotiated with Liesl [1] about our apartment here and don't want to—if I should have to leave I couldn't make a long-term lease to anyone, in view of the current world crisis—will have to let the apartment stay unoccupied or allow a responsible friend to occupy one room. I am taking the boat-train to Paris (an airplane has just crashed) and have a lot of things to do there. Have to see publishers, Hella, [2] then friends (Romains is getting married some day soon, [3] but, of course, I never go to any such festivities). I shall get to see Duhamel before I leave London. Yesterday J. Ch. paid me a visit. I am terribly sorry for him, but even sorrier for a lot of other people. The things I hear every day are depressing; I am glad I'll be out of reach of people for a short time anyway.

Please don't try to keep me in Vienna; I can't do any work there and my stay there, because of all the people, would be more expensive than the finest apartment on the Riviera. I have finished all the preliminary research and now shall have to get down to hard work, and concentrate. This is not the time to sit around and gossip—ten days in Vienna will be plenty, in fact too much; the city depresses me terribly; then some more days in Paris, and another week of getting ready for the trip. At fifty-five years one has to ration one's time.

In haste and affectionately,

St.

[1] My niece, who had married and was living in London. [2] Alzier Hella, who had been translating his books into French for years. [3] Jules Romains, like Romain Rolland, had married his young secretary.

(To Salzburg)

Zuerich, Sept. 19th, 1935

L.F.:

Arrived according to schedule. I didn't wait to get something to eat, but took a sleeping pill and went right into the pullman and to bed, for I wanted to sleep off all the disturbing aftermath of our leave-taking. Rolland is expecting me next Saturday, but I called him up and asked to come tomorrow, so that I could be sure of a chance to look through the library in Geneva on Saturday. I am eager to get to work,[1] and for nothing else, and would like to get through with Paris as quickly as possible. I am having lunch with Kesser today. Except for him I don't want to see anybody. Anything else of importance I'll let you know about either by wire or phone.

Affectionately, Stefan

[1] *Castellio Gegen Calvin.*

Montreux Excelsior, 9/20/35

Brilliant weather—I'd love to stay here! Unfortunately the visit to Rolland was not very gratifying, he looks tired and old; at the discussion about the "demonstration"[1] Rolland and I were dumbfounded. Madeleine, like myself, wanted the whole affair to center around Rolland's works. Under the circumstances I am not particularly inclined to go along with this plan and hope to be able to cut Paris short. Tomorrow I shall be in Geneva, trust I shall be able to get through with everything; also will call up the Wertheimers.

Please have Susi enlarge the enclosed photographs; I couldn't get a shot of Rolland; Corbusier came and, besides that, they were very much upset. I was terribly sorry for them.—What a pity, what a pity!

Affectionately

[1] Stefan didn't want the "demonstration," which was to center around Rolland, to be at all political in character, but this discussion seemed to indicate that it was headed in that direction.

Lauzanne, Sept. 21st

I have just arrived here from Geneva, where I obtained all the material—pretty exhausting, so many things to do, and

273

conferences. I shall be in Paris tomorrow, Sunday, and hope to make my stay there as short as possible, since I perceive this business is taking a direction I don't approve of. Well, I've done my duty and mustn't allow myself to be forced into a "demonstration" which is contrary to my inmost convictions.

S.

Café de Rohan, Place du Palais Royal
Paris, Sept. 25/35

L.F.:

I have made a change in my plans, am going to London with Schalom Asch, will be there on Friday. He seems well, but below the surface, like all of us, is a little (or very much) upset, also only wants to work, in order to save himself from life. Roth has become a complete drunkard. Ernst Weiss [1] gives him up too.—I am getting through the accumulated mail here in London; please forward only the most essential things. Take care of the rest of it with the polite excuse that I am away and engaged on some important work.—I had them all together at lunch (noon) today, Vallentin, Roth, Asch.

In haste, St.

[1] The writer and physician. He later committed suicide.

Paris, Sept., 35

L.F.:

Was with Masereel, who is *splendid,* better, more lucid, more virile than ever. On the other hand Roth, a beloved Alp weighing us down, is drunk as a Russian Mujik, that's to say, all the way; talks like one bemused.—Grasset reports that he has sent *La Peur.*[1] The city is enchanting, bright and pleasant, for I'm not taking on many people. I still ought to see Jean R. Bloch, but I am too lazy to travel down to Poitiers to visit him.

Best, St.

[1] The short novel *Fear.*

(The following are selected from among seventeen letters written between September twenty-seventh and October twenty-eighth. I went to London in November to help reach a decision about renting an apartment in Hallam Street. These letters reflect Stefan's increasing suffering, caused by the constantly darkening outlook and my failure to get him to feel more optimistic about Austria, which friends like Toscanini, Bruno Walter, Franz Werfel, Zuckmayer hadn't yet despaired of. The sale of our beloved home would be made easier by my being there [in Vienna] and, moreover, Stefan wanted me to be near his mother and my daughters and was alternately for and against my doing as he had done, burning my bridges behind me. It was difficult to get rid of the house, because well-to-do people wanted to drive right up to the door in their autos, which, on account of the steep grade, was impossible at Kapuzinerberg. The political and economic crisis, moreover, brought all business to a halt. Although I and my children were very much attached to our home, nevertheless I tried my best to sell it, though Stefan doubted this. My desire and never-ceasing endeavor were to hold his moods of depression down to a minimum, but owing to our frequent separations, my endeavors no longer could be as effective as they had been in the past, especially as events so completely justified his pessimism.)

Portland Place, London, 9/29

L.F.:

　　Am writing this right after my arrival. Very agreeable crossing. Unfortunately, a glance at the newspapers very distressing; Hungary's sudden about-face after Italy,[1] worries me. It looks bad! I, at any rate, am convinced that our hopes for security are in a bad way.—Leave the ledger which shows how many times we were together this year or that, unopened. In view of my determination to battle for my work and freedom, it is better for you not to begin anything and quietly let me make all the necessary arrangements. I repeat, we can be together again after my work is finished, but I can't say now whether I shall be through by the fifteenth or the thirtieth of November and the feeling that someone is waiting for me would be stifling.—You don't have to feel ashamed of giving in.

Affectionately, St.

Nothing but trouble with the publishers.

1 The Abyssinian War.

October 1st

I have had some splendid days here, that is to say, complete quiet; nobody knows yet that I am here and by tomorrow

I shall have finished the spade work and will then be able to start in on the main job, which means getting it into more or less final shape. Yesterday I went with Asch to see a jolly Russian film (charming), then was with Sokoloff, head of the Zionist movement; I am to meet Victor today, and will go with him to the play for which his wife did the sets. Carr [1] I am to meet tomorrow, if he doesn't cancel the date because his wife is to be operated shortly. I am also to meet Flower.[2]—Desmond has a son. Also, I'll be at Siegmund Warburg's on Thursday.

The political situation depresses me, above all England's refusal to assume any obligations and newspaper comment has it that this refusal was made with a view to a specific eventuality. Of course, my outlook, unfortunately, isn't very optimistic although I am convinced of its soundness. Even when I was in Zuerich I knew that the Abyssinian business would have dire consequences. Naturally, it will also cost me some money, because Mondadori, my publisher, will pay me in currency that has depreciated in value by one half at least. I often think of our friends there.

Affectionately, S.

I might have the prospect of a flat here. It apparently has an additional room which was an important consideration, and would have been agreeable to you as well, but as I've said before, when you get right down to it, I wouldn't want to tie myself down here just now, though I realize I won't be mobile and free again until I have acquired a fixed base once more.

1 T. H. Carr, at the time Vansittard's secretary, and an author; I had become acquainted with him and his wife in Geneva, and they invited me to visit them in '39 to enable me to acquire English citizenship.   2 His publisher's (Cassell's) son.

L.F.:

What I'm looking for now is some provisional arrangement, safe quarters, an address, a place where I can put my most important belongings. Let Salzburg continue as long as you get any pleasure of it—as a summer home, and just as long as it serves any other purpose; I have no intention of robbing anyone of a home.—I have only one desire: peace throughout the world and in my own home.

St.

Mary Stuart came out today. You will see it advertised in the Sunday papers; there have been more advance sales than for *Marie Antoinette*.

October 2nd/1935

L.F.:

The political situation depresses me extremely. The latest news reports are really gloomy; the war and, therefore, the catastrophe can hardly be averted any longer and the consequences are unpredictable. My Jermiah instinct, unfortunately, proves right again in these crazy times. And our poor friends in Italy—how will they fare? Too bad Carr had to beg off his date with me; his wife is to be operated. But I was at Cassell's and visited with Madame Budberg, will see Warburg tomorrow. My work is getting along now; I wish it weren't interrupted by all these distractions. I will be glad to give something for X., but a collection wouldn't get very far; everyone has to look out for himself these days; if only people would realize that they are being idealistic at the expense of others, and less and less at their own. Though he is such a wonderful human being! My phone is silent all day long and I feel as if I were in paradise in this flat as long as I can just read and work. This is written in haste; your mail doesn't get in until nine o'clock in the evening.

St.

L.F.:

Today war begins and when will it end? I am inquiring about a flat here. The film deal, if it works out right, will take care of a year's rent. There is still plenty of time for all that, for no one can tell what will happen in the next few months, except that it will be a terribly tense time. Please, therefore, don't tell me your decisions—I am completely conditioned by my work and the fate of the world, and so *my* plans are the more important. But as yet I don't know anything, except that

I hope to get the better part of the book done in the next six to eight weeks.

I shall be with Lakin[1] on Tuesday. Asch said goodbye today.

With all my best,

St.

1 Editor-in-chief of the London *Sunday Times*.

October 5th, telegram

Don't worry. Will call you this evening.

L.F.:

As I wrote you, I put off reaching any decision about the flat 'till November. You know how I put out feelers way back in Milan, and then the Abyssinian affair came up.—This hither and thither and hoping and disappointment gets on a working man's nerves.

Franckenstein returned my visit. I am to see Rose Walter tomorrow, but she was terribly upset by Germany, like everyone else who has been there recently. As for the rest, you know what the world looks like, since war has broken out. This time I was something of an optimist and didn't believe it would happen. But we are going through some tough schooling and it is useless to fool ourselves with renewed hope whenever there is a momentary break in the dark clouds.—I would have phoned by this time, but I don't know when you will be home.

In haste, St.

11 Portland Place, October 8th

L.F.:

I have to write you a somewhat more detailed letter today. Difficulties have come up in connection with the film. I have had a whole bundle of offers from house agents, but I absolutely want to stay downtown in the city. For the first time I have seen something that might do, in a house that has recently been finished, just around the corner, in Hallam Street. I intend to return by the end of November or December and then I shall supervise everything connected with the business of moving. I would be grateful if you could find out just how we are to go about it. Perhaps you could make a list of the things that would be usable. There is so much in the house, it could be left pretty completely furnished. These are the furnishings needed for here: a large work room, a bedroom, a dining room and a living room—the fourth room could serve both as bedroom and living room. I see how everybody arranges things here; Frischauer, Kortner, Toller and everyone else earn good money here. At the same time the general atmosphere is pleasant and peaceful and you don't feel there is the least bit of nervousness.—No one here thinks of war, only, in a general way, about developments in inner Europe. They have only one goal: to keep out [1] and that is what I, as a writer, am doing too.

[1] This was what turned out to be so tragic for Europe, and we in Austria were aware of it.

October 10/35

L.F.:

I am terribly depressed: for one thing, the situation is constantly getting worse; secondly, the frightful letters that I am now getting from Germany, these shrill appeals for help from the Jews who delayed too long and now want to get away, that is to say, must get away, but can't. This awful business of E. H.; you have surely read about it; one of the noblest human beings I have ever known—and at the same time Judge N. (who had one of the finest Goethe collections, second only to Kippenberg's) writes me asking me whether I could get his son a job as a *waiter* here, and a hundred more similar things are told me. There was never anything as frightful as this that has resulted from the hate-laws in G. Unfortunately, I foresee things like these perhaps too soon, long before they happen, which is a fault in me, but I can't change that.

Please put aside all private worries now. Don't say anything about my affairs [1] except that I am now settled in London because I have the best library available and can work most profitably there, and that I have gotten settled and have definitely given up Salzburg. Always be completely clear-cut about the really important things.

Affectionately, St.

[1] Just a week before I had received directions to do the exact contrary.

L.F.:

Just received your letter. I talked with Franckenstein for a moment today while I was in his house about a passport matter. Of course he is very busy, because of adverse criticism of the position Austria has taken in opposition to the fifty other governments.

I have already written you about arrangements to be made. It would be important for you and your daughters to go through the whole inventory again, so that they will know where everything is, and be able to find whatever is wanted when asked for it.

I regret to state that my work goes along slowly, because what is happening has affected me so deeply.

Affectionate greetings, St.

I went to London for a short visit in order to take the job of househunting and making decisions off Stefan's shoulders; we rented an unfurnished apartment in Hallam Street.

London, Oct. 28/35

L.F.:

I am glad you had a pleasant trip. Here lots to do, mountains of letters, meanwhile that tremendously gifted Felix Weiss has trapped me into letting him do a bust of me (before I get fat again).

I'll be at Warburg's again tomorrow. His uncle, Max Warburg, will be there; he has a lot to tell. He found that things were much worse than four weeks ago.—I hope we shall be spared this sort of calamity as long as possible. Only that is important, nothing else, and one mustn't make one's own ego the center of everything any longer. Good God, what terrible letters are littering up my desk again today.

St.

(From London to Vienna)

Just a line in haste! There is tremendous excitement here and a sort of stock exchange crash as a result of the Affaire Mrs. Simpson.—There is no thought of Spain now, nor of Europe, only this Affaire (the aftermath was terrific, the postponement of the coronation played havoc with those businesses that had made great preparations for it).

The world and foreign situation are beyond imagining. Even the most learned optimists are growing despondent and I envy all the jolly folk who don't worry and go on quite care-free from day to day.

Thank Alix for her letter.

With my best, St.

<h1 style="text-align:center">1 9 3 6</h1>

From now on fewer of the letters I sent Stefan and which he formerly used to bring back with him from his travels for safe-keeping in Salzburg, survived. Also, to leave more space for his letters, I am including almost none of mine in the following pages. The reader will get my reactions from his answers to my letters. The year 1936 was punctuated by short visits to Vienna and Salzburg and we were together in the summer. In January, after a stay in Nice, I went on ahead to London to install the furniture, pictures, books that had come from Salzburg, in the apartment in the as-yet unfinished house on Hallam Street. Several months before this Stefan had, though emotionally much shaken, helped in the work of cataloguing and partial breaking up of his letter files, library, his manuscripts and notes for literary projects. I tried to make his workroom in Hallam Street an exact replica of his library in Salzburg, with the red wallpaper he was so fond of, the landscape by Masereel above his book cases, which, however, contained only one-tenth of the 10,000 volumes he had in Salzburg. I went back to Salzburg in May.

London, May 11th/36

L.F.:

I am happy to learn that you traveled so comfortably. Have a lot to do here; the people in *La Peur* [1] are, I find, at least in some respects, pretty good. Also I shall talk to Ould [2] about South America. Here every visit takes up half a day.

In haste, St.

I sent some money to Roth, which will give him a chance to work in peace for six weeks at least. But this sort of thing can't go on indefinitely; today a letter came from X. in Paris; they are having trouble making their payments; I was to come to the rescue; another letter about going security for J., and still another from a third party. These endless appeals are soul-shattering.

281

1 Making a movie of the novel, with Gaby Morley.   2 The international secretary of the Pen Club who was making arrangements for the Congress in Buenos Aires.

L.F.:

   I have a lot to do just now, have to confer about the translations with Paul.[1] Otherwise nothing of importance. People here are watching the latest developments with intense interest. I wish they were really the latest and last.

St.

1 Eden and Cedar Paul, who had been his translators for years.

May 21st

L.F.:

   Just received your postcard. No, I didn't see either the *Freie Presse,* which to my great annoyance, and without my knowing about it, printed something out of *Castellio,* nor the *Neue Züricher Zeitung;* haven't any idea of how Zuerich[1] turned out, will ask Fuerstner. *Castellio* is probably already in Salzburg. Still no news from America; out of Germany only shocking news. But I feel calm and well and am in good mood for work—that's the only thing that matters.

St.

(A long letter in his own hand, from eighty-year-old Freud. I am seeing Drinkwater next week.)

1 Performance of *Die Schweigsame Frau.*

London, May 28th/36

L.F.:

   Unfortunately my plans are uncertain because I don't know when Huebsch and that Hollywood person are to be here. I am negotiating about the South American lectures.— In any event, I should like to get away for a time. I haven't had a real walk since Nice. At the moment I am working well, enjoy my quarters. But I am surely going to pay Mama a visit some time in June and will be passing through Salzburg then.

St.

L.F.:

      May 26th

Nothing new to report, except that Huebsch arrives about June first. So I shall be leaving here in the middle of June and then, toward the end of June, I shall pass through Salzburg on my way to Vienna. As far as I, personally, am concerned, things are going along all right, but I am unhappy about the times we live in. After Germany, Palestine! It is impossible to figure it all out. I'd like to creep into a mouse-hole and never see a newspaper again. In great haste,

      St.

      May 28th/36

L.F.:

Do forgive this hasty, unamiable, dictated note. I wanted to answer you right away. It's all right for Mrs. Meingast to leave at Whitsuntide. Later on I shall have plenty for her to do. There will be a manuscript which will run to eighty printed pages and some shorter ones, to be copied. You can see from this that I haven't been lazy here.—I still have that conference about the Argentine and Brazil before me. The Brazilian Government has again sent me a most urgent invitation, and I shall go there first, in any case, because Brazil interests me very much. I'll take in the others perhaps on the way back. But I have accepted only on condition that I needn't make any speeches and that there won't be an official reception. My plan is: to leave for Zuerich on the fourteenth or fifteenth then Salzburg and then, if you want to, a trip together to Vienna. By that time, if everything goes according to schedule, I shall probably have proofs of the second volume of the novellas, plus *Sternstunden,* in other words, my entire narrative prose works brought out in two big volumes. We are still wrangling about the price, for I am insisting on a very moderate price. So it would be important for me to correct these proofs before I disappear from Europe. Because I didn't read the final proofs, a few small but annoying errors were left in *Castellio.* If I had these two volumes behind me, then only a third would be left, for my selected essays, and then the whole Opus will have been brought under one roof.

I should leave from Southampton because my packing for the trip, dress-suit, etc., must be done here.

Tomorrow I am going to have a tough fight with Nancy Price who nags me dreadfully about *Jeremiah*. But that production of hers that I saw didn't impress me at all and really I haven't any desire to overemphasize the Jewish aspects.

I met Professor Bonn at an evening party we arranged for Max Hermann-Neisse at which I made a short speech. But the fourteen days that still are left me will be full of work and I am glad of it, because work is all that is still bearable in these disgusting times.

My best, St.

L.F.:

I am in a dreadful mess. *Castellio* has impressed the people whose opinion counts, but one page, due to being shifted, is not historically correct. I am having the entire section reprinted, but meanwhile the review copies have gone out and all this will take some time—so this book which I considered one of my most important, has caused me the most heartaches. It is enough to drive one to the verge of insanity. Yet nobody could have helped me, because nobody else was familiar with the material.

I've told you already that I'll be in S. for a day and will then go on with you on the seventeenth to Vienna. I would like to get a thorough rest for once, and Vienna seems to be quite depressing; we live in a frightful era. But, at any rate, I'm working hard and that's the one thing that helps me.

St.

June 2nd

L.F.:

At the moment I have a lot to do, revision of the English translation (the burnt child fears the fire). All in all, I am terribly weary of this never-ending grind—never once to the theater, no fun, one doesn't really live. I am getting everything ready for next week. Will be in Salzburg about the thirteenth.

All my best, Stefan

L.F.:

Just a line in haste. Despite my irritation about the *Castellio* matter, I have been working well and am still at it. Of course, it was a mistake to let myself be pressured by Reichner. Hereafter I shall let every book stay in galleys for at least a month, so as to get it into proper perspective.—I had concentrated on it completely and was prepared to do whatever might have had to be done.[1] Now we have this drop in the valuta, a very touchy business abroad too, in the countries where we make our money, now that Germany is out of the picture.

A world in chaos: I am dreaming a lot about the trip to South America.

In haste, Stefan

[1] *Castellio gegen Calvin* was the first book he wrote and put the finishing touches on away from his regular workshop. The more vehement controversies about the errors that had crept into the text but could have been corrected in the definitive edition, didn't develop until some years later after the French edition appeared, at a time when the clash over fanaticism and dictatorship had become less of a burning issue. It was at that time no longer being read in the old spirit of partisanship. Pastor Jean Schorer defended Zweig's *Castellio* in his *Jean Calvin et sa Dictature* and the way he did it was most gratifying.

L.F.:

A lot of work went into revising *Castellio,* and the revisions will be inserted into at least fifteen copies. Meanwhile am working at some new things. In the past year everything has become more difficult; Poland, Hungary etc. want the books but can't pay for them, and this is a trend that is spreading to other parts of the world. If I were only allowed to do my work! But this moral obligation to stand up for people and causes—the Freud [1] business alone cost me a tremendous lot of work! I had a very agreeable visit with Huebsch. I don't want to stay too long in Vienna. There are very few people left there who are close to me. Moreover, there is the dentist and a hundred business matters, and I must fill out that Volume II of the novellas.

Affectionately, S.

The important thing is for you to have all those things, mail, etc., ready and in proper shape for me when I get to Salzburg, all non-essentials weeded out, so that I can get through in a hurry.

1 Freud was in London at this time; he had been rescued and brought there, and was being fêted everywhere.

June 9th

I had a most interesting hour with Axel Munthe yesterday; he has gotten back his eyesight, thanks to Joyce's doctor. To-day, negotiations with my Swedish publisher.

Affectionately, S.

(From Salzburg to Ostend)

July 31/36

Dear Stefan:

Let's not discuss your trip abroad or make any decisions at the present time. Certainly it wouldn't be wise to talk about problems concerned with material things or try to look too far ahead in this connection. Now you are the optimist, when you talk about a steady income in Austria. So I'll simply say: let's wait and not despair. Let's just hope you'll have a fine, care-free trip. Raoul Lange ¹ raves about South America. I am delighted that you are so popular there. You can't imagine what a crowd of tourists has invaded Salzburg. It seems as though all the motorists and all the sensation-seekers in the world had no other goal save the Festival Plays. Despite the fact that the German frontier is still closed. Our house is an oasis of tranquility, and my few visitors seem to breathe more easily here. The lunch for the artists' children, which I wrote about, was delightful. Klaus Mann was full of enthusiasm and invited Lix and Susi to a farewell party for tomorrow eve-ning. Paul Valéry's little son is perfectly charming, and Marina Chaliapine entrancingly pretty. But I find I can't enjoy the Festival Plays very much, because my throat is choked with tears all the time. I implore you think of your health.

Affectionately,

F.

1 The actor.

L.F.:

My stay here will come to an end tomorrow. I have been more content than in a long time, despite the dubious weather, and have finished another *Sternstunde*.—I have managed to get Roth into much better shape, he eats something every day now —only nobody can make him come on walks or go swimming. I have made provision for him, sufficient to take care of him for some time to come, but foresee for him, and for all authors, a black future; sales are declining steadily and difficulties will increase.

Affectionate best, St.

Just had a fine swim in the ocean.

(Trip to South America)

R.M.S. *Alcantara*, Aug. 1/1936
Mailed on the high seas

Today, Monday the tenth, was terrifically interesting; the ship was ordered to take on refugees in Vigo (Spain); we stopped over for four hours and only three people ventured into the city, which is occupied by Fascist troops—naturally I was one of the three. So once again I got a close-up look at a revolution; also took some snapshots, it was incredibly interesting; of course, you see more life on a single street than here on board ship in weeks. The water supply [of the city] had been cut off; they were doing some recruiting (new, foreign uniforms) and, aside from that, life there, wonderfully picturesque, went on as usual. Tomorrow, Lisbon.

Best to all, Stefan

On board, Aug. 21st

I am writing this just before our arrival, so that I can mail it right away in Rio, and to report that I have arrived in good shape. The trip was very pleasant. Calm ocean, wonderful air, I've read a lot and made notes for future projects. I was able to choose my company because I hadn't allowed them to put me on the passenger list, and so, for instance, there are two ladies who had brought several of my books in the French translation along on the trip and have been reading them in-

287

tently; they hadn't any idea that I was nearby. Very interesting was a professor who lectures on evolution, and who is under contract in Brazil; I took a course in biology with him. Then there was the head of the English educational system. Also an American mining engineer who had developed gold mines in Abyssinia and South Africa and is returning to Brazil. He told me a lot. I do exercises every morning on the upper deck and bathe in the tubs filled with sea water set up in the sun, which transforms the ship into a seaside resort, and then one is surfeited with the ladies' naked backs. Naturally I didn't take part in the idiotic Equator baptisms.

I am looking forward with anticipation to Brazil and haven't much appetite for Penargentine [1] but, as they have paid for my sojourn on this floating sanatorium, I can't do otherwise. Please send a few books to London: (1) Schopenhauer, (2) Casanova, (3) the South American novels of H. E. Jacob, (4) a small book about Magelhaes.[2] I hope you are having as good a rest as I am having on this trip and hope to have on the return.

Affectionately, Stefan

[1] He refers to the Pen Club Congress which he was to attend as a "Senator."   [2] Magellan or Magelhaes. The trip inspired him to do the explorer's biography.

Rio de Janeiro, August 21/36

Arrived in Rio, took part in this fantastic and exhausting fairy tale, not to be imagined. The entrance [to the harbor] magically beautiful, beyond all expectations no matter how great. Four gentlemen from the ministry of foreign affairs were waiting for me at the dock, and because of that, the Austrian Chargé d'affaires was there too—the Minister being away in Buenos Aires. I have my quarters in four rooms in this marvelous Copacabana Hotel, right at the water's edge; you go in your bathing suit straight into the water, and the view is such that you don't want to go to sleep. There is a grand auto and a chauffeur to drive it always at my beck and call; a charming Attaché from the Ministry is in attendance all day long. I found a heap of visiting cards waiting for me, because my daily program is printed in all the newspapers; so I had to visit: the Minister of Foreign Affairs, with whom I posed for a photograph in the resplendent old Ministry; the President of the Academy; the President of the Pen Club; as well as interviews with a horde of reporters; tomorrow I'm going in "my" auto and with "my" attaché, to Petropolis, after having already seen a lot of wonderful things here today; in the evening with the Austrians; on Sunday the Foreign Minister is giving an unfortunately big dinner for me at the Jockey Club; Wednesday a reception at the Academy; Thursday I shall have to deliver a lecture (in French—when will I have time to work it up?); Friday drive with the Minister to Sao Paulo and visit the factories, if I haven't collapsed by that time. I fear I shall not have a chance to enjoy the city's enchantment enough. I have never seen a more bewitching place, one could wax poetic about it. What a glorious city—and at the same time, shopping ridiculously cheap if one had time for it; it would pay to make a trip here just for that; and what super-abundance of fruits and colors.—I received your letter. Please give Mama my best; I can't write letters. Address as per former communication.

Affectionately, S.

Letter per Condor, Zeppelin, Lufthansa, Aug. 25/36

L.F.:

Writing is out of question. It's too mad a rush. Today, after working all night on a lecture, I must: (1) visit the President of the Republic; (2) the Historical Museum; (3) reception at the Academy where I am to make another speech. After the dinner at the Foreign Minister's we autoed out to the most beautiful house and the most beautiful landscape I have ever seen. It is enough to drive one out of one's mind, magnificent; but I am being made mincemeat of, torn to shreds. I am shedding a pound a day; but Brazil is *incredible*. I feel as if I wanted to howl like a sick hound, because I shall have to leave. And with it all, a *courtoisie* as of ancient days. It is obligatory to leave cards everywhere, but the people are enchanting and the women unbelievably beautiful. But I shrink from the publicity—new pictures of me every day in all the newspapers. Please write Alfred. I haven't the fraction of a minute to spare. I am very happy to have been here.—I scarcely dare describe the reception they have given me; for from six to eight days I have been Marlene Dietrich.

Duhamel, Romains, Pierard will be at the Pen Club—
that will indemnify me a bit.—If I could only give them back
the money and stay here in Rio. This is written while eighteen
photographers are snapshotting. Tomorrow I am to deliver a
lecture in a closed meeting for the refugees. Please give my
best to Mama.

St.

August 26th

L.F.:

I can't write, it's just one mad rush from morning till
late at night. The beauty, the color, the enchantment of this
city are indescribable—there is nothing on earth that can com-
pare with its variety. Today, went to the Islands on the Government's private boat. I've never beheld such a paradise. The
people are enchanting and—a mercy on this earth of ours—this
is the only place where there isn't any race question. Negroes
and whites and Indians, three-quarters, one-eighth, the wonder-
derful Mulatto and Creole women, Jews and Christians, all
dwell together in a peace that passes describing. The Jewish
immigrants are in seventh heaven; all of them have jobs and
feel at home.

It is impossible to give you the least idea of what is happening to me. If I should want to deliver a series of public
lectures here, I could fill Albert Hall four times over. At the
Academy reception people were standing in line for two
blocks; the Foreign Office didn't know which way to turn, because attendance at the lecture being by invitation only, they
were overwhelmed from early morning till evening with demands for tickets and only had two thousand seats. Today I
gave a more intimate reading (there weren't any notices in the
newspapers) in German for the Hilfsverein,[1] and 1,200 people
came; half of them stood all through the evening. Unfortunately I am compelled to write 500 autographs every day and
am close to getting writers' cramp. The visit to the President
of the Republic was *very* interesting. The Minister of Foreign
Affairs is going with me to Sao Paulo. All the notables show up,
the Naval Commander and the Ministers, one after the other,
to get a picture of me or my autograph—and you must consider
that this isn't a village, but a city of a million and a half and

a country with a population of forty million. I have received a heap of presents, not to mention invitations. But that, heaven knows, isn't why I like the country so much—it is simply the most enchanting place on earth. And one thing is sure, this isn't the last time that I'll be here. Just the country for me: divine coffee (about five farthings a cup), the grandest cigars, the most bewitching women, the loveliest landscape. If I only knew something about photography—actually I'm a regular Charlie Chaplin about things like that. The people here are wonderfully tactful and correspondingly sensitive themselves (a servant leaves his job if he has been spoken to in unfriendly fashion). That is why this oriental politeness must always be reciprocated. I met Rochefoucauld who visited us in Salzburg; he is just as bewitched as I am. Pity that I have to leave. Of course it is mid-winter now, and in the summer one would be completely leached out. Please write Mama that I'm well.

Affectionately, St.

1 The proceeds amounted to 1000 Swiss francs. Here this was equal to ten times as much.

Esplanada Hotel, Sao Paulo, Sept. 3rd/36
(I've got only three rooms here instead of four)
From the loveliest madhouse on earth, greetings. I am leaving Brazil. It was incredibly beautiful, but overplus of enjoyment, painful. I had some crazy experiences again today. I visited the world-renowned prison in Sao Paolo, one of the grandest and most humanitarian institutions of its kind on earth; while there I was, as happens daily, photographed forty times (they make everything in the prison, and when I innocently inquired what crime the photographer had been guilty of, I was told that he was a three-time murderer). Meanwhile the band, consisting of thirty inmates, marched into the courtyard; I came over to review them, and thereupon they played the Austrian national anthem—the first time in my life that it has been played in my honor; two-thirds of them were murderers, one-third thieves, etc. All of which has something grotesque about it. Yesterday I spent with the Minister of Foreign Affairs on a coffee plantation and came back with the Archbishop. It is fantastic to think of the experiences I have had

these last twelve days in this indescribably beautiful country where I'd like to live for years. I regret to say that I am leaving four-fifths of the presents behind; for instance, the Coffee Institute sent four kilos of the most wonderful coffee and a huge coffee machine; the books came in hampers; [1] I just this moment received an engraved cane from the Minister of Foreign Affairs, made of the costliest Brazilian woods, cigars from the government, enough to poison me with nicotine eight times over at least. But because of the duty I will be able to take along home with me only some of the things. Today in the Snake Institute—exciting and beautiful, indeed I can't possibly give an account of everything that I have learnt—I missed having a secretary, although the Adjutant assigned me by the Minister is a splendid, highly cultured man, belonging to one of the oldest families and has been extraordinarily helpful. The whole thing has a dreamlike and improbable quality, like this indescribable country itself.

Best, St.

[1] As a matter of fact, big boxes of books and presents soon began to arrive in London where I was waiting for Stefan.

On Board the Royal Mail Liner, Sept. 5th/36

Just before arriving in Montevideo; the only thing to report is that the ship has been delayed a day. I am having a fine time with Duhamel and his wife here on the ship; they have brought their charming seventeen-year-old son with them to show him the world. It is really *remarkable* how Duhamel and I understand each other. He is clever, humane, and there is nothing of the Academician about him. It's also very nice to be with Emil Ludwig and his wife and there are some very pleasant Hindus and Scandinavians. All of us are at work, take notes and leave each other in peace, but the pessimism about politics is *frightful.* I am glad that others will do the talking at the Congress, so that I will have quiet and can remain in the background after the super-highlights of Rio. I will, at most, just give a private reading from the *Legend* [1] for the benefit of the refugees, to get some money for them. No doubt I shall be able to do a little work of my own during

the return trip. I am looking forward with pleasure to my
quiet London flat after all these beautiful days.

Affectionately, S.

1 *Der Wandelnde Leuchter.*

Buenos Aires, Sunday, Sept. 12th

L.F.:

I didn't get a chance before to write you a line from
Buenos Aires. The air isn't as good here as in Rio. The Congress full of conflicts between Fascists and others, and also
deadly boring—everything gets translated into three languages.
I haven't done any talking, have refused the Presidency—it is
not for me to make a play to the gallery. At the very end I
may perhaps address a few words of thanks to Wells, so as to be
able to boast that I opened my mouth at least once. But it's
no good being so cautious, the newspapers pursue you from
morning till night with photographings and "stories."—I was
pictured more than life size, *weeping!* as I listened to Ludwig's
speech.—Yes, there it was in gigantic letters. The truth is I
felt so disgusted because they played us up as martyrs that I
hid my head in my hands so that I couldn't be photographed,
and they invented that ridiculous caption for it—I am letting
other people attend to everything—the really fine people at the
Congress like Kalidas Nag are doing the same. And that has
made me the confidant of everybody and, by underground
conciliatory tactics, I have prevented a big smash-up. It was
wise of me to keep myself altogether in the background, although that will be misinterpreted too. I shall be glad to get
aboard ship again, although I saw a lot of interesting things
today, after the others had adjourned, the slaughter-house,
something quite unique.

Affectionately, S.

Buenos Aires, Sept./36

L.F.:

Received your airmail letter. I am pleased at Weingart-
ner leaving, for Walter's sake. Now, doubtless, the terrible mess
in Salzburg is ended. I am writing during the Congress's sessions. I stand apart, although I am overwhelmed with requests

to make speeches. Ludwig does all that for me and in the most praiseworthy manner; his vitality, his erudition really phenomenal. Romains delivered a magnificent opening address, very keen, very beautiful and, in my opinion, very full of a feeling of comradeship; he also quoted me. Duhamel, again, is wonderful in his humanitarian feeling—too bad, from my point of view, who am in the middle as it were, that they are on such bad terms. Both are clever, courageous human beings, both my close friends, which puts me on a spot. Buenos Aires is tiresomely lovely; wouldn't dream of comparing it with divine Rio with which I have fallen in love. I'll write an article about Brazil when I get back onto the ship.

The recesses between sessions always gave me a chance to rest up a bit after this Berlitz school. If words could accomplish something, then a lot would have been accomplished here, because they never stop passing peace resolutions, and then everyone waxes terribly dithyrambic. I am in a whimsical mood, go quietly to the Argentinian Pucheros to eat. Yesterday Professor Salomon paid me a visit, very interesting. In Buenos Aires you seem to be living in Birmingham or in a Genoa without the pictures and palaces.

I hope to be in Southampton by the sixth of October. Meanwhile my best to everybody. Please write Mama that I am well.

Affectionately, St.

This is my last letter from our apartment in Hallam Street in London; I never went back there.

London, September 29
To Mr. Stefan Zweig
Passenger per *Almanzora*, Vigo
Dear Stefan:
I think it's worth taking a chance and hope this letter will reach you. The mail brought nothing important, except a movie offer that came to Salzburg. I hope, with my whole heart, that you are well and that your work didn't suffer because of the news from Europe. Let's hope that your newly accumulated spiritual riches will survive all possible devaluations. People here don't seem to be impressed by the fact that pounds and dollars stay so steady. Of course, it's hard on me;

but I try not to think of it. I am making up for all the books I have missed; for instance, have been reading Luc Durtain's work on South America, it has made me look forward to your descriptions which will be more interesting to me than his. You'll find everything in good order here. It was a great joy for me to stay here in London and feel so close to you—in spite of the vast ocean between us. I'll meet you in Southampton, so that we can be together as long as possible. There's much to tell. But everything is overshadowed by my eagerness to have you fill in your letters with verbal reports. I wish you a happy home-coming. Many, many greetings from your

Fr.

(To Paris, Hotel Louvois)

London, October 14th

L.F.:

I am doing heavy penance for going away just this once. I have just received the two volumes of the novellas from Reichner. It is done all wrong. Instead of the title *Collected Tales,* Volume I and Volume II, with the subtitle, he has simply omitted the main title, and called one book, *Kaleidoscope* and the other, *Die Kette,* and nobody will realize that, and some people will be annoyed because these stories are merely the old stories, whereas there would have been a big public for my *Collected Tales.* To top all this, the binding is horrible—I am in despair. How wonderful everything used to be at Insel's.

Affectionately, St.

Things are not going along any better for me here. Cassell has sent the book. Despite what I told him, Calvin's picture is at the top and thus plays up Calvin and not Castellio. I am desperate because I can't stay away for even eight weeks. The Pauls have made an even sorrier mess and Castellio disappears altogether. Oh! one always has to do everything oneself.

Affectionately, St.

I envy you your enthusiasm about people. I, unfortunately, have nothing but annoyance and trouble—the past four years seem like forty and have correspondingly aged me spiritually. Lucky that work offers some distraction.

L.F.:

I met La Cebotari yesterday. She is to sing *Die Schweigsame Frau* in Vienna in a year from now. A year is a long time and all sorts of things can happen in the meantime. I didn't see Maestro R. Str. and didn't do anything in that direction. The American movie has come a cropper. Willi Maass is coming tomorrow to stay for three days. I am invited to Miss Rose Stanfield's for Monday. I shall dine with Bruno Frank on Sunday.

In haste, St.

Nov. 10th (To Salzburg)

L.F.:

Thanks a lot. Please take the light-weight fur coat along to Vienna. If I pass through Salzburg I shall wire Johann to meet me at the station, if only to shake his and Mrs. Meingast's hand. An invitation came for you from his Excellency Franckenstein to the Archduke Johann ball on December third. Please write to say that you regret you will have to be in Austria on that date.

In haste, St.

(From London to Pension Atlanta, in Vienna)

Nov. 30th

L.F.:

Thanks for your congratulations. The arrival of the goose liver has been announced by the customs authorities and it should reach me by Monday. In the matter of the house,[1] the lawyer is still acting like a clodhopper. And in other matters there also is no lack of annoyances and troubles; it has been a really disagreeable year as far as all these "external" affairs are concerned, and I shall begin the new year with little confidence. A person grows a bit weary of these constant difficulties and complications after he has reached fifty-five and after thirty-five years of work. I would love to be able to have a bit of anonymous existence somewhere and get off this relentlessly onward rumbling armored tank.

Affectionately, my best, St.

[1] Reference to the Salzburg house.

I have eliminated all the letters of this year that contained controversial matter, such letters as Stefan frequently wrote during this period of outer and inner stresses. I have done this in such a way that the reader will not be aware that our relationship had suffered shipwreck. During the years that followed, the life of my comrade of twenty-five years became overcast and sad, although it had theretofore often been full of cheerfulness. His attitude toward me also changed, as though I were partly to blame for the sins of the whole era. My affection for him never diminished, nor my sympathy; I strove, despite all the things that tended to embitter him, to rescue and rehabilitate his old "I", and myself with it. The evil that he suffered was not made more bearable for him, the friend of mankind, by the fact that he had many comrades in misfortune who had lost even more than he. Then came the immeasurable injustice done him by the country to which he had dedicated himself, and then, as a postscript, even before Hitler's invasion, his own native land struck at his freedom, which he valued above all; he saw himself hemmed in by foes. I sought in vain to keep him from exaggerating things. A house search, not aimed at the family, at the time when concealed weapons were being hunted down, during the uprisings of the opposition, wounded him deeply. My subsequent protests which produced an apology from the Crownland's highest officials, merely embittered him the more against me. He wanted to drain the cup to its dregs and turn his back stubbornly on the city where so many fine things had flourished. (How he loved it, and the whole country when he was far away from it and had lost it forever!) Up till now his seismographic way of seeing everything in the blackest hues had been kept in balance by my credulous optimism; this had been a vital element in our lives. But henceforward, his pessimistic outlook was to become the dominating one.

(Naples, February 2nd, to Vienna, where I was staying in a bungalow with my friend Yella Hertzka)

L.F.:

Notwithstanding your request, I can't write much, and unluckily only disagreeable things. Today I had a letter from Frau X. asking me to lend her 500 sch. I *gave* her this sum outright two years ago and am not able to do anything more now. And on the same day J. asks for exactly the same amount. I have also already helped him out with considerable—it's frightful, this saying no, and on top of everything else, to have to make excuses. But I can't do any more of this in view of the present situation; this open-handedness has merely led people to believe that I have an enormous income, which I haven't got by a long shot. I must point out that the others should come through once in a while. I can't take care of everybody. What annoys me especially is that one gets dubious about human beings, because many of these people never show up until they need something. Please, therefore, don't give my address to anyone while I am abroad. That is another reason why I couldn't live in Vienna, aside from other considerations; just a stamp from there and it somehow depresses me. Also my relations with R.[1] are bad in every respect except in the matter of my work; I have really had a lot of unhappy experiences with people since 1933, and you have to be on your guard not to let them embitter you too much. How we have to struggle to be allowed to work a bit in peace and quiet, and you must constantly ward off all the demands that are made upon you. After all, one doesn't want anything of anybody, only to work quietly, and remain in obscurity. I shall stay on here for the rest of this week, then three days in Rome, two, three days in Milan, perhaps one day in Zuerich and then London, where I hope I will be able to finish the book [2] in two months and then work at whatever I please.

You are right to stay in Vienna;—the house must be terribly unfriendly and it is better to have Susi with you.

Affectionately, St.

1 The publishing house.   2 *Magellan.*

L.F.:

The second version will be finished by Monday. Yesterday, hardened by my experience with the two Marys, Stuart and Antoinette, I was easily able to kill off poor Magellan and am now at work on what followed. The third version will be finished in London. I think to be in London about the sixteenth to the twentieth. It seems to be as cold in Vienna as it is sunny and becalmed here, certainly better here. Don't move into that freezing Salzburg house before spring.—I regret to say that I have lots of mail and, therefore, can't write you more in detail.

Affectionately, St.

298

L.F.:

I drove per auto up Vesuvius with the worthy Mrs. Selden-Goth—indescribly lovely—and now we are sitting in a little Trattoria in Torre del Greco by the sea. Had news at my hotel today; Jannings and his wife are coming to make a film here, right in the hotel where I'm staying, instead of the Excelsior, although his friend Goering stopped there.

My very best, S.

We are sitting in the sunshine and rejoicing at how beautiful life is.

Affectionately, your Gisella

February 3rd/36

L.F.:

I am leaving Sunday for Rome, shall be in Hotel de Russie there and about the thirteenth in Milan, Hotel Excelsior.

There was an incident. A Monsignore found out I was here through Mrs. G. and an invitation came right off by phone from the Crown Princess. But I couldn't accept, because I was just leaving for Capri to meet Axel Munthe and Albertini. Then I was again invited for the next day. It was really touching, for the Royal Chamberlain, etc. begged me not to tell anyone that she was receiving me, because she had denied herself to all sorts of people, even important ones—as a matter of fact, she is in her very ninth month, it won't be more than a few days now and the country will perhaps have its much-desired heir-apparent. I spent quite a long time with her in the splendid palace, one of the most beautiful in the whole world, and she really was deeply affecting because she was so close to her time. I was a bit touched by her receiving me in that condition, when generally a woman only lets her most intimate friends visit her. We talked of many things. It was most interesting.

Jannings and his wife have been in the hotel the last two days; I haven't seen them yet, only had a few words with

Ruth: strange situation. But it is not for me to speak to the Senator and Privy Councillor, that might embarrass him.[1]

Best, in haste, St.

[1] Jannings, whose star in Hollywood had been fading, had accepted the honors and the chance to continue with his work offered him by the Third Reich. We had been very close to him and his action disappointed Stefan very much.

(Postcard from Naples)

February 5th/1937

After an immoderate meal, salutations from

Stefan

Rickchen [diminutive for Friderika]: we are thinking of you with love and friendship.

Gussy (Jannings)

We are very happy and are imbibing a bottle to your health.

Emil

Orvieto, 11/12

L.F.:

I am compromising Lavinia[1] a bit; we are traveling about together to hidden but wonderful places, like Orvieto,

Stefan

[1] Lavinia Mazzuchetti, Stefan's excellent translator and our good friend.

Carissima:

It's shameful that I never write you, but you know how it is when you are traveling about. We have had some very lovely and rewarding days and I'm returning renewed and thankful.

Your Lavinia

Florence, February 14th/37

I was to dinner at the Selden-Goth's in Florence today on the way through Florence with Lavinia, will stay two days in Milan, will see Maestro Toscanini and Wallmann[1] tomorrow, come back on Wednesday and will be in London about Friday.

Weather was glorious.

My best, St.

[1] Margaret Wallmann, the choreographer.

(London, 2/15 to Vienna, at Yella Hertzka's)

Just arrived by plane, found everything in excellent shape, so I can get right to work tomorrow—the only consolation under this gray sky. Maestro was grand as always, and Milan was better in other respects this time too, because I had things to do at the Ambrosiana. My best to Mama to whom I will write soon, and Mrs. Hertzka.[1]

Affectionately, Stefan

[1] The Advocate of peace, one of our best friends, the widow of Emil Hertzka; as the head of the *Universal Edition* she promoted the works of modern composers.

(From London to Vienna)

February 28th

L.F.:

Just received your airmail letter. I am awfully sorry about your sister and your poor health. Let's hope things will get better. As to Czokor, please, of course, get the thing going in my name. After all, he is one of the decentest of the lot. And there are so few friends left.

As to Johann [1] I don't know what to say. I have been fighting these three years not to have to keep the Salzburg house cluttering up my brain. That's why I wanted to get through with it at any cost. Johann is your affair. So please wind it up yourself.

I am lying low here; as yet nobody knows that I am here. I would like to get rid of the book [2] and back to my more important work.

Affectionately, and a happy recovery, with best,

Stefan

[1] Stefan's servant, who served us faithfully for seven years and about whose pension I wanted to talk to Stefan.   [2] *Magellan.* The next work was a novel entitled *Ungeduld des Herzens.*

(London, Hallam Str. to Vienna)

March 4th/37

L.F.:

I wanted to phone on Sunday, but summertime begins today and I didn't want to talk about things in a daze, right after waking up. Please, without fail, be at home between eight and nine this evening. After that I must visit the Salzburgers, at Franckenstein's. I talked with Paumgartner [1] at the concert. —I would very much like to leave in four or five days and spend two days in Salzburg, to get things in shape or to burn them up, call up Hinterberger,[2] then a few days in Vienna and so be back right after the coronation. I have a frightful lot to do, if I am to get finished before then, edit some other translations. When that is all done, I'll be ready for my own work— I pushed this book ahead because it might find a ready market; after that I could have a bit of leisure at last, especially if these various business matters stopped bearing down on me. I haven't had an hour for a walk these last weeks, not since Naples; at fifty-six I am starved for an interlude of not-being-harried from pillar to post.

[1] Bernhard Paumgartner, director of the Mozarteum, an excellent musician and a Mozart biographer. [2] The Viennese antiquary, Heinrich Hinterberger, a trustworthy business man and friend, to whom Stefan entrusted the sale of valuable books and auctioning off of manuscripts. My own situation, due to the proposed breakup, was approaching a crisis.

(London to Salzburg)

April 30th

L.F.:

I hope to arrive in Salzburg on the fifth. Will stop over at the "Traube"; [1] would like to have a simple midday meal at home, so as to waste no time, and not meet anyone. I hope that a fairly good part of the things will already have been sold. Perhaps you will set aside such of my clothes, underwear, etc., as are to be disposed of, from those I shall want to take with me.

I don't know whether you have kept up to date on the catastrophic developments of the last few days, for you are so preoccupied by Salzburg affairs. It is the greatest financial crash in years. People are completely stunned by their terrible losses, and moreover, there are dangerous political repercussions. You ought to be aware of this in Salzburg too. Today's newspapers report that half of all the reservations by Americans for trips abroad have been cancelled. Even people like Warburg are pessimistic—he has given up his house here and taken a flat, in order to be more footloose. So you see other people regard "security" differently from what you do. Please get as much as possible ready for me. I shall have a few difficult days. I have five or six meetings in Vienna, am battling with Reichner. On the whole it's a good thing that I'm leaving here. A whole host of my acquaintances will soon be arriving; also there is the threat today of a bus strike—a disaster in London. I was very wise to engage my seat in the plane fourteen days ago, as all accommodations for outgoing as well as incoming planes have been sold out.

1 Stefan wanted to stay in Salzburg at a hotel. He now made arrangements to have our joint affairs completely liquidated.

(To Kapuzinerberg, Salzburg)
                                    Hotel Regina, Vienna, about May 11th/1937
L.F.:
    I have just had word from Dr. M.¹ that you will call on him on Friday and that you and he will then definitely settle matters with my lawyer. I would come to this second meeting only if you particularly wanted me to be there. I hope you will be calm and clear-sighted; I shall try to be in a similar frame of mind, although the last few days have been very trying for me as well. My really sincere desire is that the settlement shall be made in an atmosphere of mutual trust and friendliness. As for me, I shall do my best.

                                                Affectionately, Stefan

1 I had chosen one of Stefan's friends for these negotiations, so that no quarrel should develop.

(To Kapuzinerberg, in Salzburg)
                                           Hotel Regina, May 12th/1937
Dear Fritzi:
    I wouldn't want you to think that this has been a happy hour for me—on the contrary, I am writing you after a sleepless night full of thoughts of the good time now gone forever. We both made mistakes and I would wish that things had

turned out differently.—By God, in my heart I feel only sorrow at this external parting which isn't an inner spiritual one at all as far as I am concerned, but rather, perhaps, a drawing closer together again, for we shall no longer be so harried by petty and disagreeable things. It is not conceit on my part when I say I know how terribly hard it will be for you to be without me—but your loss really isn't very great. I am no longer the same. I have become unsocial, introverted, one whose only pleasure now is in work. You know how many things I have put away from me; I realize it is my fault that the increasing silence and emptiness around me has tended to isolate me more and more; the blow dealt us by Germany has wounded us more deeply than you are aware of, and all things festive and joyous now seem weird and ghostlike. No, you won't be losing much and my inmost being is certainly not lost to you—I know exactly who you are.—Please believe me, I only want to see you content—and I wish your children all the luck in the world, also. If I sometimes was dissatisfied with them, that was because I didn't discern [in them] any of that burning eagerness to learn that both of us know so well and which was the glory of our youth. I repeat, there isn't a drop of bitterness in me toward you, only a great compassion. The present age depresses me horribly. Please forgive me because I spoilt many an hour for you by this sort of pessimism, but you know I couldn't take things lightly; and I have made it hard for others —aside from a few happy interludes—to be cheerful while they were with me. I beg of you, with all my heart, don't lose faith in me. I am full of faults and shortcomings, but one thing you know, that I have never forgotten a single human being whom I had ever become fond of, and how is it possible that I should be alienated from you, who were closest of all to me. You know how much I value friendship, that I never deny its obligations, even when friends have done me grievous wrong (as is the case with Roth just now).—Please never harbor the idea that you have somehow "lost" me, and don't pay any attention to people. If they condemn me, they are at least partially justified; for the rest, they don't know how much I have suffered in recent years because of the Salzburg situation.—But no one will pass adverse judgment on you, and whoever takes your part will be beloved of me and dear to me. (At the moment I loathe everybody who seeks to aggravate the tension between us.) I, for my part, almost believe it better that things have turned out as they did, although it has caused me much anguish; what does anything we still have to face in the future signify, after all? The best has gone beyond recall and we had it together; a lot of it was real happiness and I was blessed in my work. Let's think of this when we are depressed, and believe me, I am grateful to you for everything and am remembering it all now when the little bothers that often confuse us are forgotten. You too must forget how often I was unfair to you. Don't believe for an instant that I am lost to you, and think of me as your best friend—I hope to have many an opportunity of proving this to you; and forgive me for all the pain that this parting has caused you. Your grief is my grief too, and if I can be with you or aid you at any time, that will be a happy time for me, even though it may be overcast by melancholy. I want to thank you for everything and am not forgetting the good life we had together during all these years and will never forget it.

Ever yours, Stefan

(Since the arrangements between us didn't envisage a divorce, it seemed proper for me not to claim a separate domicile. After the old house had been sold in May, I leased a villa at Nonntal, in Salzburg, in my daughter's name and moved my own library of about 2,000 volumes, valuable books and furniture, carpets, silver, my personal belongings, after a part of the furnishings had gone on to London and a part had been sold, into this cottage. To welcome me in my new home, that was hardly a home, Stefan had sent me the original manuscript of the *Mailied* by Goethe which, however, didn't reach me till later when I was abroad. The rest of the contents of the old house were taken out of storage, when I didn't return to Austria, and confiscated by the Gestapo and sold at auction. However, the correspondence published in this book and the Romain Rolland and Rilke letters were rescued and hidden away by our dear friends, Magda Grasmayer and Josephine, which appeared to make it certain that these precious documents would eventually be gotten out of the country intact. To me the most precious of all the items taken by the Gestapo was the original manuscript, in Stefan's own handwriting, of *Jeremiah,* prefaced by the poem dedicating the play to me. My complete collection of his works including those of them that had been translated into other languages (about 600 volumes), which had been beautifully bound for me, with printed dedications, by Inselverlag, were taken by the Gestapo right after Hitler's invasion. The boxes filled with his notes, also in his own handwriting, for his various literary projects, and specially dedicated copies of his books, suffered the same fate.

I stayed in Paris until January 1938 with my daughter who was working there as a photographer; I wanted to meet Stefan after his trip to Portugal. I remained in Paris until the Germans came in. My attempt to bring Stefan's mother to Paris to stay with me proved unsuccessful. She died a year later in the house of her sons.

The following letters were nearly all written by Stefan from London and addressed to Salzburg where I had stayed, with the interval of a visit with him in Klosters, Switzerland, and in Vienna. I had intended to return from Paris to Austria but never did, as Hitler had by that time invaded Austria.)

(To Nonnthal, Salzburg)

London, 6/1

L.F.:

I haven't much time for a long letter. I didn't get out into the country, although I needed to *desperately*. That nervous breakdown hasn't run its course as yet. I am still tired all the time, and *distrait,* yet I have urgent jobs to get through.— Soon the proofreading will commence, and that will be in addition to my other work; you have no idea what a load I am carrying. Today, Sunday, when everyone else is weekending, I had to waste half a day going through maps for *Magellan* with an expert in this line. There is some sort of interruption every day, so that my real work suffers—it is too much for one person, especially if at the same time he is harassed by personal matters.

I invited Toscanini together with Franckenstein. Otherwise I would hardly have had a chance to see him as much as I should like to. I can't always be at the rehearsals, it takes too much time—six concerts alone mean six evenings. And I have to get together with the Brazilians at least once, and with Victor. I really need a little rest—just like what other people who travel for pleasure have, whereas my three trips every year to Austria are exhausting and nerve-wracking. I don't believe I shall go to Marienbad, even though it would do me a lot of good—it is really too far, because I would find the regular route via Germany impracticable and I can't pass Salzburg by and yet I don't want to stop over there either.

I would like to get away from here for a few days, but don't want to play hookey from the Toscanini concerts—and Bruno Walter is due again; he will have a hard time competing with T.

My affectionate best, Stefan

L.F.:

For the present there's no chance of a vacation; today, however, there was some relief; in the forenoon an hour at a Toscanini rehearsal, lunch at Lady Colfaxe's with Harold Nicholson and (as a surprise) Furtwaengler, afterward with Nicholson to the House of Commons, in the evening with Baroness Rothschild at the Toscanini concert (I gave my ticket away because she invited me). So it was a day devoted to "social life." Please, my best to Roth.

On the whole, I am beginning to recuperate—it was really time.

All my best, Stefan

Today *Schweigsame Frau* in Prague; it is to come to Vienna too.

(Excerpts from June and July letters of 1937)

Dear Fritzi:

Just received your airmail letter. Yes, now at last there must be an end to the tension between us. Your feeling of independence had become too pronounced—not that, from an intellectual point of view, you didn't have a right to it—but it was too much for me and I hadn't any strength left to go on with the subconscious struggle against it. Even at the very end of the settlement negotiations you couldn't trust me; perhaps you were right, for I don't trust myself either any more. I am getting to have doubts of myself, because I see how my oldest friends like Roth, Rolland, have become estranged (on account of political differences) and perhaps it is really difficult to get along with me.—The blow dealt me four years ago went deeper than you thought. It is better that it happened the way it did, that is my hope, for at least you have peace and security and, in addition, I swear to you, my most affectionate friendship, which will be proven to you far and away more effectively than in these dead letters.

I am very much exhausted, managed to listen to Walter's fine concert with only half an ear, Wallmann took me to the Philadelphia ballet, also saw Burghauser. Huebsch is here, I am having some long talks with him about new projects;

on top of that there will be, in the next few weeks, in addition to my regular work, the proofs of *Magellan* which I haven't looked at yet, and the proofs of the book of essays. I don't as yet know where I shall go after that. Perhaps, I'll have to pass through Vienna after all—and in that case we would meet toward the end of August or the middle of August. I have an idea that there are a lot of things that have to be thrashed out between us.

You haven't a notion of how much I have to do. Everything is getting to be more difficult and financially less productive.—I would like *so much* to concentrate altogether on the new book.

Affectionately, S.

July 4th

L.F.:

I am returning Leonhard's [1] moving letter. I telegraphed him at once to please wire me if he is arriving via Southampton by July 15th.—I have been trapped for a five-minute interview tomorrow on "Television"; they have a series there and it is quite amusing to talk to people who can see you but whom you can't see. All my engagements have unfortunately not been taken care of yet. I have to be at the Legation on Thursday at the reception for the Vienna Philharmonic, then to an evening benefit for Drinkwater's child (D. died poor as a beggar). And all the time proof corrections (which you can't take over), two new *Sternstunden,*[2] work on the new book, conferences about *Magellan,* which I have still to put in final shape. That's really quite a lot, but at least it helps one to half-forget *how* dangerous this era we live in is (much worse than before 1914). The newspapers here are very much wrought up, the exchanges in accelerating declines. I am glad I didn't go to the Pen Congress in Paris, despite the free plane flight and free stay there. It was held at an unlucky time. As to our being together this summer, I shall give you a date as soon as I can look ahead a bit.

Affectionately, St.

[1] Leonhard Adelt, who was badly hurt in the smash-up of the Eckener dirigible in New York; he had written me a very detailed report of the

tragedy and asked for our news.   [2] His most successful historical short
stories

L.F.:

It's symbolic how all these things pile up on me this
year at the same time and inconveniently for me. I received
a letter today from Leonhard saying that he is passing through
Southampton on the fifteenth. Now I wanted to leave on the
fifteenth.—I suddenly got the book [1] from Roth. I had just
written him about it. It is really remarkable how his brain has
remained intact. He is the same great artist that he always was;
perhaps the material has lost some of the freshness and
novelty that it formerly had. It does really seem as if he might
still be saved. R. needs a dragoon of a wife and not all those
others who encourage him in his alcoholism.

I gave the letter to Huebsch. We are on very cordial
terms, but only meet once or twice a week, because we are
both too busy.

Affectionately, St.

[1] The story *Das Falsche Gewicht.*

July 7th

L.F.:

I wanted to let you know right away that I have made
a reservation for the morning of the sixteenth for the trip to
Marienbad; but, I am sorry to say it isn't at all certain that
I can leave by then, because the political situation is so
dreadful—any moment now things may take a very different
turn. The Spanish conflict is a continuing danger to world
peace.

Fuchs,[1] modest as ever, is here, and we are working
hard together. He is your loyal adherent and the very model
of discretion. Let me take this opportunity to tell you that
in case of my death (and not before) he will hand you a
(sealed) letter which will contain various dispositions and
arrangements on your behalf which I don't want known in
certain quarters just now. You can always rely on him. Perhaps he will travel via Salzburg. It was sweet of you to invite
him. But I implore you, don't be too improvident with your

invitations, (although I know it's none of my business). You are too sincere, too spontaneous and never realize how great are the burdens you assume.

Affectionately, S.

1 His trusted assistant from Salzburg who was at this time with the publishing house of Reichner. I never got the letter mentioned.

L.F.:

Unfortunately I am no better off than you—I get tired easily. I need more time than I used to, because nowadays I can't work more than two hours at a stretch without stopping for a rest.—A second sympton, one that frightens me: two days after meeting people, I don't recognize them any more. Thirdly, my English is much worse than it was three years ago. I, like almost everybody else, have been very much distracted by current developments. Yet I must give my work the utmost concentration if I am to maintain its quality. So, I feel terribly exhausted. I couldn't endure anything like festival performances.

Affectionately, S.

L.F.:

Thanks a lot for your fine letter. I am leaving on Friday, will send my address from Marienbad, but our meeting will not be until we are in Switzerland. You won't admit that Salzburg has been a nightmare to me for the last four years and that I can't bear it there.—And especially now, with all the prying and gossip.—I have had a sweet letter from Asch. The situation seems to be improving a bit. Do take *good* care of yourself.

Affectionately, S.

Marienbad, Villa Souvenir, 7/17
L.F.:

I had a very fast trip to Prague by plane, visited with Max Brod a few hours. Marienbad is madly overcrowded. I went right away to see Dr. Auerbach, but don't start with the "cure" till later, because I am fearfully tired and I am not dangerously overweight. I want to live in complete retirement and to work, and not overdo the "cure."

All my best, Stefan

(After Stefan's stay in Marienbad, we were together for a time in Luzerne. Stefan then spent some time in Tessin and then returned to London. We met two more times, in Paris. The letters of the period that followed, including those in which he notified me of his marriage (the fall of 1939), were lost in various ways. Those which I received during my stay in Paris and some of which were concerned with the business of our divorce, I entrusted, before our flight to the south of France, to a Frenchman who, in turn, handed them over to a friend for safe-keeping. The latter, for fear of the Nazis, burned them. Only two postcards have survived. In the meantime Stefan had bought a house in Bath and installed his new household there. This house reminded him of the Kapuziner establishment. He wrote me that it was about time that we saw each other again, and that his guest room was ready for me. With the help of our friend Julien Cain, and that of the organizer of the Conferences des Ambassadeurs I secured permission for Stefan to make a trip to Paris; on this occasion we met in harmony and with perfect understanding. He selected Vienna of the past as the subject of his lecture, and spoke with affection of his native city. His radio talk also evoked considerable sentimental reactions. He addressed his talk to his friends over there who were condemned to silence. The postcards below were written a short time after this, our last meeting.)

1 9 4 0

(From Bath, England to Croissy, Seine-et-Oise)

(In French)

L.F.:

At last your letter of May sixteenth received. I hope you can stay at Croissy. And the children? I am waiting for news from you. Poor Otto Pick is dead. I am afraid it was suicide. Robert Naumann is in a concentration camp; one can no longer help anybody. And it is all pretty unimportant, compared with the big things that are happening. Tell me whether you can stay and whether a first of July money remittance to Croissy would still be possible. Werfel and Trebitsch [1] are already at Vichy. As for me, I have an offer for a lecture tour in South America, but you know I am in two minds about that. I know nothing about Landauer; [2]

nobody can do anything any more. The main thing is "ueber-stehen" [to survive] to quote Rilke. Kind regards,

Stefan

1 Siegfried Trebitsch the author, and translator of Shaw.   2 The pub-lisher, later killed by the Nazis.

(To Croissy)

Bath, Lyncombe Hill, June 5th/1940

Dear F.:

Thanks for your letter. I dare not now even think of all our friends. Now you will understand my sadness; I have always felt that the war hadn't begun yet. I have offers to lecture in South America and people seem to think I ought to take it on. As for me, I don't like the idea very much, not because of the perils of the trip, but because I feel tired out. And it is such fine weather here. But if I decide to do it, I'll let you know at once. The prospect of leaving home and my books and the projects I have begun, for an indefinite period, is not an agreeable one, but everything is hard nowa-days for everybody. Don't say anything to our friends because it's only a possibility, and who can make plans in these times?

Your faithful, Stefan Zweig

Three days before the Germans entered Paris we succeeded, as if by a miracle, in getting away into the South, to Montauban, in the vicinity of Toulouse. At that time I didn't know whether Stefan had already left England or not, nor where he was. In the town in which we had taken refuge a group of seasoned Austrian and German Social Democrats were congregated; they were certain that some sort of rescue project would be launched. A report reached me that Hermann Kesten and Erica Mann had organized a committee in New York to bring refugee intellectuals and writers whose lives were in danger, to the United States, and that I had been chosen to serve on this committee. He, Kesten, meanwhile had been joined by Stefan, who at the time was stopping over in New York en route to South America. Stefan obtained my address from my nieces in New York and sent me a number of cables. Here are his first telegram and letter to Montauban.

(In French)

Have done everything possible to have American and Mexican visas delivered near future in Marseilles. Necessary to go there under all circumstances.

Zweig

Also, at his request, Antonio Ferro, a high Portuguese official, sent a telegram which assured us of the right to cross over into Portugal.

Here is the first letter, dated July thirtieth, sent from New York, Hotel Windham.

(Also in French)
Dear F.:

Today I read your letter of the thirtieth of July to Monath [1] and sent you three cables to reassure you and let you know that we have put you (with your two daughters) on the list forwarded to Washington.—Perhaps I shall get visas for all of you at Rio. It will be easier to wait there because it is twice as cheap as New York—prices here are ruinous. I don't know how long I shall stay. Perhaps I'll have to go to Chile and Venezuela. Will I ever get to see my house, my books, manuscripts, my notes again? I have left *everything* behind. I wasn't even able to take my working notes [2] along with me.

It is terribly hot, but everything is better here than elsewhere. I know how you must feel—alas, your optimism will always be disappointed in this world and even my pessimism has been surpassed by actual events. Try to be strong—perhaps everything will turn out well.

Your old Stefan

[1] Husband of my niece, Dr. Paul Monath.   [2] Balzac biography.

(Also French)

c/o Viking Press, 18 East 48th Street
Dear F.:

We have tried everything. Possibly a few special visas will be granted; I tried to get one for you and, if possible, for your daughters (which is more difficult, for the visas are for writers only). If only I could manage to bring you over, the other matter would be easier—not very easy, for I haven't been able to get a visitor's visa even for myself, but merely a transit visa which expires in three weeks. I have had you put on all the lists of people for whom visas are being requested, and one of them will certainly come through, I hope. As for me, I must travel on to deliver lectures in South America and I don't know whether I can come through here

313

when I return. I am worn out and I dream of my house, my books, my work.

I shall also inquire what can be done in Brazil and the other countries I am going to. I beg you to realize that if there is a delay, don't think it is our fault. What a life!

Regards, Stefan

Meanwhile I had made sure of visas to Mexico for myself, my daughters and sons-in-law and a large group of artists, by applying to the Mexican Ambassador when he passed through Montauban. Also in Marseilles I succeeded in getting my sons-in-law entered on the list of the Emergency Rescue Committee, a list that had been approved by President Roosevelt. (My daughters had both married friends of their youth in France).

(Also in French)

New York, August 8th
Dear F.:

I received your letter just before leaving. My next address is Rio, Edition Guanabara.—I applied for a visitor's visa for you as a writer. Schalom Asch will make the affidavit. I am almost certain that I can obtain five visas for you for Brazil when I get there. I am sure my friends Jaime Chermont and Caio Mello-Franco in the Foreign Office will help me. Only I don't know whether you want to go there.—I have lecture tours in Uruguay, Chile, Argentine, Venezuela.—In the last analysis I have a horror of these enormous journeys. Forgive this letter being altogether about practical affairs, but it's essential to be clear and precise. Paul and your nieces promised me they would do everything you told them to.

Regards, Stefan

(Also French)

Hotel Paysandú, Rio (until October 15th) to Lisbon, Sept. 18th/40
Dear F.:

I trust that when you receive this letter you will already have received from the Libraria Civilazao [1] and Paul whatever is needed to permit you to stay in Lisbon and even permission to leave. I know how difficult everything must be down yonder, but one has to be satisfied with a minimum of personal liberty. I have no reason to complain about things here, the city is magnificent, I am overwhelmed with invitations, but, alas, the heat begins here toward the end of

October—except for that Brazil would be a paradise. I have visited your brother once and will see him again the first day I am free. I heard about the death of Arnold; [2] it might have been better for him if he had stayed in Europe, that's still a good place to die in, but not for living. I am practically certain that everything I have in England, my books, my manuscripts, my savings will be lost, but I had at least one good year free of daily terror and I hope to spend my last years somewhere—God knows where? I hope to have news from you—and good news at that.

Your Stefan

[1] Stefan's publisher in Portugal who, while I was staying there, acquired the rights to my biography of Pasteur. [2] My beloved brother, an excellent physician and humanitarian, Dr. Arnold Burger. Another, older brother, was living in Rio at this time. Stefan was very much attached to him.

(Also in French)
Dear F.:

I am writing this in a hurry. I am lecturing here, then about the middle of October at Buenos Aires, Montevidéo, then to Chili; in January I hope to be in New York, and my present dream is to get back into England.—If you have a free day you should take the autobus to Cintra—the gardens there are an unforgettable sight and one has need of a bit of beauty in this world filled with disaster. My lectures are well paid so that I can live decently from their proceeds and return to New York.

I am happy to know that you are safe; I am waiting impatiently for your letters. I want to know where you are going—unfortunately one is a foreigner [1] everywhere and you will miss Europe just as we all do.

Your Stefan

[1] A curious paradox now developed. Stefan while abroad became homesick for Austria, while my children and I soon felt quite content in the United States where we were never treated as foreigners.

Rio, Sept. 26th
L.F.:

I have just been at Teresopolis for eight days boarding in a Czechoslovak *pension* where I was ruined by a diet of dumplings, ham patties, roast chicken. One can escape the heat up yonder.—I had hoped to have some word from you here in Rio; I am leaving by plane today for Buenos—doubtless you sent your letter there direct. It is unlikely that you'll get an answer to it from me, because it's going to be a madhouse down there. Yesterday I lectured here in French, two Spanish lectures for Buenos (and in a few other places), one in English, one in German, and a dozen people are lying in wait for me; all in all nine lectures in fourteen days, at Cordoba, Rosario, Montevideo among other places. It will be hard work, but after that an end to this lecture business for a long time. These big social affairs play havoc with my power of concentration. I only occasionally get a chance even to think of work on my books, which is my real job. I hope to be back here by the seventeenth of Nov. and then shall work for a whole month, then perhaps to New York in January. There isn't any sense making plans for more than four weeks ahead.

With my affectionate best, St.

(To Paris)

Buenos Aires, October 30th

L.F.:

In great haste. Yesterday my first lecture in Spanish was delivered under very trying, though rather flattering circumstances. The hall, jam-packed with 1500 people, was literally stormed, so that at first 3,000 people crowded into it and the police had to be called in. I was urged to repeat the lecture, and the hall is already nearly sold out. In fact, it's a sensation here, an author talking in Spanish, and, wonder of wonders, I spoke well. The audience was fantastic—crowded close together, no hemming or hawing, not a sound. After it was over I was shut up in a reading room to protect me from all the people. I felt as if I were a tenor.

But a more important matter: I may perhaps have a chance to obtain two or three visas here in a few days and when I talk to the important person who wants to meet me, I'll request them for Landshoff and Landauer. If I succeed, I'll telegraph you right away care of Kesten. As to Chili, I may be able to do something about that in Rio; I am acquainted with the Consul there: the poetess Gabriella Mistral.—I still have to do a radio talk today, and in the evening a lecture in English.

All my best, St.

Just this minute Alfredo **Cahn** phones me that he can sell your *Pasteur* at a price that would be considered good in this country.

Santa Fé, Nov. 9th/1940

Your letter was forwarded to me in Buenos. Alfredo **Cahn** has been traveling with me. The whole thing is fantastic— you speed by auto (after an all-night train trip) over the pampas without seeing a house and meet perhaps a few children riding to school (everybody travels horseback: there are still hundreds of thousands of horses here and they cost between three and six dollars apiece). The most trying thing, however, is the hospitality—a renowned author from Europe who not only ventures into the interior, but, what is more exciting, lectures in Spanish, is to them a unique phenomenon. You have to go through with it all—meet the local bigwigs; the Jews arrange special receptions in every little town and some of them come in from distant points traveling five and six hours. But what moves me most is the common people.— The barbers won't take any money, the waiters won't accept any tips; every Tom, Dick and Harry recognizes me in the street, because they have seen the innumerable snap-shots of me.—I am so weary, not from riding, but because of this constant Spanish-talking, which is as deadly as chopping wood. For that reason I begged off Uruguay. But they misinterpreted my motives and doubled my fee and offered me an airplane to accommodate three people for the round trip, so I've got to go there on the thirteenth, have to do a radio talk on the fourteenth, and fly back the next morning (eight hours) to Rio. It's a miracle how I do it, at fifty-nine, and in addition the interviews in Spanish, and the lectures often begin at ten o'clock in the evening and finish at one o'clock. However, the net return, not to speak of the moral values, is considerable, but it would have been easier for me to have earned the money by working quietly at home. The fall of France, after

317

Italy, Holland, Rumania, Norway, etc., etc., is truly shattering. —I suppose no one else had become so influential as a writer, internationally—not to speak of Germany [as I]—and now all that is wrecked by this mentally deranged creature.

I can't send anything to U. I can't single out individuals any more. I have delivered two lectures here, each yielding a net of three hundred dollars, which I donated to English and German philanthropies; this is more than I, in view of my present circumstances, can afford. You will guess from your own loss in pounds,[1] what a beating I have taken, and now that I am cut off from all languages, or at least most, the prospects of earning a living are dim. My chief worry at present is about whether I can work in Brazil during the hot season. This lecture tour was, after all, a duty tour. From now on I would prefer not to do anything more of the kind and to work only for and by myself. Everything else is vanity and waste of time.

Affectionately, S.

The Argentine is somehow exciting because of its super-abundance which cries for more people—a liter of milk costs a cent. Hundreds of thousands could live on what they throw away here, and they won't let anybody into a country like this that is bursting with a wealth of everything.

[1] Because I was making my escape on the very day when I would have had to exchange my pounds, I lost a good part of the money which I had set aside to keep me going.

On the train, in bed by two, and got up at seven
I have just returned from Rosario; the entire trip was a remarkable experience; it could easily turn one's head. A whole caravan of autos came from Santa Fé to Rosario to the lecture; they wanted to listen to me again; among them was the Provincial Minister, all the government officials—they surely couldn't have gotten back home again before four o'clock in the morning. Now I still have La Plata before me for tomorrow. I am on exhibit, in all the movies in Buenos Aires at the same time as I am lecturing.

All this would have been gratifying, but, unfortunately, my pleasure has turned to ashes. I had, in these, my later years, acquired a wonderful friend in Rio, Hernandez Catá, the distinguished Spanish author and Cuban minister—he came to pay me a visit on my first day in Rio, and we saw each other practically every day thereafter. He was of a wonderful humanity, nobility and goodness, such as I have seldom encountered in any other human being; his wife, his daughter were like sisters to me. At the very time I was lecturing in Santa Fé, he was killed in a plane crash while returning from Sao Paulo—I was really plunged into despair. For perhaps I was to blame: I told the people in Sao Paulo that they ought to invite him to lecture there, he was a splendid speaker, and on his return trip after his lecture, the horrible accident occurred. Ernst Weiss's suicide has also hit me hard, he was a close friend and I had managed to keep his head above water for years. Always the decentest! the best! To cap it all, the news that Russia and Germany have reached an agreement.—What more can the future hold for us? I believe I shall never return to this Europe, and everything of mine there, my books, and above all my *Balzac* (three-quarters written and put in shape) is lost, as well as the countries where I had won a footing, for the English and American world is not my own world after all. And this hotel existence destroys all possibility of working.—At any rate, I have secured permission for permanent residence in Brazil, in order to have one country where I needn't be constantly begging for a visa. As yet all the South American countries are open to me, all of them want me to come, but that can all change suddenly, as in France, where only four months ago I was an important gentleman and today am outlawed, I and all my books.—The people here were really touching; women told me, with tears in their eyes, that they had never dreamed of meeting me in their provincial towns. Some came from their ranches eight hours away. The hotels refused to take my money. I had autos at my disposal everywhere, and received presents.

(To New York)

Hotel Central, Rio de Janeiro, Nov. 16th/1940

L.F.:

I got here after an eight-hour flight, am living in a different hotel because here I have a terrace overlooking the sea. Today is a day of rest; work begins tomorrow. I brought along with me a jolly film which was being shown in all the movies there, me, in person, delivering my lectures, and also a pile of newspapers. For your especial consideration: I observe how differently we have been developing.—You are becoming more and more active, meet thousands of people, while I, for my part, breathe a sigh of relief if I can just sit quietly in my room and ward off everything. I warn you, don't get to be the whole world's dogooder. There won't be much difficulty about Masereel; he is a Belgian and a Christian; but will he be able to live here?—For the present I don't want to go to New York, I am afraid I should find all Berlin, Vienna, etc., there. I'd rather cope with the heat here. But please, don't you save the world, but look out for yourself and yours—nowadays, believe me, this is a big enough job.

Affectionately, S.

Nov. 30th/1940

L.F.:

First and foremost, my congratulations on your birthday. You still have two years to go before your sixtieth, while I am seeing my fifties for the last time. When I recently had to apply to the police for an identity card, the pretty young lady wrote on it: "Hair gray." No wonder.

You don't understand the Balzac [1] mess. How can 600 pages of *German* manuscript, 2,000 pages of notes and 40 annotated books be gotten past the censor? If the house is blitzed, then a lot of other things will go too—correspondence, contracts, my own books, the manuscript collection.—Everything I own has been wiped out by the currency depreciation anyway. No "salvaging" possible now. And things are going badly indeed. *The Tide of Fortune* has not appeared in England, because Casell's entire fall output, inclusive of my fully printed book, was at the bindery when the latter was destroyed during an air raid.

I don't care about German books at present and shall wait until this chaos is over. The main thing now is to work. I shall certainly write your publisher Scherz about *Marie Antoinette* but *The Tide of Fortune* is identical with *Stern-*

stunden and belongs, in part at least, to other publishing houses.

I have never ceased having a deep sympathy for the refugees, have given them more help than most everybody else. The fact is, I can stand only just a limited amount of sociability. It exhausts me to see five, six people a day and this prevents me (Paris was an instance) from seeing the people and things that *I* want to see. The telephone rang from early till late at night in New York and Buenos Aires; what I am afraid of is that people terribly overestimate what I can do for them: I am asked to get Huebsch to take this book or that, arrange about newspapers, etc., etc. Certainly when I *can* do something, I do it of my own free will. I now am acquainted with from 200 to 300 people in New York; all of them would be hurt if I didn't get to see them. I must, because of increasing exhaustion, salvage at least half of every day for my own affairs. After all I have business with my publisher, the dentist, other errands in New York—it's impossible to see everybody; and they call that snobbishness. I haven't acquired Mann's shrewd time-economy; he gets rid of each visitor inside of an hour.—All my people stay at least three hours.

I wangled Argentine visas for Landshoff and Landauer; it wasn't easy. But how are they to get over? You have to have lived in England to realize that this is the most horrible siege in the world's history. None of you have any conception of it. You don't understand that nothing like it has ever been known. It is more horrible than in the trenches, because after six or eight days you were relieved and brought back to safe quarters and sleep. But in England there is no interlude for recuperation, rest.—It is gradually getting warmer here. But Rio is magnificent, so one can endure it for the time being. The beauty, the variety of this city are indescribable, you can never see all of it. If the heat doesn't become intolerable, I shall stay till the end of January.

My affectionate best, Stefan

1 I constantly advised that he have the Balzac manuscript sent him. Working on it would immediately have distracted him. It finally arrived, eight days after the tragic end.

L.F.:

There isn't much to write about; it is getting hot and that, paradoxically, induces thoughts of Christmas greetings: all my best, therefore, in case I shouldn't write again soon. One way or another, I must go down to Bahia again, "only six hours" by plane. As soon as I have finished the little book on Brazil, I shall want a good library for the *Autobiography* and will go to some small university not more than two hours from New York. I'll no doubt have to "X" out my house, my books, and manuscripts. Bristol is being bombarded daily and we aren't any further away from it than Brooklyn, indeed much closer. But at any rate, I salvaged my own old bones. All of which is so horrible that I wouldn't want to see any people. Of all my friends I have had no word— Victor, Warburg, Felix and so many others still in that inferno. Mail has been at a complete standstill for weeks. One couldn't help them anyhow. I find people who can make or talk "literature" nowadays incomprehensible; it seems to me to be a shortcoming of human nature rather than a virtue (but perhaps art is really always conditioned by such shortcomings).

My affectionate best, S.

Hotel Central, Rio (but don't send any more mail here)
12/31/1940
L.F.:

I must hurry! It has become terribly hot, which interferes with work, but has one advantage, I am losing weight. I am leaving for Bahia during this greatest of hot spells, also to Pernambuco, Belem (on the Amazon River), where I shall stay for ten days (I need it for the book, and after all the expensive trip to the frontier is free). Then slowly to New York—not all of a sudden, for it is dangerous to jump from 107 degrees above to 5 below.

Now to New York. I have a dreadful lot to do there for the first few days. I shall see you of course; shall get in touch with you as soon as I arrive at the end of the month. I am pretty well exhausted by this furious traveling about in unendurable monkey heat, and so let me tell you right off: although I always used to be ready and willing, now I can't do anything for anybody. I need this one, scant week to get myself settled, because unless I have at least two months by myself, I won't be able to go on. I prefer to tell you this straightaway and beforehand. Please don't let anyone know that I am coming.—I paid your brother a visit yesterday; he seems happy and content.—So I hope I'll be able to come; but one can never tell from week to week what may happen and I beg you to understand me when I say that during these few days in New York, and after all these exhausting experiences, I shall not be at all sociable.

Affectionately, Stefan

(Now something strange happened that made a deep impression on both of us and seemed to be evidence of the almost mystical bond between us— another one of those inexplicable encounters that began with our childhood and were repeated throughout our later years. As I and my daughter Susi went, in this city of seven million, to the English consulate to get a navycert for the luggage that was being shipped us, and came out of one of the elevators, there, waiting to get into it, stood Stefan. He had arrived just an hour before. We hadn't expected him until a week later.)

The Wyndham, 42 West 58th Street, New York
Thursday, Jan. 23, 1941

L.F.:

It was astonishing to meet like that the first thing after my leaving the airplane—while I was on the way to notify the English consul, as in duty bound, of my arrival.

I am like one utterly shattered; had to get up at four: thirty every day for the last ten days, traveling to catch the plane, then the trip into the interior, the frontier red tape, the receptions—last night traveled by plane, without a spot where I could lie down, from Miami. I'd already flown from the northernmost tip of Brazil, leaving from there at six in the morning, and flying until five o'clock. (Another plane, making the same flight according to what I have read, was wrecked.) This is a travel record that I don't ever want to chalk up again. Because I have arrived ahead of time, nobody knows I am here, and I earnestly beg you to tell nobody that I *am* here, *nobody*—and there are to be no exceptions. I need a couple of days to get established here; these quarters are only temporary and I want to get settled somewhere. Perhaps

you will telephone me Sunday.—In three days, traveled three
times as far as to Europe and back!

Affectionately, Stefan

Hotel Taft, New Haven, Conn.
February, 1941

L.F.:

Thanks a lot for the letter and the notes. I am plenty
busy here; visited Thornton Wilder yesterday; tomorrow
Landshoff is coming for a conference.

Affectionate best, Stefan

L.F.:

I am living here quietly, see no one, in this rather
old-fashioned hotel, and I appreciate the library card which
allows me not only to pick out the books that I want, but
also to take them home with me. I am sending on one copy
of the short story and would like Alix to make three copies
on thin paper, which can be sent by air mail. I want to send
them to the last countries left me, Sweden and the Argentine.—
The opportunity for you to take out your "First Papers"
won't be too long delayed I imagine; the Mexican visa ought
to be important in getting you permission to reenter.[1]

I hope to recuperate a bit while I am here; books are
better company than humans just now and I have had to
do without them for a long time.

With my best, Stefan

[1] This refers to the fact that if you are a visitor, you have to leave the
United States and come back as an immigrant, if you want to stay permanently.

I have had news from London that my good friend Max
Herrmann Neisse is dead—all younger than I.

Affectionately, Stefan

(New Haven to New York)

March 3rd, 1941

L.F.:

I can't write very much. It is bitter cold outside and
the rooms are devilishly overheated, and this comes right

after the tropics. I had some important things to do in New York, but must postpone them. The blessing and consolation here is the library. I have lapsed into a rather gloomy mood. The only compensation is that I don't have to listen to those idiotic optimistic blowhards.—I am terribly clear about what is going to happen in Europe in the next few weeks. This will be the most frightful year in all history and everybody who, unlike the great majority, is not lucky enough to be able to ignore whatever doesn't touch his immediate interest, is suffering horribly. I *know* what is going to happen now and that, at times, upsets me fearfully.

It's a good thing that I have hit upon a little job [1] (almost a scientific research) unrelated to anything else; any other type of subject would be impossible just now, but this has an insulating effect. I see few people here, although several wanted to visit me.—I don't like to see or be seen when I am in this kind of mood.

Please pay Alix eight dollars for me. It's possible I'll be able to give her some work, since there is a lot to copy and correct.

Affectionately, S.

[1] *Amerigo Vespucci.*

Dear Fritzi:

I was in New York for only a few hours to a conference with Huebsch and Romains. They are planning some sort of big banquet for the International Pen Club, to give it a better standing. I haven't gone out for a walk for days, actually not for weeks, was to a fine play for which Viertel [1] did the sets, and will be at Van Loon's on Friday and Bermann-Fischer's (in Old Greenwich).

Kind regards, Stefan

[1] Berthold Viertel, the poet and producer.

March 13th/41

L.F.:

I have just learnt through indirect channels that my dear Erwin Rieger has died—I was always wondering about never receiving any answers to my letters. He was uphappy to the point of losing his mind, in Tunis, and perhaps his death wasn't brought on by natural causes. The space about me is rapidly thinning out and I say to myself that Roth [1] and all of them were perhaps the cleverest. His last years were really tragic, he was another "exceptional case." Did he finish his autobiography? As far as I am concerned all that is a part of the past, something that has vanished.—He was always faithful to me and a true friend. Probably Scheyer is also on the other side by now. I hope the Friedmann [2] business will go through successfully. Here, of course, he is considered old already, because he is fifty-six.—The Jules Romains are coming on Saturday.

Affectionately, S.

[1] Stefan was of the opinion that Roth's drinking was rooted in a suicidal complex.   [2] Prof. Wilhelm Friedmann; Mme. Henri Focillon was trying to get him into the country as an immigrant. Because of mistaken identity, similarity of names, his visa was delayed and he fell victim to the Nazis in France.

L.F.:

The death roll grows from day to day. Oscar Loerke has died in Berlin. All younger than I.

I wouldn't worry about the confiscation.[1] It is almost better to lose everything right off than to battle to keep it and then lose it at last anyway—I have written off everything of mine in England, too.

I go out very little, I can't talk to people about the hideous state of things: America will be late coming in. Everywhere they put faith in the same mistaken idea that one can stay out of it by just keeping quiet. We have to get used to living in chaos till the very end. The younger generation will just have to cope with the new conditions by itself.

Best, Stefan

I shall telephone you in the next few days.

[1] The reference is to the auctioning off by the Gestapo of all my property and mementos.

(While Stefan was in New Haven and later, when he was in New York, we exchanged letters almost daily, indeed much oftener than we phoned each other or met. We communicated with each other most frequently about the agonized pleas we both of us received, begging us to bring friends from Europe to the States. I ran errands for Stefan to various offices and managed to persuade him to speak at a well-attended dinner for the benefit of the Emergency Rescue Committee; this brought in a good deal of money for the rescue work and also helped some few of our own "clients." Milton Koblitz gave us more effective support than anyone else. He had given up his law practice so that he could devote himself to helping needy [refugee] intellectuals and artists, in the States; and all of this he has continued to do to this day, serving entirely without compensation.)

(The following are excerpts from various letters)

L.F.:

That lecture, although only ten minutes long (indeed because of that) isn't at all easy, for I *will* not say a word that could be interpreted as urging American's entry into the war, not a word that foretells "victory," nothing that would be a justification of war or exalts it, and yet I must at the same time give the thing an optimistic twist. But I couldn't get out of it, and who knows what mischief someone else taking my place might not do.—I hope you had a pleasant trip. I remember the picture gallery in Boston with pleasure.

Best, Stefan

L.F.:

You needn't have any regrets about the dinner.[1] I dread it, because they will make a "collection" which I feel is unworthy of the occasion. I shall speak only for the European radio, not the radio here. Then, of course, the whole affair is tied up with a rat-tail appendage of conditions. The "Leftists" think they aren't sufficiently represented. Wherever you touch human vanity there you discover how shabby human beings are. I tried to give up my "part" to someone who is more vainglorious than I and has less "disgust" for such theatricals— it is horrible to know what really goes on behind the scenes of these ballyhoo affairs.

This week is, unfortunately, full, but I shall be with you very soon.

Affectionately, Stefan

[1] I felt it would be more tactful if I stayed away from the dinner.

L.F.:

I scarcely see anyone these difficult days; it's all too horrible to talk about and I can't stand people who are always wanting to have other countries and races fighting for them and yet won't lift a finger to help anyone else, or make a single sacrifice. I shall see Milton Koblitz about Lucka [1] next week, the money for the trip must still be gotten together and so I must bring my own influence and the influences of whomsoever I can enlist into play.

Stefan

I would like to see Beer-Hoffman and Roda, Toscanini, all old friends, but can't bring myself to it.

[1] The Austrian philosopher and writer, Emil Lucka.

New York, The Wyndham, May 1941

L.F.:

I am having a cocktail party for our Austrian and German friends next Wednesday, June 4th, here at Hotel Wyndham, and want to inform you that you are most cordially invited.

Received a letter here from Victor which should interest you. I am sending him a food package and am having some money forwarded to him—but what a life!

My affectionate best, Stefan

I shall visit Koblitz Friday in Atlantic City.

(I had moved to Ossining on the Hudson early that summer. Our friends, René and Erika Fueloep-Miller and Albrecht Schaeffer were living in nearby Croton, where the latter's wife had a children's home in which a young relative of Stefan's was boarding. Stefan rented a pretty villa in Ossining; one of his reasons for doing so was that he could confer with me there about various details he wanted for *Die Welt von Gestern* (his autobiography), details he no longer could recall himself, and, no doubt, also because he wanted to be near me. We visited each other, and my children were made welcome too. Because he was harassed by a terrible restlessness and had the status only of a visitor in the States, he cut short his stay even before he needed to have; he sought peace, unfortunately in vain, in Brazil where he was so warmly accepted.)

(Last letter from New York, before the stay in Ossining)

July 24th

L.F.:

I have just had two phone calls from Monju Scheyer's niece; she told me about a plan to have the Red Cross in

Switzerland get him out of the camp in Orleans where he has been since May. We shall have to make another attempt to do something about Masereel. Hermann Broch will bring further pressure to bear on the Emergency Comm. We must also try to push Koblitz into doing something about Lucka. And now, after today, Ossining, 7 Ramapo Rd. God grant that I can work there for the next two months without being interrupted. This daily piling up of other people's worries onto one's own gradually wears one down. I hope your affairs are gradually getting into shape; as for mine, for the moment I don't even want to mention them; I regret each wasted hour. But first, back to work, perhaps my last spell of work— who knows? There are so many things yet to be faced in the dreadful future.

Affectionately, St.

On Board S.S. *Uruguay*, August 20th/41

L.F.:

I am writing this en route. Very calm trip. I am only just becoming aware of how tired I was, because I loaf around practically all day. But I am on the mend now that we have left New York, also feel spiritually freer.—The thought of having to sit out another war as a foreigner has depressed me horribly. I have had to do that once before—and you had to, too. It is difficult to get accustomed to living always without any rights at all, although we have been getting lessons in this art for more than twenty-five years. I haven't spoken to anyone on the ship as yet, except Mrs. Wiener, Morgenthau's sister; I had already met her. I hope your affair [1] will come through very soon; I know how important it might be for you in the near future and I would very much want you to have a settled domicile; it would be a haven of peace for you.

Affectionately, Stefan

[1] Our immigration.

Sept. 10th/1941

L.F.:

I have just come from your brother's and am taking the opportunity offered by a mail steamer sailing tomorrow to send you this letter. I am feeling spiritually much better here, because the landscape is indescribly lovely, the people charming, Europe and the war farther away. If there were a good library it would be good to live here, although prices are going up noticeably, and national feeling is becoming more touchy. The turning point is my resolve to rent a little house in Petropolis, whose chief feature (for me the decisive feature) is a gigantic veranda. I hope acquiring even this shadowy status of a resident will be good for me. Petropolis is a little Semmering, only more primitive, like the Salzkammergut of anno 1900, the hotels and houses in about the same category except for the chateaux. As yet there isn't any large middle class here, you have either very rich or very modestly circumstanced people. It is an hour and forty minutes by bus or train from the city. So I can last out the hot summer, and who wants to make plans beyond March and April. I want to work the autobiography over and begin something new.[1] Meanwhile you have doubtless received the book about Brazil which, you will be surprised to hear was not considered enthusiastic enough by the local people—they don't like the very features of the country we like, and are much prouder of their factories and cinemas than of the marvelous colorfulness and simple, natural way of life. If they had one of those libraries from up yonder, it would be paradise. Well, for a time at least one can cut down one's reading to Shakespeare and the like. I regret not having the Fueloeps and Hermann Broch here from America. But now the main thing is to survive this era.—News from France and, indeed, generally, emphasizes the fact that eating and sleeping peacefully are great achievements. You simply have to reduce your standards to absolute zero, forget who you were, what you wanted, and be utterly modest in your demands. You'll soon have news from Petropolis—no matter how primitive, at least for five months no more living in hotels, no more looking at stacked-up luggage!

My very best to you all,

Stefan

[1] *Die Schachnovelle. (The Royal Game.)*

330

L.F.:

Migrated here without mishap. It is a tiny house, but has a big, covered terrace and wonderful view, plenty cool, considering it is winter, and the town is beautifully deserted, like Ischl in October. At last a place to rest for a few months with the trunks safely stowed away. There will be some small vexations, because one can't always get the Portuguese help to understand what one wants, but they are touchingly willing, and I pay five dollars a month for two maids and a gardener who runs the errands! True, the house, relatively speaking, isn't cheap, because Petropolis is the only summer resort near Rio, but life here is paradisically comfortable; we just drank divine coffee in the local cafe for two cents. If I could only forget Europe and be reconciled to the idea that all my belongings, house, books, are lost forever, and be thankful that I may live quietly here in this divine landscape, while Europe falls to pieces in hunger and misery, then I should be content.— You may imagine what consolation is to be extracted from nature here, which is full of color on every side, and where the people are so touching in their childlike ways. I have been wandering around the streets of Rio again these last days. I had a very cordial meeting with Ferro and Secretary Pereira de Lavalho, who have arrived here from Portugal. My book has gotten a lot of attention here and is being much discussed; people believe it was commissioned and paid for by the Propaganda [Bureau]. I have word from Masereel that he would rather come to Brazil than Colombia, but I hope he won't delay much longer, for they will make life in France more and more difficult [1] for him. I hope you will win peace and quiet for yourself. I, for my part, hope to attain to inner spiritual detachment here during the coming months. I am looking much better already. The news from Europe is horrifying. This will be a winter of frightfulness such as the world has never before witnessed. I want to edit and put more intensity into the autobiography *(The World of Yesterday),* this month; also I am planning an unrelated little novella, and so I won't want for work, given a bit of peace. I only wish I had those American libraries handy! In any case I shall merely make an outline which I shall organize in a general way as soon as I have a chance. All in all, I can't congratulate myself enough on my decision to leave America; you live more to yourself here and are at nature's heart; you hear no talk of politics; and, even though it may sound egotistical, it is after all a question of physical as well as spiritual survival. We can't forever be spending our lives paying for political follies that never gave us anything but always took from us, and I am content with the narrowest metes and bounds provided I have peace and quiet for work. I hope your children have found outlets for the exercise of their talents, and let us hope that you will receive the definite decision at last which you have been looking forward to.

With all my best, St.

Give my regards to the dear Fueloeps, I miss them a lot here.—I hope Huebsch sent you the book.

1 If he had been with Stefan, the tragedy would have been averted. Unluckily nothing came of his trip to Brazil.

(From Petropolis to New York)

9/29/1941

L.F.:

Just received your letter. I have noted down the new address and hope you are all right there. The weather here isn't as yet just what it should be, but nevertheless I take a lot of walks. The black Doña is very nice and intelligent and we are teaching her the art of cooking, which is difficult because people here have never eaten anything but manioca and black beans; even rice and potatoes are luxuries for them. But they are so very willing, you overlook everything. She always comes into the room barefoot, in the old slave manner, takes off her wooden slippers in the kitchen. The "Café Elegante" is just beyond the garden and in the green little plaza there are always several dozen donkeys who keep up a rhythmic waving of tails; I have an extraordinary fondness for them.—You have no idea how colorful and at the same time restful life here is. There is no hurry about anything, not even the mail, but the people are touching; despite their unmitigated poverty (nobody has a whole pair of pants) nothing is ever stolen; it is a kind of primitive society, a grandfather age. But how wonderful to live in one that doesn't remind you of the present.

I am busy editing the autobiography, have worked out a project for a little chess novella [*The Royal Game*]; I got the idea from a book about chess that I bought, because, living as I do in complete isolation, I found relaxation in working out the games of the great masters.—I haven't yet seen the English edition of the book on Brazil. Some people here don't consider that it praises everything sufficiently, because they believe machines and new buildings are more important than, and are inclined to be ashamed of, the picturesque aspects, which the next generation will rediscover, no doubt, just as we destroyed the old Burgtheater and the house where Beethoven died, only to mourn their loss afterward. But you would be enchanted every hour of the day here; the street is a stage-play and the little colored children like sweet animals you want to take up in your arms. It is a comfort to know that for some months I shall have a steady "domicile" somewhere, and have no truck with the authorities or be bothered with publicity; an old Goethe, a Homer, a Shakespeare suffice for the time being as reading matter. I can borrow anything else I want—although the New York libraries are irreplacable. So that appears to be all for now, and for the present my best wishes for your new home.

Affectionately, Stefan

You should phone Hermann Broch or Kesten again about Lucka.

(To New York, One Sheridan Square)

Petropolis, October 14th/1941

Dear F.:

I assume that you are in your new living quarters and finding them comfortable as I do mine here. Although the weather has been rainy, I am very fond of this little bungalow, especially because it isn't in the fashionable quarter, but on the periphery, close to little Negro shops and donkies and enchanting children. It is living in Paradise. Today was received in the bistro across the way like a king; a roast with

rice, bananas and coffee, two milreis per person, ten cents!
I scarcely ever get to Rio; I enjoy reading Montaigne, Goethe,
Shakespeare, and working, leading my normal life, in short,
which had been impossible during the years since the war.
The worries, too, which tortured me in New York, have lost
their intensity—everything is so far away and the war so
terribly long drawn out; it is impossible to guess what will
come afterward. Everything one has struggled for, will not
matter a bit then, and we will have to begin an entirely new
life, provided we still have the strength.—We have invited
your nephew to occupy our primitive guest-room as soon as
this worthy youngster's vacation begins. Otherwise nothing to
tell, have worked the autobiography over from the ground up
and the end of it is in sight.

My affectionate best, Stefan

I haven't had a letter from you for some time, probably our
letters crossed each other.

Petropolis, October 27th/1941

L.F.:

Thanks for your two letters which reached me promptly.
We have sunny weather here already. I don't imagine you
could endure such an isolated and uneventful existence as
mine. It does me a lot of good, at least for the present. I feel
physically much better; personal worries don't preoccupy me
the way they did up there; on the other hand my horror of
the age we live in grows immeasurably. We are only at the
beginning, or at most, the middle of the war, which is really
just commencing now that the neutral powers have gotten
into it, and then will follow the chaotic post-war years. I feel
hampered on every side in my work.—My books, it is to be
assumed, will not appear in the original [language] any more,
yet my whole thinking and point of view is tied to the
European, indeed, the Latin mentality. Besides, I am without
material. My Balzac manuscript still hasn't arrived, and even
if it had, I would have trouble with it. I am dreaming of a
sort of Austrian novel, but for that I would have to read
through ten years of newspapers to get the details of what I
want—this would be possible only in New York and I don't

want to go back there in the foreseeable future. Add the thought that one will never again have a house, a home, a publisher,[1] and can't help one's friends any more even the least bit, since everything is gone. The best of being here is that one needs so little and therefore one can go on without scribbling for the newspapers. But I am always worried about producing; creative production must gradually be extinguished like a light without oxygen, if there is no new inflow.—I have written again about Masereel; I believe it is merely a matter of his making up his mind to go to Colombia; everything was arranged. I can't do anything here for Lucka; they aren't giving any more visas. Really I can't imagine what is to become of all of them, the Ehrensteins, etc., who can't be translated and who have no productive capacity. I am glad that I am now polishing off the last of the autobiography; it has become somewhat livelier and somewhat more concise— where and how it is to be published still remains a problem. I hope your matter will soon be put through and I am glad that you are settled in your own room—nobody knows better than I how these temporary situations weigh one down. What good can old age bring now? Formerly it brought tranquility, rest, remembrance and honor; today, being hunted down, avoided, hated. I am really quite desperate, and it is only this wonderful quietude and isolation which keeps me in some sort of balance. There might be a great deal of improvement if I were able to begin a new, big piece of work, but every such project is hampered by the lack of documentary material. I was very much tempted to write about Montaigne, whom I am now reading steadily and with great enjoyment, another (better) Erasmus, an altogether heart-warming soul. But there is practically nothing about him here and I don't know whether I could get the books I require even in America, for you need the whole extent and content of an era, to understand a human being belonging to it. I am always saying, survive the war and then make a new beginning. But before it is over and I can settle down somewhere, at least two, three, four years will have gone by, irreplaceable years, and besides, security in the matter of material existence is gone. This war, I am convinced, will destroy utterly everything that former generations have built up. The one thing I still have is this

335

simple, removed existence without newspaper reviews and visits. I read a lot, and, for the first time, really carefully—*Wilhelm Meister* and the like. But will this interlude of contemplation be possible much longer? I am glad the radio gives out only Brazilian news. I read through newspapers in a matter of three minutes—it is horrible to think of all the misery. Montaigne speaks with infinite sorrow of people who live the sorrows of others in imagination, and advises them to withdraw and isolate themselves. A small share of egotism and lack of imagination would have helped me a lot in life; it is too late to try to change one's self now. Moreover, I *implore you,* don't tell anyone about my birthday. I love everybody who doesn't remind me of it, and consider him a real friend.

All my best,

Stefan

Wrote Huebsch about Soma Morgenstern and recommended the novel to him.

[1] His prophecy concerning his house and publishers didn't come true. His beloved Inselverlag would have been available to him again and Bermann-Fischer made good on his (S. Z.'s) works. His house in Bath was only slightly damaged and awaited him, as it were, with everything in it intact. And even Austria would not have closed her doors to him.

Petropolis, Nov. 20th/1941

L.F.:

Thanks a lot for your letter of November thirteenth. I am confounded by your having gotten up a commemorative book for me; [1] this is not a time for commemorative festivities and my friends, where are they—out of reach, like Rolland, Masereel; others in the earth like Roth and Rieger; and one doesn't even have a particularly high opinion of oneself anyway. But the intention was touching and I thank all of you very much! Also think about giving Chambrun the information he wanted. With regard to Da Ponte [2] I myself have plans, even a novel, and if it is to be a biography, let it be one on which I have set my heart, Balzac and Montaigne. Montaigne avers that in one's later years one should do only what one likes to do (acquire knowledge in youth, in manhood be active in some profession) and his words always carry the weight of truth. Nothing new to report from here, my life is completely monastic and without variety, though I am at work, but don't ask to what end. The autobiography is already on the way to Bermann-Fischer and Huebsch; this boulder is off my chest at last. I am terribly sorry that your affair in connection with permission to immigrate has been held up—I had a similar experience two years ago and then it arrived too late or didn't come through at all. But your business will eventually be arranged in proper shape; we are in the midst of a maelstrom of history and should be glad if our souls aren't drowned in it. Letters arrive seldom, very few from England, and from the rest of Europe not at all. When I recall what mountains we had to plough through ten years ago [3] and what we lived through during those ten years, then the whole thing seems unreal to me, and nevertheless the worst is still to come.

So my very best, and a thousand thanks! I hope your children will achieve success in whatever they undertake and that they will be a comfort to you and bring you joy.—In these times as never before one needs to have work to do. Many thanks also for the Montaigne bibliography. There is a library here with a few French books, which are, in any case, a little fodder for an aged reader.

Stefan

[1] The reference is to a fine commemorative book by Jules Romains.   [2] I had begun collecting material for a Da Ponte biography and offered it to Stefan in case he was interested.   [3] His fiftieth birthday had brought hundreds of letters. The contrast now was significant and he mentioned it to other people as well.

Petropolis, Brazil, 11/24/41

L.F.:

Now it's my turn to be the congratulator, for time passes quickly, and now you too have only one year before your sixtieth! Celebrate the day properly, for after all you have your children with you, and that is very unusual these days. Thanks a lot for the Montaigne references—it happens that Fortunatus Stronski is living in Rio, and perhaps he will lend me his book.[1] Meanwhile I have been making notes on material I have found in St. Beuve.—On the fateful day, [his birthday] I shall go out to Friburgo, an old Swiss colony, in my publisher's auto, to escape all visits, in case anybody here should remember.—Am looking forward to the book with anticipation and will thank Romains immediately. I regret to say that I still take a gloomy view of our era; never before have so many human beings been murdered and made unhappy on the earth; it is almost beyond bearing to imagine that this may go on for years and years. What good fortune that you have your children with you—everything else by comparison is irrelevant. Here there is unheard of prosperity, the country is growing rich,—too rapidly to suit me!—and self-conscious, but it is just now a paradise for quiet people (if it only had some books!).

All my best, Stefan.

1 One of the books about Montaigne which I had referred Stefan to and which put him on the track of the French biographer of Montaigne who was living in Rio.

Petropolis, 11/29/1941

L.F.:

Survived the fateful day happily; we wanted to go to Friburgo, but the highway was in such poor condition that we had to return to Petropolis after having spent the day in Teresopolis. I succeeded in suppressing any publicity [about his birthday] so that there were telegrams from England and America only. I received the following presents (in addition to the Romains book); a complete edition of Balzac from Huebsch, which will be a great help; from my publisher, to enliven my lonesomeness a bit, an enchantingly cute and darling wire-haired fox terrier, very affectionate, very well-trained, but of course without the intelligence or the masterful persistence of Kaspar. He (the new arrival) felt quite at home inside of a day, and he gives our little house a homey feeling. Also my publisher made a movie of the house and view; I hope it will turn out well. The dog comes from the highest diplomatic circles—the Rio Branco family—has won the second prize for looks, and has a mile-long pedigree which doesn't impress us descendants of Abraham as much as his nice manners. An animal is a good substitute these days when humanity has become so repulsive. I am going down to Rio on Tuesday; Fortunatus Stronski has gotten together the best of the Montaigne books (his own). It is really a lucky coincidence, my having the greatest authority so close at hand.—So there you have it all, you can see from the details about the dog and Balzac that, due to my mounting scepticism, I am more and more inclined to isolation, at least for some time to come. You have to arrange your time so that it will deny the times as much as possible. The superabundance here is overwhelming—the little bit of rice we give the dog would be a feast over there for a whole family, and on my birthday I received a Hungarian goose liver which was as truly genuine as if it had originated in the second district of Vienna. My sincere thanks to Alix and Susi for their congratulations, and all my best,

Stefan

(Believing he had to do so on account of the war, Stefan wrote nearly all his letters after this in English.)

Petropolis, 12/15/1941

Dear Friderike:

Thanks for your letter. I am afraid that owing to the war letters will sometimes be delayed especially by boat, so I hope you will at least have this one for Christmas. It will be a sad Christmas for us all who love peace and I hope you will have at least the satisfaction to have your children around your table. Let us not think too much of the coming years, they will bring destruction of so many things we are longing for—quiet life and a certain security—and also after the final destruction of Hitler the world will still have her problems to find a new way and every one of us.—Life will be terribly hard for all of us and with my literary work I see not much chance especially because I cannot continue my old plans like Balzac: perhaps the Montaigne will take form in a few months. Poor Scheyer, what must he suffer—I do not understand how all these people insist to continue such a life; even if he could still come over to the U. S. he would come without nothing and you know how proud he is. Here all is still quiet and no excitement at all, but also this country will be involved one day; my dream would be to sit quiet somewhere but houses have gone up fantastically in prices and one had to go in the interior where one is entirely cut-off from books and friends. In any case I have a lease till to the end of April, but alas, time runs with frightening rapidity. How far it seems to me, that I had a house, my books and I know already that all this is gone for ever.—In January your brother and Clarissa [1] will come for a few days to escape the heat of Rio: he has good news from his son, who had made some important scientific discoveries.

I suppose that you see less people as everybody will be occupied now with his own worries and that you can continue your book. Now it will take a long time if we shall see each other (if ever) and I am glad that you have your children and relatives with you. Petropolis will loose in the next two months its solitude and I am rather frightened by the thought of meeting people again—I do not like to talk now, because nobody can understand our position. One must have gone through things by own experience. Now they will better understand what we have suffered since years and that one looses with his home more than one can imagine. Kindest regards to all and a quiet Christmas. (I have not the courage to say: a happy one.) Love

Stefan

[1] Unfortunately the visit never took place.

(This letter was in German.)

Petropolis, December 28th/1941

L.F.:

I am hoping that typed letters arrive at their destination more promptly. So I want to thank you for your postcard and trust that meanwhile you have received my letter in which I gratefully acknowledged receipt of the two Montaigne books. I am a bit nervous just now about letters, for since the infamous Japanese attack and because of the Christmas jam, letters here are subject to very annoying delays.

I needn't comment on current events. This is the first time in history that a war has involved the whole world, and also it may last many years more; this thought is soul-shattering for all of us as human beings. It is horrible to think that the crimes committed by this one man Hitler have these many years been destroying the lives of hundreds of thousands and millions, and one would despair entirely were it not certain that the majority, the innumerable majority which opposes him openly or secretly, will succeed in wiping out once and for all him and his.

I am hoping that your affairs will soon be properly settled and that all of you will have an opportunity to develop useful activities. Here no change in my loneliness. I was horror-stricken for a week or two about my work because of an apparently incurable absent-mindedness and defection in attention to my work, but I hope to get back into form gradually. Brazil will be the center of important conferences during the next few weeks, but I shall see little of all that, because I hardly ever get down to the city. To compensate, I am looking forward to having your brother with me soon.

With my best, Stefan

1 9 4 2

Dear Friderike:
I did not write all these days because there was nothing to tell, life continues in a quiet and rather monotonous way, reading, writing, walking, without interruptions by concerts, theatres and society—there are no news except those in the newspapers which have nothing reassuring in the sense that the victory will be a rapid one; on the contrary we have to be prepared that this war will be a very long and exhausting one. For me it becomes more and more sure that I will never see my house again and to remain everywhere but a traveling guest; happy those who could begin a new life where ever. I had a beautiful letter from Roger Martin du Gard, the best letter I have read since years, expressing the same what I feel, that we in our age have only the charge of spectators in the great play (or better tragedy) that the others the younger one have to play her part. Ours is only to disappear quietly and in a dignified way. I have finally got also the third Montaigne

book (by Gide) and thank you very much for it(—it is not very important and I hope I have more to say about him). I have seen your brother Siegfried and he will later come for a few days—he likes Brazil but we are all too old to get quite accustomed to foreign languages and countries. I hope your children feel allright and also the Höllers have found an occupation.— It is necessary today more than ever. It is a nightmare to think what happens in Europe: Lucka and all the others in France. And here is no more opportunity; hermetically closed and God knows for how long. We have at least beautiful weather and my only pleasure, the long walks, afford always new variety. Love and kindest regards.

Stefan

The little book on "Amerigo" (Vespucci) will be published next month.

Petropolis, 11/4/1942

Dear Friderike:

It is now a good long time I did not hear from you but all mail to Brazil seems to have been delayed by the conference which occupied the clippers with mail and members. There is not much to tell. I am rather depressed by the perspective that the real decision and ultimate victory will not come any more in this year and that the greater part of our best years has been passed for our generation in these two great world-convulsions. All will be changed after this war, which spends in one month more than nations earned before in years and I am afraid our old days will not be without anxiousness and difficulties—there is no more security in our time than in those of the Reformation or the fall of Rome. I was worried by the idea that your son-in-law and Susi will be hampered in their occupation and will have to look for other possibilities; also here are many restrictions in employment and certain nationalistic measures. I enjoy now the beautiful summer and have while the heat makes Rio to a furnace, cool nights and splendid days; from the physical point of view it could not have been better. There is season now in our Ischl but I live not less retired than before, reading, working and walking with the little dog which is very sweet, not so intelligent as Kaspar was but very affectionate as if I would have him already for years. Letters become more and more scarce, everybody has his own worries and one does not like to write if one has nothing important to tell—and what in our little and reduced life is still important in comparison with the world-events. My autobiography was sent by air mail to Sveden and I hope the manuscript has safely arrived. Hübsch will publish soon my little study on the Vespucci question and I wrote on the Montaigne but all this with a lack of real intensity—when one does not feel like once the response inmidst the thunder of the guns one has not the right passion. Reading is my best help and only reading good old, if I may say, *proved* books, Balzac, Goethe, Tolstoi; but what we miss is good talk with people of our level. Most of the people we meet do not understand what is going on and coming, they believe that the coming peace will be but a continuation of the peacetime; one must have gone through certain things to understand them and Europe is mentally as far to them as China has been to us in the last terrific times. I hope your work [1] goes ahead, I would not advise to send it to me now as books etc. take many weeks to arrive and there is no security. The country itself is still untouched by the war, there are only some restrictions for the Axis, aliens forbidding to speak Italian or German on public places and to carry printed matters in those languages. Food and all material things are here in this unexhaustible country in aboundance. I am not yet sure if I can rent the bungalow longer than April, in the case of a changement I shall let you know it in time. Love and friendship

Stefan

[1] *Wunder und Zeichen,* important figures of the middle ages, which I had already begun in Paris and which Bechtle Verlag in Esslingen brought out.

Petropolis, 11/18/1942
Dear Friderike:
    I have not more to write to you than kindest thoughts. There was now the fantastic carneval in Rio but my mind is far away from festivities and more distressed than ever. There will be never return to all bygone things and what is expecting us will never give more what those times had to offer us. I am continuing my work but with a quarter of my strength;

it is more continuing an old habit than really creating. One must be convinced to convince, to have enthusiasme to stimulate the others and how to find this now! All my best thoughts are with you and I hope your children find good opportunity to work and to go ahead; they will still see the better world after this one. I hope you are in fairly good spirits and in perfect health and that New York with its variety gives you at least sometimes of his artistic wealth—here I have [1] but nature and books, old good books which I read and reread again. Yours ever

Stefan

[1] The word "have" is illegibly written. It might also have been "had" and thus indicated that he was saying farewell.

Petropolis, 11/22/1942

Dear Friderike:

when you get this letter I shall feel much better than before. You have seen me in Ossining and after a good and quiet time my depression became much more acute—I suffered so much that I could not concentrate any more. And then the security—the only one we had—that this war will take years, that it would take ages before we in our special position could settle again in our home was too depressing. I liked Petropolis very much, but I had not the books I wanted and the solitude which first had such a soothing effect began to become oppressive—the idea that my central work, the Balzac, could never get finished without two years of quiet life and all books was very hard and then this war, which is not yet at his hight. I was too tired for all that. You have your children and with them a duty to keep up, you have large interests and an unbroken activity. I am sure you will see still the better time and will give me right, that I with my "black liver" did not wait any longer. I send you these lines in the last hours, you cannot imagine how glad I feel since I have taken the decision. Give my love to your children and do not complain me—remember the good Josef Roth an Rieger, how glad I always was for them, that they had not to go through these ordeals.

Love and friendship and cheer up, knowing me quiet and happy

Stefan